VIRTUAL REALITY AND ENVIRONMENTS

Edited by **Cecília Sík Lányi**

Virtual Reality and Environments
Edited by Cecília Sík Lányi

Published by InTech
Janeza Trdine 9, 51000 Rijeka, Croatia

Publishing Process Manager Jana Sertic

Technical Editor Teodora Smiljanic

Cover Designer InTech Design Team

Additional hard copies can be obtained from orders@intechopen.com

Virtual Reality and Environments, Edited by Cecília Sík Lányi
p. cm.
ISBN 978-953-51-0579-4

For EU product safety concerns:
IN TECH d.o.o., Prolaz Marije Krucifikse Kozulić 3, 51000 Rijeka, Croatia,
info@intechopen.com or visit our website at intechopen.com.

Meet the editor

Dr Cecília Sik Lányi studied Mathematics and Computer Science (B.S.) – József Attila University (1981) - Mathematics and Computer Science (M.S.) – József Attila University (1984). She became Teacher of Mathematics - Berzsenyi Dániel Teacher Training College in 1988. She obtained the degree of Dr Univ. at the University of Veszprém, Hungary in Physical-chemistry (1993), and the degree of PhD at the University of Veszprém, Hungary in Computer Science (2000). She has worked as a software engineer and as an associate professor for program languages at the University of Pannonia. Currently she is focused on virtual reality and its application, user interface design, computer graphics for informatics engineering students and using multimedia in the education for teacher training courses. PhD and Masters' supervision has an emphasis on multimedia/ virtual reality for the rehabilitation of children with disabilities and patients with mental health issues. She got the "Master teacher" award of the Hungarian Ministry of Education in 2001. She has published more than 300 refereed articles and conference papers, and worked as guest editor for many renowned journals. She was the secretariat manager of EDeAN in 2009. She is the representative of Hungary in IFIP Technical Committee 13: Human-Computer Interaction (TC13).

Contents

Preface

Virtual Reality is clearly interdisciplinary research area. It has, not only Information Technology importance but social, educational, economical importance too. It combines multiple disciplines for the development of virtual reality systems in which the user has the immersive feeling of being in the real world. Virtual reality has several applications in almost all fields of real life. The most typical fields for the application of virtual reality are health-care, engineering and game industry.

The objective of this book is to provide new knowledge to the readers.

The reviews in this book describe the latest Virtual Reality-related knowledge in three fields: virtual reality tools, virtual reality in education and rehabilitation and ergonomic design.

The chapters selected for this volume offer new perspectives in terms, tested practices and solutions. Our book may be a solid basis for the novice and advanced engineers who would like to develop user friendly Virtual Environments for education, rehabilitation and other applications of Virtual Reality.

The main features of this book can be summarised as follows:

1. The book describes and evaluates the current state-of-the-art in the virtual reality field.
2. It also presents several applications of Virtual Reality in the field of Immersive and non-Immersive Virtual Environments, Educations, Collaborative work, Ergonomic design, and Neurorehabilitation. Last but not least, it introduces the commonly used Virtual Reality hardware and software.
3. The contributors of this book are the leading researchers from Academia and practitioners from the industry.

This book provides a resource for wide variety of people including academicians, designers, developers, educators, engineers, practitioners, researchers, and graduate students.

We would like to thank the authors for their contributions. Without their expertise and effort, this book would never be born. InTech editors and staff also deserve our sincere recognition for their support throughout the project.

Finally the editor would like to thank her husband Ferenc Sik, her sons András Sik and Gergely Sik for their patience and Professor Janos Schanda, the Head of the Editor's Laboratory for his wise advices.

Dr. Cecília Sík Lányi
Associate professor at the University of Pannonia,
Veszprem,
Hungary

1

Virtual Environments in Physical Therapy

Felix O. Akinladejo
University of Technology,
Jamaica, West Indies

1. Introduction

This chapter examines virtual environments which usually represent computer simulated environments, otherwise called virtual worlds or virtual reality and its application in physical therapy. Virtual environments present computer-generated three-dimensional (3D) representation of a physical presence of places in the real world as well as in the imaginary world. Users mainly interact with virtual environments using virtual reality headsets. Many of the current virtual reality environments are primarily visual experiences display either on a computer screens or through other stereoscopic displays. Applications of virtual environments are mainly focused on artificial reality that projects users into a 3D space generated by the computer with some sort of tracking devices which may be the virtual reality headsets worn or another 3D tracking device attached to the body of the user such as the electromagnetic tracker system. Research in virtual environments has made significant impact in the entertainment industry and in the training field such as the flight simulator (Stern, 1995).

Source description: Hospital Corpsman 2nd Class Tim Sudduth, from Vashowish, Wash., demonstrates the Virtual Reality (VR) parachute trainer, while Aviation Survival Equipmentman 1st Class, Jackie Hilles, from Ekland, Penn., controls the program from a computer console. Students wear the VR glasses while suspended in a parachute harness, and then learn to control their movements through a series of computer-simulated scenarios.

Fig. 1. Virtual Reality Parachute Trainer. Source: http://www.news.navy.mil/view_single.asp?id=3523 Courtesy: The work of the United States Federal Government under the terms of Title 17, Chapter 1, Section 105 of the US Code.

In another view, some researchers like Strickland, Hodges, North and Weghorst (1997) describe virtual environments as computer presence and feel of another place with tracking of what the person does in this imaginary scene. They argued that when the headsets are used to remove the real background of the user, the mind is fooled and the senses are made to accept as reality this new imaginary environment. Some simulations of virtual environments add more sensory information to depict the imaginary world as close to reality as possible and advanced haptic systems are now being coupled with tactile information (force feedback) to create systems for medical and gaming applications. Advances in telecommunications have enabled remote communication environments which now provide virtual presence of users with the concepts of telepresence and telexistence (Liang et al., 2006; Szigeti et al., 2009). The example above demonstrates the use of virtual environment in parachute training. The system provides a parachute simulation where students learn how to control flight movements through a series of computer-generated scenarios.

2. Applications of virtual environments

The use of virtual environments in real life applications has grown tremendously in the last decade. A growing number of educators and researchers are reported to have found virtual environments useful for teaching and research, despite its challenging technical requirements. Many of the properties of virtual environments are viewed to be conducive for good learning as they tend to be interactive, engaging, and provide safe places for students to learn by doing and experimentation. There is also ample provision of scaffolding and immediate feedback to measure if learning has actually taken place. The report reveals that over 74 universities and colleges already have a presence (virtual campuses) within Second Life, an online virtual world created by Linden Lab, where a host of client programs (Viewers) enable Users (Residents) to interact with one another through avatars. The Residents can explore the virtual world, meet other Residents, socialize, participate in individual or group activities, trade virtual property and services with each other. Second Life, taunted as the Internet's largest user-created 3D virtual world community, has been used for distance learning, museum-style exhibits, corporate training, broadcasting information, or simply as an interactive supplement to traditional classroom environments. It is envisaged that virtual classes and virtual classrooms will become more commonplace, as the number of schools that hold online classes within Second Life continues to grow. As simulations and designed experiences, , researchers believe that virtual worlds are useful for experiential, exploratory learning and for teaching various content areas like business (e.g. virtual real estate, intellectual property), economics, art design and architecture, science, among other topics. It is also reported that Second Life already has over a million active users.

In the use for therapeutic applications, the field of motor rehabilitation, especially after a stroke assault, is one of the fields that have benefitted significantly from virtual environments applications. A number of virtual environment-based systems have been developed along the theory underlying neuronal mechanism targeting recovery. It is assumed that recovery could be facilitated by harnessing mechanisms underlying neuronal reorganization. O'Sullivan and Schmitz (2001) argued that motor recovery evolves from a complex set of neurological and mechanical processes that inform postures and that the brain normally provides signal that help with balance, coordination and orientation necessary for movements, especially walking. Molnar (2002) argued that stroke impairs these complex set of processes involved in walking. Liepert and his colleagues in 2000 along with Jack and his fellow researchers in 2001 showed indications that virtual environments can be used to simulate artificial images that trigger biofeedback mechanisms that can aid in motor recovery.

In the work of Jack and his colleagues (Jack et al., 2001), a PC-based desktop system was developed that employed virtual environments for rehabilitating the hand function in stroke patients. The system uses two input devices, a CyberGlove and a Rutgers Master II-ND (RMII) force feedback glove, that allow users to interact with the virtual environment. The virtual environment presents four rehabilitation routines, each designed to exercise one specific parameter of hand movement e.g., range of motion. The authors used performance-based target levels to encourage patients to use the system and to individualize exercise difficulty based on the patient's specific need. Three chronic stroke patients were employed to carry out pilot clinical trials of the system daily for two weeks. Objective evaluations revealed that each patient showed improvement on most of the hand parameters over the course of the training.

In 2002, Boian and his colleagues used a similar virtual environment in a different context to rehabilitate four post-stroke patients in the chronic phase. The system developed was distributed over three sites (rehabilitation site, data storage site, and data access site) and connected to each other through the Internet. At the rehabilitation site, the patients underwent upper-extremity therapy using a CyberGlove and a Rutgers Master II (RMII) haptic glove integrated with PC-based system that provides the virtual environment. The patients interacted with the system using the sensing gloves, and feedback was given on the computer screen. The data storage site hosted the main server for the system. It had an Oracle database, a monitoring server, and a web site for access to the data. The data access site was a 'place-independent' site, being any computer with Internet access. The therapist or physician could access the patients' data remotely from any location with Internet connections. The patients exercised for about two hours per day, five days a week for three weeks, within the virtual environment to reduce impairments in their finger range of motion, speed, fractionation and strength. Results showed that three of the four patients had improvements in their thumbs' range of motion and finger speed over the three-week trial while all the patients had significant improvements in finger fractionation, and modest gains in finger strength.

Similarly, in the same year, Alma S. Merians, with some members of Boian's research group continued related work using the CyberGlove and the RMII glove, coupled with virtual reality technology, to create an interactive, motivating virtual environment in which practice intensity and feedback were manipulated to present individualized treatments to retrain movements in three patients who were in the chronic phase following stroke. The patients participated in a two-week training program, spending about three-and-half hours per day on dexterity tasks using real objects and virtual reality exercises. The virtual reality simulations were targeted for upper-extremity improvements in range of motion, movement speed, fractionation, and force productions. Results showed that one of the three patients, the most impaired at the beginning of the intervention, gained improvement in the thumb and fingers in terms of range of motion and speed of movement. Another patient improved in fractionation and range of motion of his thumb and fingers. The third patient made the greatest gains as that patient was reported to have gained improvements in the range of motion and strength of the thumb, velocity of the thumb and fingers, and fractionation.

These evidences showed the usefulness of virtual environments for rehabilitation therapy to improve movement performance and/or functional ability and add to other research efforts such as the study of computerized training in a virtual reality environment as an enhancement to existing methods of retraining the hand in patients in the later phase of recovery after a stroke (Merians et al., 2002), robot training using a virtual environment to enhance stroke rehabilitation (Krebs, Hogan, Aisen & Volpe, 1998), and Professor Baram's work on a virtual reality device that helps Parkinson's and stroke patients walk better (Garbi, 2002). Curtis (1998) and Merians et al. (2002) observed that the field of virtual reality was still in its infancy, especially for special needs; however, crossovers with fields such as computer graphics, Computer-Aided Design (CAD), acoustics, and human-computer interface, which are much better established, are currently making the creation of virtual environments more viable. Advances in technology, in terms of computer processing power and graphics hardware, have made it possible to create virtual environment on cheap computer platforms (e.g., 486 or Pentium IBM compatible PCs). These were previously only possible on high-end workstations such as silicon graphics machines. Breakthroughs in LCD technology are already being delivered in the form of cheaper and higher resolution virtual reality headsets, which are required for fully-immersive virtual environment. Global Positioning Satellite (GPS) technologies, such as compact gyroscopes, promise mass production of three-dimensional (3D) input devices, similar to those already found in the Phillips 3D mouse, to facilitate interactions at a very low cost, and fields such as Human Computer Interaction (HCI) have long been focused on the use of virtual reality as an alternative means of interaction (Snowdon, West & Howard, 1993). Telecommunication networks currently can deliver via the Internet high bandwidth graphical information required by virtual reality, and technology solutions are now being implemented using virtual reality for special needs (Boian et al. 2002; Smythe, Furner & Mercinelli, 1995). Web page designs can now utilize 3D capabilities using the Virtual Reality Mark-up Language (VRML), and the ability to extend healthcare's reach has been advocated (Plant, 1996).

3. Forms of virtual environments

Virtual environments are generally classified by the degree of immersion it provides through level of user interactivity, image complexity, stereoscopic view, field of regard and the update rate of display. A careful and complex combination of all these factors determine the level of immersion achieved as no one parameter is effective in itself.

3.1 Fully immersive environments

Virtual Environment can be fully immersive, where, in this sense, the user feels they are part of the simulated world. All the senses of the user are engaged, sight, sound, touch, smell, taste, with technology such as panoramic 3D displays for full sense of vision, surround sounds for auditory immersion, haptic and force feedback for tactile feelings, and smell and taste replications for olfactory and gustation experiences. This form of environment. Fully immersive environments provide the most direct experience of virtual environments and have been reported to be probably the most widely known VR implementation where the user either wears a Head Mounted Display (HMD) or uses some form of head-coupled display such as a Binocular Omni-Orientation Monitor or BOOM (Bolas, 1994).

3.1.1 Head Mounted Display (HMD)

This is a headset used for full immersion. It can contain a pair of goggles or a full helmet. In front of the eyes are two tiny monitors that present images in three dimensions. Most HMDs include a head tracker so that the system can respond to head movements. The small monitors placed in front of each eye provide stereo, bi-ocular or monocular images. The Stereo images come in a similar way to shutter glasses as only a slightly different image is presented to each eye. The major difference is that the two screens are placed very close (50-70mm) to the eye, while the HMD optical system keeps the image which the wearer focuses on much further away. Bi-ocular images can present identical images on each screen while monocular images are formed using only one display screen.

The most commonly used HMDs employ small Liquid Crystal Display (LCD) panels which provides enough screen resolution for many applications, but the more expensive ones employ Cathode Ray Tubes (CRT) that increase the resolution of the screen image. Fully immersive systems usually exclude the user's view of the real world and enhance the field of view of the computer generated world. The advantage of this method is that the user is provided with a 360° field of regard giving them a visual image in whatever direction they turn their head. The HMDs are central to achieving the sense of full immersion; hence their resolution, the update rate, and contrast and illumination of the display are critical factors.

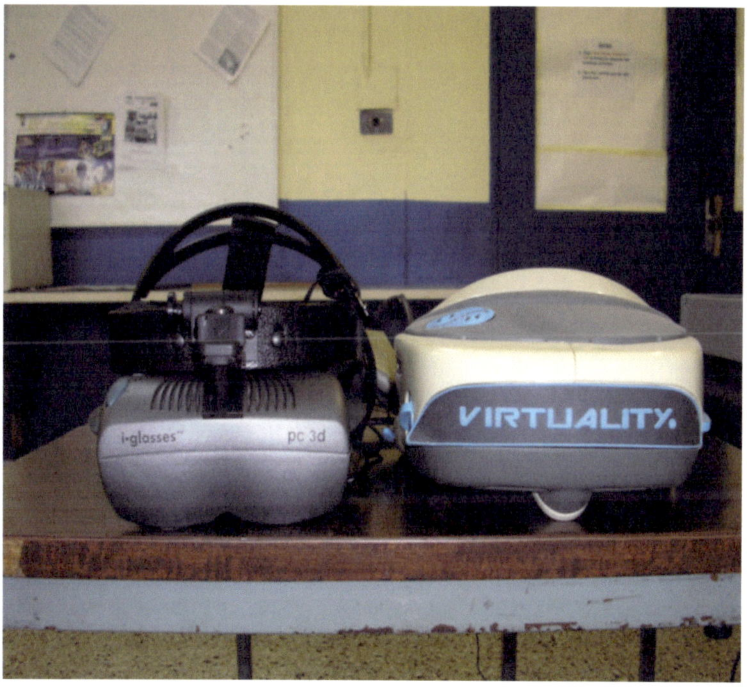

Fig. 2. Virtual Reality Headsets

3.2 Non-immersive environments or desktop systems

These are the least immersive implementation of virtual simulation techniques. With Personal Computers on the desks, the virtual environment is created through a portal or window by utilising a standard high resolution monitor. Users interact with the environment through conventional means such as keyboards, mice and trackballs, which can be augmented by using 3D interaction devices such as a SpaceBallă or DataGloveă.

The non-immersive systems are more economical to set up as they usually do not require the highest level of graphics performance and without any specialized hardware requirements. They can also be cloned on high specification Personal Computers. These are the lowest cost VR solutions that are being employed for many virtual environment applications. The reported drawback, however, is that they are usually outperformed by the more sophisticated systems. They are confined within the limit of the existing 2D interaction device and thus provide little or no sense of immersion hence of little use where the perception of scale is an important factor. It is expected that the growing use of Virtual Reality Modelling Reality Language (VRML), which is also being adopted as a de-facto standard for the transfer of 3D model data and virtual worlds via the internet, should fuel the use of non-immersive virtual environment applications. It is argued that the advantage of VRML is in its ability to run relatively well on personal computers as opposed to many other proprietary VR authoring tools and the growth in its use that can result in the current trends of commercial VR software having VRML as a tool incorporated in them to explore the commercial possibilities of desktop VR applications.

3.3 Semi-immersive virtual environments

In semi-immersive virtual environments, the viewer becomes partly but not fully immersed in this environment. These systems borrowed considerably from technologies developed in the flight simulation field and are a relatively new implementation of VR technology, which often consists of a large, concave screen, projection system and monitor similar to the large screen experiences seen at IMAX cinemas. They usually involve high end computer graphics. A flight simulator, for an example may present a semi-immersive simulation of an aircraft cockpit where the set up would consist of a physical display of the cockpit and chair with three dimensional images. The trainee does not need to wear virtual reality gear such as a data glove or head mounted display (HMD) and is still aware of the real world outside of the virtual environment. Semi-immersive systems present a few advantages over fully immersive systems such as a CAVE, an automatic virtual environment system, which includes cost, ease of use and logistics. But it has its disadvantages as well which include limited range of interaction devices and problems with multi-user applications

A semi-immersive system can be set up with a relatively high performance graphics computing system which can be coupled with a large screen monitor, a large screen projector system or a multiple television projection systems. They provide a greater sense of presence than non-immersive systems and also a greater appreciation of scale. Because the images can be of a far greater resolution than those of HMDs, semi-immersive systems possess the ability to share the virtual experience. This has been argued to be its advantage, especially in educational applications as it allows simultaneous experience of the virtual environment without the need for head-mounted immersive systems. Also, stereographic imaging can be achieved, using some type of shuttered glasses in synchronisation with the graphics system. According to vrs.org, Shutter Glasses are Liquid Crystal Shutter (LCS) glasses which consist of a lightweight headset with a liquid crystal lens placed over each eye. Stereopsis works on the principle that in order to perceive depth in a scene, the observer must see slightly different images of the scene under regard in each eye. In the real world this occurs because the two eyes are placed slightly apart in the head, and so each eye views the scene from a slightly different position. Multi-user issues have been reported as one of the main advantages of these systems and designers must consider the handover of control between users as this technology develops.

Virtual environments applications continue to grow. Developers are coming out with new technologies that can simulate effects such as wind, vibration and lightning to enrich the virtual environment for a true model of reality. Virtual environments are being successfully used for applications such as driving and flight simulators and we are now witnessing some entertainment environment like the simulated Viruga Mountains in Rwanda to explore a tribe of Mountain Gorillas.

4. Some barriers and issues in virtual environment applications

Despite all the strides in virtual environment applications, research still shows inconsistencies in the reports on research efforts in virtual environments. One main contention is whether skills gained in virtual environments transfer to real-world conditions. This argument has come to the forefront in the widely use of virtual environment for therapeutic applications. For example, efforts to promote functional recovery through therapeutic interventions like neurofacilitation techniques, progressive strengthening, biofeedback and electrical simulation, after the occurrence of stroke, have yielded inconsistent results (Duncan, 1997; Feys et al., 1998; Merians et al., 2002; Richards & Pohl, 1999). O'Sullivan and Schmitz (1994) argued that these inconsistencies stemmed from inadequate training and skills in performing these procedures in order to ensure the validity and reliability of the tests. Wilson, Foreman and Tlauka (1996) reported that internal representations resulting from exploration of simulated space transferred to the real environment. Kozak et al. (1993), Deutsch, Latonio, Burdea and Boian (2001), argued that although subjects trained on a motor task in a virtual environment demonstrated the ability to improve performance in that environment, the learning did not always transfer to the real-world task. Jack et al. (2001) attributed this problem to the current paucity of investigation into the use of VR for motor skill training. These inconsistencies indicate that research in motor task training and transfer of that task to the real-world environment is neither fully understood nor entirely conclusive (Jack et al., 2001). These conflicting findings need to be more carefully explored in order to ascertain the usefulness of VR as an enhancement to traditional therapy. Fox and Fried-Oken (1996) also observed that many questions relating to the generalization of new learning to the natural environment remained largely unanswered.

Recent studies have shown that virtual reality technology can be used to provide this treatment approach based on its capability to create an integrated, interactive, motivating environment in which practice intensity and feedback can be manipulated to effect functional recovery or improvements in patients following stroke (Liepert et al., 2000; Merians et al., 2002; Taub, Uswatte & Pidikiti, 1999;).

5. A virtual environment case study

The author conducted a case study to justify his own belief on this inconclusive subject. The research undertaken also aims to justify or not research efforts in virtual environments applications as alternative intervention techniques for motor rehabilitation for researchers and clinicians involved in rehabilitation engineering. The study specifically focused on the effect of using virtual environment to improve ambulatory function in stroke patients, and investigated whether the skills gained from the environment transfer to real-world conditions. A virtual reality system was developed to train stroke patients with lower extremity problems (Akinladejo, 2005, 2007). The product of the research study was developed using the i-glasses PC 3D HR Head Mounted Display and the Polhemus electromagnetic tracker system.

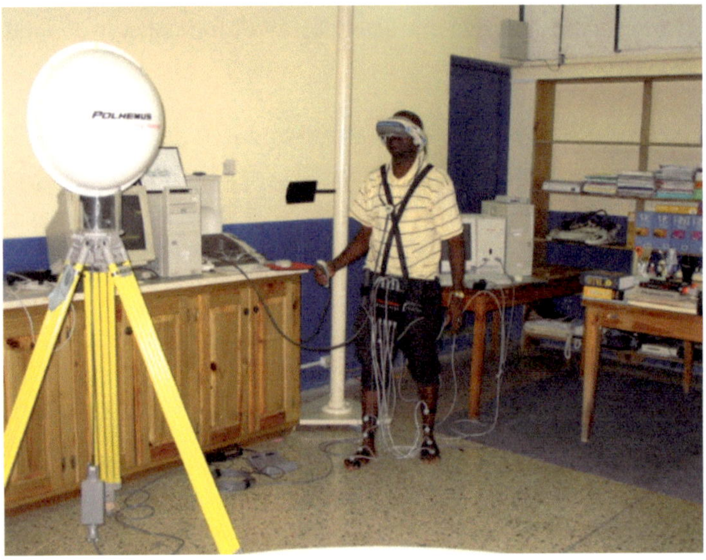

Fig. 3. The Author with the i-glasses PC 3D HR Head Mounted Display and the Polhemus electromagnetic tracker system (Akinladejo, 2005)

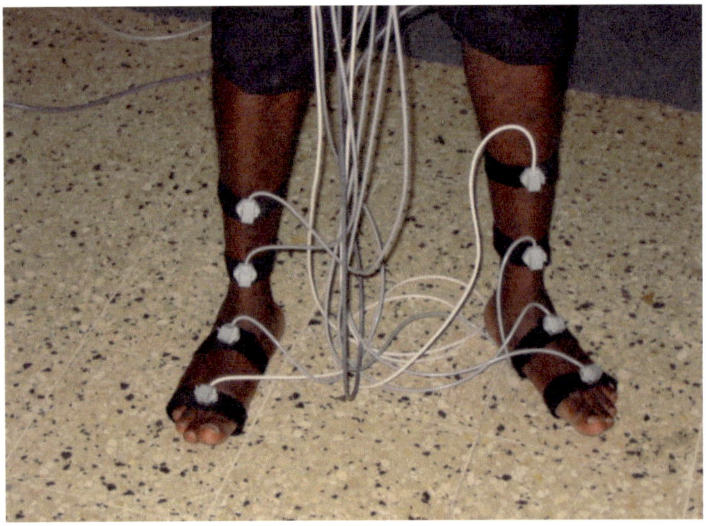

Fig. 4. The Author with sensors of the Tracker system on his legs. (Akinladejo, 2005)

Information about a scenario of interest to the patients was gathered. The VR system was used to present this scenario in the form of an environment where the patients performed a VR-based exercise in order to induce the therapy needed to correct their gait problems. The VR system was employed to present the patients with VR tasks (in the form of a painting exercise) closely linked with the therapy needed to correct or improve any abnormality in their walking patterns. This stage model phase modeled all the primitives, visual and audio, of both the task-specific exercise and the VR environment as formalized in the scenario stage. The virtual reality task was based on a painting exercise, which served the purpose of inducing the therapeutic movements needed for the functional recovery or improvements of the lower extremities of the patients. The VR-based painting exercise was employed for the purpose of simulating visually immersive therapy exercise on a PC without having to physically use real paints, brushes, boards or papers.

Research has recently been focused on the painting process and virtual reality technology (Lin, Baxter, Scheib & Wendt, 2004), and the clinical community for the work agreed that the painting task is capable of inducing the movement patterns that are closely linked with the therapy needed to correct ambulatory problems, especially in ankle and foot movements. The painting exercise induced in the leg the complex strokes associated with physical painting in the real world. A graphical user interface provided the therapist with a simple and minimal set of keystrokes with which the VR exercises were manipulated for the appropriate level of exercise difficulty for each patient. The VR-based painting exercise presented the patients with windows of different sizes to be covered. The patients were required to cover the windows with 'red blinds' using their hemiplegic legs. The window's color, initially cyan over a blue background, becomes red over a blue background when completely covered. The therapist viewed the painting process on a computer screen as the patient performed the exercise within a virtual environment using the head mounted display. The author designed a 'LegMouse' and a 'LegPad' (Akinladejo, 2005), which the patient used to accomplish the painting exercise. The LegPad was attached to the patient's hemiplegic leg for movements on the LegMouse. The LegPad was designed, in consultation with the clinical community, with a hemispheric base in order to allow dorsiflexion, plantar flexion, inversion and eversion movements of the ankle joints. As the patient moved his or her leg with the LegPad over the LegMouse, the painting program caused the cursor on the computer screen to 'paint' a defined window. There were four different window areas, each corresponding to the task difficulty level that the patient was performing. The painting process stopped whenever the cursor moved outside a window area. Thus the patient was constantly challenged with the task of keeping the cursor within the window area in the virtual environment, and also with the task of moving his or her hemiplegic leg in all directions for the painting process to continue. These movements (e.g., dorsiflexion and plantar flexion movements) helped to induce in the leg the therapy needed to correct or improve ambulatory problems in the ankle joint thereby leading to better walking skills. Some images that present the patient's view of the systems is presented. The painting exercise was modeled using OpenGL, an environment for developing portable, interactive 2D and 3D graphics applications. This application programming interface (API) is widely used on a number of computer platforms for innovative developments through its broad set of rendering, texture mapping, special effects, and other powerful visualization functions available for application developers (http://www.opengl.org/about/overview.html). OpenGL is a truly open, vendor-neutral, multiplatform graphics standard that provides consistent visual display results on any OpenGL API-compliant hardware irrespective of the operating system. It offers complete independence from network protocols and topologies. Application developers are well shielded from underlying hardware as OpenGL drivers ensure proper encapsulation of hardware primitives, thus giving them ample flexibilities for innovative designs. The OpenGL standard provides language binding for C++ and Java, the two main languages employed for the research study. The virtual exercise system incorporated performance-based target levels to increase the patients' motivation (Jack et al., 2001). Feedback mechanisms informed the patients on the target levels and their actual performance on the VR system, and the therapists employed the GUI-based interface to tailor exercise difficulty to the patients' specific problems. The feedback provided an avenue for encouraging the patient to accomplish more trials in the virtual environment. To encourage motivating environment, the author identified, through interviewing the patients, that music will make the scenario of interest to them, and combined an audio system with the painting exercise, in a way that presented an interesting and motivating environment where the patients were unaware of the technology behind the VR-based exercise, just because they wanted to 'play the game' on the computer and enjoy the music.

6. A clinical trial

Qualified physiotherapists from the clinical community were employed for the clinical evaluation of the VR-based rehabilitation program. They also helped to recruit the research subjects for the work, and supervised their training sessions. The patients were required to use the virtual environment for regular rehabilitation for about half an hour per day, five days a week for a period of four consecutive weeks. A computer screen provided the therapists with feedback on the performance of the patient on the system, and the therapists were able to adjust the level of difficulty of each exercise based on the specific need of the individual patient. Adjustment was in terms of what the author termed Task Difficulty Level (TDL), which ranged from 1, the easiest to 4, the most difficult. The therapists observed the progress made by the patients while they performed the VR tasks, and also guided them in producing more refined movements to reduce movement errors. The clinical trial was carried out at the Sir John Golding Rehabilitation Centre, popularly known as Mona Rehab. Mona Rehab is a unique center for the rehabilitation of persons with physical disabilities in the Caribbean, and it is only a short distance from the researcher's place of work, which made it easily accessible. The researcher installed the system in the Physical Therapy Department. The patients' gait variables were obtained prior to and after the treatment, and were analyzed and used to ascertain the usefulness of virtual reality technology in rehabilitation program directed towards lower extremity problems in post-acute stroke patients. A test was carried out to determine whether skills gained within VR environments transfer to the real world.

7. The virtual environment system

The VR system executes and displays a welcome screen where user of the system will have to enter a password in order to gain access. The screen dump below shows the first interface of the system which the users, in the clinical trial case, the physical therapists, will use to gain access to the systems.

A valid password has been stored in the memory, which the system compares with the user's supplied password. A mismatch will allow the user two more attempts before the system logs out. A match will lead the user to the Patient Information Screen. The user will be required to

Fig. 5. The Interface for the Clinician. (Akinladejo, 2005).

supply a patient research number (PRN). If a PRN is not found, the system will give opportunity to either re-enter another PRN or add the current PRN to the database. There is an optional button to exit the program. If a PRN is found or is added, the system then leads the user to the Task Difficulty Level (TDL) screen where the user will specify the appropriate VR-based task that the chosen patient will undergo. The tasks range from one (1) the easiest to four (4), the most difficult. If an invalid TDL is entered, the system will default to TDL1.

The clinician can opt to change the patient from this screen or exit the program. The appropriate TDL choice leads to the exercise mode, where the patient performs the chosen exercise at its TDL level. The exercise mode displays the name of the current patient, the exercise type he or she is performing, the target time for that exercise and the time the patient starts the exercise. The exercise is to cover a window area with a blind, in the form of paint. The TDL of the VR exercise presents the patients with four different rectangular windows that they need to cover with a red blind. As the patients move the cursor over the window using their legs, the window is being covered with the red blind; hence, the patients paint the window area with the mouse until the window is completely covered. The system informs the patients once the window is completely covered, and displays the target time to complete the chosen TDL, the patients' start time, stop time and time taken to cover the window. The user can reset the exercise for the patient or exit the system using the exit button. On exit, the system writes the patients exercise data in an output file, which the author exports to an external application for analysis. The task difficulty level is influenced by the fact that the windows are of different sizes and the 'paint brush' has varying sized tips. These pose challenges in terms of the time and effort required to cover the windows. For example, TDL 1 has a wider window size and a thicker paintb\rush, while TDL 4 has a smaller window size and a thinner paintbrush.

Fig. 6. The patient views this window in the virtual environment using the 3D i-glasses. (Akinladejo, 2005).

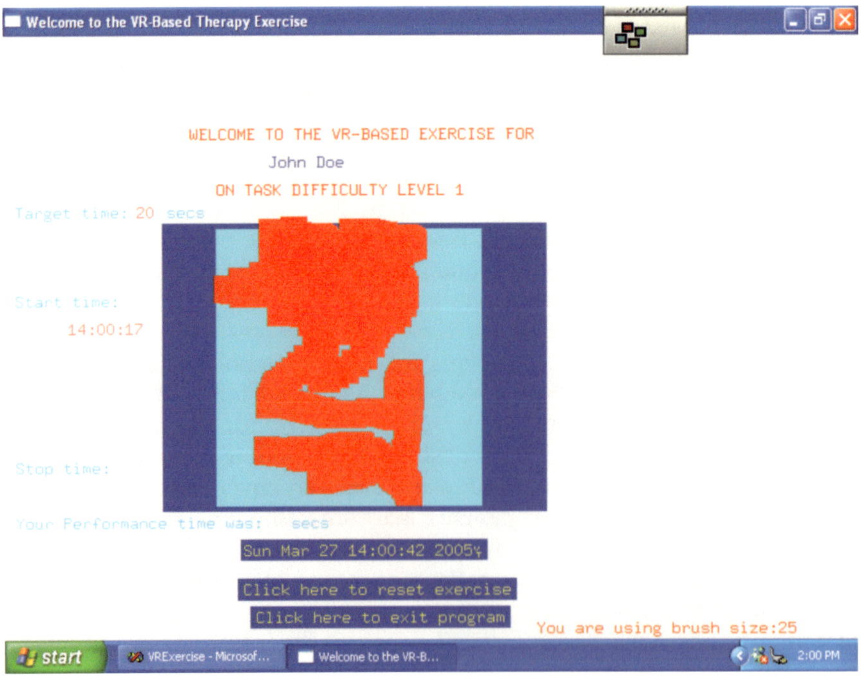

Fig. 7. A sample of an exercise being performed in the virtual environment by one patient. (Akinladejo, 2005)

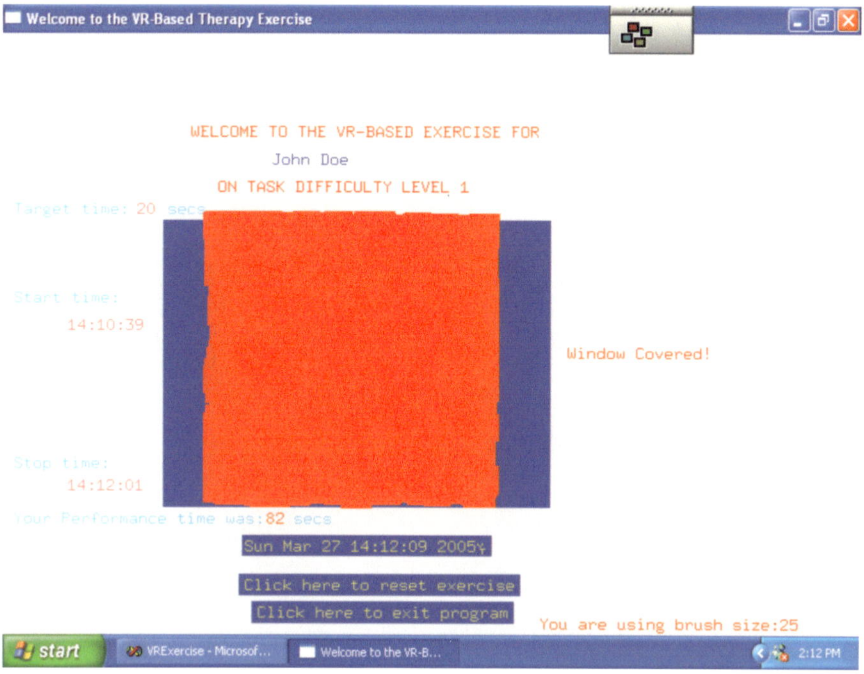

Fig. 8. A Completed Task of Difficulty level 1 by a Patient in the Virtual Environment. (Akinladejo, 2005).

Fig. 9. The Clinical Site. (Akinladejo, 2005).

Fig. 10. A Physical Therapist Guiding a Patient in the Virtual Environment. (Akinladejo, 2005)

Fig. 11. Another Patient in the Virtual Environment. (Akinladejo, 2005).

8. The research results

A number of analysis were carried out during the study and results obtained, details of which have been presented as in Akinladejo (2005). This chapter presents two results on two of the patients who used the virtual environment.

8.1 Performance results

For the exercise sessions in the virtual environment, the percentage of improvement in using the system was calculated based on the patients' performance data for the last day of week two and that of week four on the painting exercise. That is,

$$\frac{\text{LastDayData (Week2)} - \text{LastDayData (Week4)}}{\text{LastDayData (Week2)}} \times 100\ \%$$

The table below summarize the data.

Patient	Time taken on TDL 1 in secs	Time taken on TDL 2 in secs	Time taken on TDL 3 in secs	Time taken on TDL 4 in secs	Total time on exercise for the day in secs	Total time on exercise for the day in minutes
RB1	1007	594	545	885	3031	51
EO2	831	416	691	472	2410	40

Table 1. Last Day Data for Week Two

Patient	Time taken on TDL 1 in secs	Time taken on TDL 2 in secs	Time taken on TDL 3 in secs	Time taken on TDL 4 in secs	Total time on exercise for the day in secs	Total time on exercise for the day in minutes
RB1	365	302	161	449	1277	21
EO2	165	225	138	212	740	12

Table 2. Last Day Data for Week Four

The following are the percentage improvements for the patients on the VR task over the four-week period (note that improvement addresses the percentage reduction in time taken to complete the task in the virtual environment).

$$\text{RB1} = \frac{51 - 21\text{x } 100\%}{51} = 59\% \text{ improvement}$$

$$\text{EO2} = \frac{40\ -\ 12\text{x } 100\%}{40} = 70\% \text{ improvement}$$

All the patients could not complete the four different levels of the VR task during the first week of the exercise. However, at the end of the second week, their performances had improved, and they were all able to complete the tasks at all the levels. Results from the analysis of the exercise data of the last day of week two and the last day of week four as in table 1 and 2 show that patient EO2 made the most improvement on the VR task(i.e. spent less time completing the task), while patient LP3 made the least improvement. EO2 diligently studied the painting movement and acquired the method of the painting process during the implementation period, hence the result. LP3, however, struggled until the last week before he started improving on the painting process. This result is significant to their functional gains as explained subsequently.

8.2 The clinical results

The gait variables of the patients were captured using the Polhemus Electromagnetic Tracker System before and after the intervention using the virtual environment, and Kaltenborn's convention (Akinladejo, 2005) was used to interpret the results. The graphs below were obtained for the two of the patients.

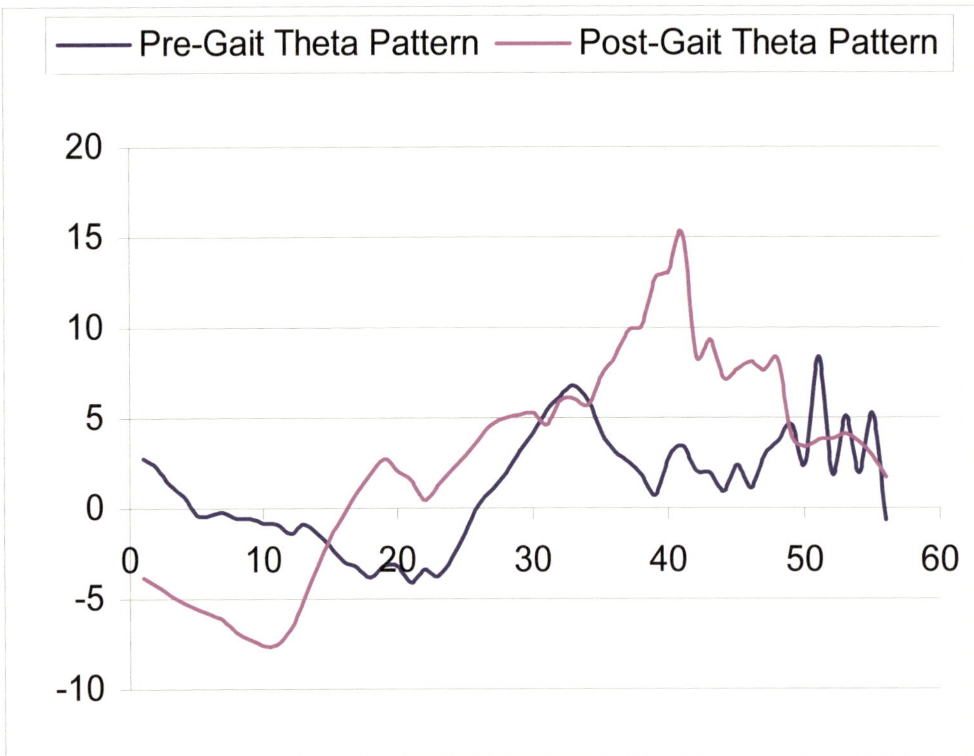

The pre- and post-intervention gait pattern for patient RB1

Fig. 12. Graph for Patient RB1. (Akinladejo, 2005).

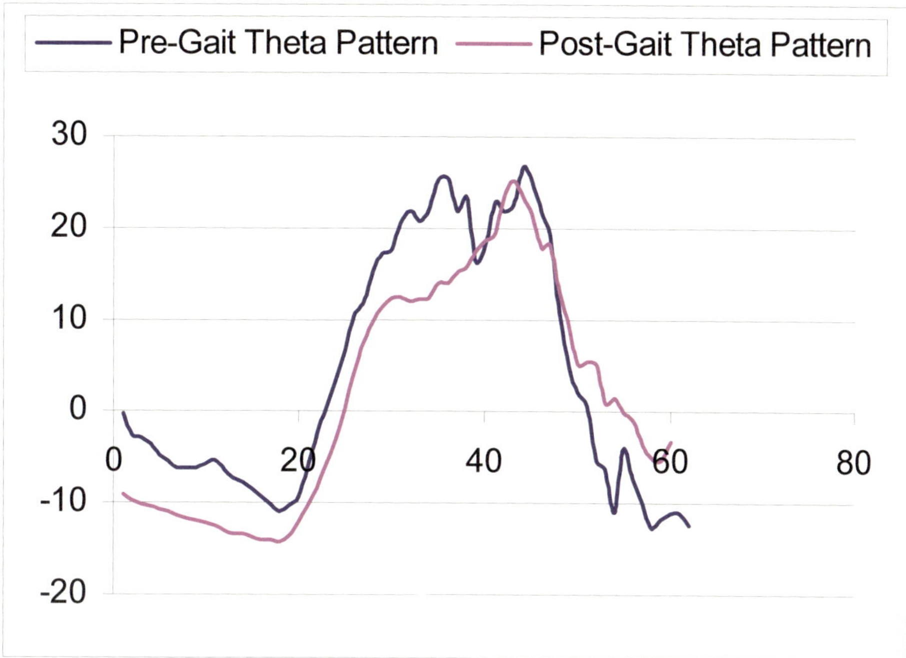

The pre- and post-intervention gait pattern for patient EO2

Fig. 13. Graph for Patient EO2. (Akinladejo, 2005).

9. Interpretation

Before the intervention program, using the Kaltenborn's convention, patient RB1's **Range of Motion (ROM) was 8-0-4 as against the normal values 15-0-20** (see Whittle, 2003 for normal ranges for gait parameters). **The ROM was improved to 15-0-8 after the intervention program.** This means that patient RB1 had reduced dorsiflexion and plantar flexion due to spasticity before the intervention program but his ankle joint gained more movements after the program.

Patient EO2's ROM was 27-0-10 before the intervention but changed to 25-0-14 (normal values are 15-0-20). This means that his excessive dorsiflexion 27 was reduced to 25, and he had increased plantar flexion. Excessive dorsiflexion has been linked with tibia tilt, which presents a challenge for normal walking, hence the improvement observed in his walking skill.

10. The transfer of skill result

The transfer-of-skill observational measurements were carried out by one of the three physical therapists that supervised the clinical trial. The patients were followed up one week after the intervention program to observe whether the skills learnt transferred to the real world. Patients EO2 and LP3 transferred similar skills to the natural environment. They initially had mass movement of the limbs due to sluggish brain activity/coordination. It was observed that these patients were able to move their ankle joints on the floor, without involving their hips. Synergy, according to the therapist, lost some of its control over the patients' motor acts during the clinical trial, and they were able to transfer these skills into the natural environment. Patient MR4, the third patient whose data was not presented here, had a smoother transition of her leg from the gas pedal to the brake during driving. This skill was similar to the movement of the leg during the painting exercise on the VR therapy. The therapy program induced increased brain activity; hence her increased reflex movement in the limb, as sensory activity from the brain was now more specific. She effectively transferred this skill to the real world condition. The transfer-of-skill analysis observed in this study supported the argument (Wilson, Foreman & Tlauka, 1996) that skills gained in virtual environments transfer to real-world conditions.

11. Conclusion

Results show that all the patients improved on their range of motion in the ankle joint due to the use of the virtual environment intervention program. These results buttressed the literature (Liepert et al., 2000; Merians et al., 2002; Taub, Uswatte & Pidikiti, 1999) that supported the usefulness of virtual reality technology in therapeutic rehabilitation. The transfer-of-skill analysis supported the argument that skills gained in virtual environments transfer to real-world conditions.

It is interesting that patient (EO2) with the highest improvement on the computer task was not the one with the highest improvement in the clinical measurement. Patient LP3, with the highest clinical gains had to struggle more than the other patients to complete the VR task. Patient EO2 was completing the exercise faster than LP3. This means that patient LP3 spent more time exercising his hemiplegic leg on the intervention program than the others who were completing the task faster than him, hence his high clinical improvements. This result suggests that the more difficult the virtual environment task is, the more beneficial it will be to therapeutic rehabilitation.

The results obtained from this research study have confirmed the usefulness of virtual environment technology in rehabilitation medicine, especially its efficacy in therapeutic intervention directed towards functional recovery or improvements of the lower extremities in post-acute stroke patients. It has also buttressed the argument that skills gained in the virtual environment transfer to real-world conditions. These results may be of particular benefit to professionals in the fields of physical therapy, physiology, sport physicians, and those involved in the study of human movement, who would want to train their clients to learn motor acts in a spatial environment for subsequent performance in the real world. The study has contributed to the current effort to provide wider access to therapeutic intervention technique using computer technology and should an asset to professionals in the field of physical therapy, physiology, bio-engineering, and all those involved in the study of human movement.

According to O'Sullivan (2001) the most pressing deficiency in rehabilitation feedback literature is the lack of controlled studies involving patients. She observed that most of the works so far have been based on normal subjects or small sample patients. Future research effort could be conducted that employ 'pure' statistical research methods using control and experimental groups with more research participants (like 40 patients) using the virtual environment. This design might likely appeal to the quantitative analysts.

Researchers are currently looking into the subject of what has been termed as Virtual Cocoon, a technology that aims to add the sense of smell into virtual environments. The quest continues.

12. Acknowledgement

The author acknowledge the support of the clinical community drawn for the study mainly from the Sir John Golding Rehabilitation Centre (Mona Rehab), Jamaica and the University Hospital of the West Indies (UHWI), Kingston, Jamaica

13. References

Akinladejo, F. O. (2005). Computer-Supported Rehabilitation Management: A Case Study of Using Virtual Reality Technology in Ambulatory Training for Post-Acute Stroke Patients. Ph.D. Dissertation, Graduate School of Computer and Information Sciences, Nova Southeastern University, Florida, USA.

Akinladejo, F. O. (2007). Computer-Based Physical Therapy: A Case Study on Four Post-Acute Stroke Patients. Proceedings of the IEEE SoutheastCon 2007, Richmond Virginia, pp. 370 - 377, ISBN 1-4244-1029-0

Boian et al. (2002). Virtual reality-based post-stroke hand rehabilitation. *Proceedings of Medicine Meets Virtual Reality*, Newport Beach, CA, 64-70.

Bolas, M. (1994). Human factor in the design of an immersive display. IEE Computer Graphics and Applications 14(1).

Cameirao MS et al. (2010) Journal of neuroengineering and rehabilitation http//www.nebi.nlm.nih.gov/pubmed20860808

Curtis, K.M. (1998). Virtual communications aids for the disabled. Research study and project of the Hebden Green School PSA. Rehabilitation Engineering Group, University of Nottingham.

Deutsch, J., Latonio, J., Burdea, G. & Boian, R. (2001). Rehabilitation of musculoskeletal injury using the Rugers ankle haptic interface: three case reports. In *Europhaptics 2001*, Birmingham, U.K.

Duncan, P.W. (1997). Synthesis of intervention trials to improve motor recovery following stroke. *Topics in Stroke Rehabilitation, 3*(4), 1-20.

Feys et al. (1998). Effect of a therapeutic intervention for the hemiplegic upper limb in the acute phase after stroke: a single blind, randomized, controlled multicenter trial. *Stroke, 29*, 785-792.

Fox, L.E. & Fried-Oken, M. (1996). AAC Aphasiology: Partnership for future research. *Augumentative and Alternative Communication, 12*(4), 257-271.

Garbi, J. (2002). Virtual Reality for aiding people with movement disorders. http://www.cs.technion.ac.il/~baram Accessed November 19, 2002.

Jack et al. (2001). Virtual reality-enhanced stroke rehabilitation. *IEEE Transactions on Neural Systems and Rehabilitation Engineering, 9*(3), 308-318.

Kaltenborn, F. M. (2002). *Manual Mobilization of the Joints. The Kaltenborn method of joint examination and treatment. The extremities.* (6th ed.). Olaf Norlis Bokhandel, Oslo, Norway.

Kaye, H.S. (2000). Disability and the digital divide. Disability Statistics Report, Department of Education, National Institute on Disability and Rehabilitation Research, Washington D. C.

Kozak et al. (1993). Transfer of training from virtual reality. *Ergonomics, 36*(7), 777-784.

Krebs, H.I., Hogan, N., Aisen, M.C. & Volpe, B.T. (1998). Robot-aided neurorehabilitation. *IEEE Transactions on Rehabilitation Engineering, 6*, 75-87.

Liang, R., Pan, Z., Cheok, A., Haller, M., Lau, R.W.H., Saito, H. (Eds.) 2006. Advances in artificial reality and tele-existence. Proceedings of the 16th International Conference on Artificial Reality and Tele-Existence, Hangzhou, China

Liepert et al. (2000). Treatment-induced cortical reorganization after stroke in humans. *Stroke, 31*, 1210-1216

Lin, M.C., Baxter, W. V., Scheib, V.E. & Wendt, J.D. (2004). Physically based virtual painting. *Communications of the ACM, 47*(8), 41-47

Merians et al. (2002). Virtual reality–augmented rehabilitation for patients following stroke. *Physical Therapy, 82*(9), 898-915

Molnar, M. (2002). Virtual reality device helps Parkinson's patients work better. http://www.globaltechnoscan.com/_vti_bin/shtml.dll/29thMay-4thJune02/virtual_reality.htm/map. Accessed November 19, 2002.

O'Sullivan, S. B. & Schmitz, T.J. (1994). Stroke. *Physical Rehabilitation: Assessment and Treatment.* (3rd ed.). F. A. Davis Company.

O'Sullivan, S. B. & Schmitz, T.J. (2001). Stroke. *Physical Rehabilitation: Assessment and Treatment.* (4th ed.). F. A. Davis Company.

Plant, T. (1996). A new dimension to weaving the web. *Ability, Journal of the British Computer Society Disability Group, 18*, 14-16.

Richards, L. & Pohl, P. (1999). Therapeutic interventions to improve upper extremity recovery and function. *Clinics in Geriatric Medicine, 15*(4), 819-832.

Smythe, P., Furner, S. & Mercinelli, M. (1995). Virtual reality technologies for people with special needs. In ROE P.R.W. (ed.). *Telecommunications for all, COST 219, (Office for Official Publications of the European Community)*, Luxembourg, 276-285.

Stern, J.M. (1995). Microsoft flight simulator handbook. Brandy Publishing. An Imprint of MacMillan Computer Publishing, Indianapolis, Indiana, 46290, ISBN 1-566-86-282-5

Snowdon, D.N., West, A.J. & Howard, T.L.J. (1993). Towards the next generation of Human Computer Interface. *Proceedings of Informatique: Interface to Real & Virtual Worlds*, Montpellier, 399-408.

Strickland, D., Hodges, L., North, M., & Weghorst, S. (1997). Overcoming phobias by virtual exposure. *Communications of the ACM, 40* (8), 34-39.

Szigeti, T., McMenamy, K., Saville, R. & Glowacki, A. (2009). CISCO telepresence fundermentals. (1st ed.). CISCO Press, ISBN-10: 1-58705-593-7

Taub E., Uswatte, G. & Pidikiti, R. (1999). Constraint-induced movement therapy – a new family of techniques with broad application to physical rehabilitation: a clinical review. *Journal of Rehabilitation, Research and Development, 36*, 237-251

The Virtual Environment Info Group (2008). Virtual Environment Information. Accessed October 4, 2011 Available from http://www.virtualenvironments.info

Vrs.org (2009). Semi-immersive Virtual Reality. Accessed October 6, 2011. Available from http://www.vrs.org.uk

Whittle, M.W. (2003). Normal ranges for gait parameters. *Gait analysis: an introduction.* (3rd ed.). Elsevier Science Limited.

Wikipedia (n.d). The free encyclopedia. accessed October 2011 Available from http://www.wikipedia.org

Wilson, P., Foreman, N. & Tlauka, M. (1996). Transfer of spatial information from virtual to a real environment in physically disabled children. *Disability Rehabilitation, 18*(12), 633-637.

2

A Survey of Some Virtual Reality Tools and Resources

Moses Okechukwu Onyesolu,
Ignatius Ezeani and Obikwelu Raphael Okonkwo
Nnamdi Azikiwe University, Awka, Anambra State
Nigeria

1. Introduction

Virtual Reality (VR) technology enables users to interact with three-dimensional data, providing a potentially powerful interface to both static and dynamic information (Ausburn & Ausburn, 2003; Ausburn & Ausburn, 2004; Baieier, 1993; Onyesolu, 2011; Onyesolu & Eze, 2011). VR has existed in various forms since its inception. It has been known by names such as synthetic environment, cyberspace, artificial reality, simulator technology and so on and so forth before VR was eventually adopted (Onyesolu, 2006; Onyesolu & Eze, 2011). Though VR has existed from the late 1960s, its latest manifestation, desktop screen-based semi-immersive type which made its first appearance in entertainment industry, has made it come within the realm of possibility for general creation and use. As a result of proliferation of desktop VR, the technology has continued to develop applications that are less than fully immersive. These non-immersive VR applications are far less expensive and technically daunting and have made inroads into industry training and development.

There have been a lot of advances in VR and VR is being applied in all areas of human endeavor (Onyesolu, 2009a; Onyesolu, 2009b; Onyesolu & Eze, 2011; Onyesolu, 2006). Many VR applications have been developed for manufacturing, training in a variety of areas (military, medical, equipment operation, etc.), education, simulation, design evaluation, architectural walk-through, ergonomic studies, simulation of assembly sequences and maintenance tasks, assistance for the handicapped, study and treatment of phobias, entertainment, rapid prototyping and much more (Onyesolu & Akpado, 2009). VR has had impact in heritage and archeology, mass-media, fiction books, television, motion pictures, music videos, games, fine art, marketing, health care, real estate etc. Today, VR is being used as powerful tool in education to simulate learning environments. Such VR environments have been very valuable instructional and practice alternative (Onyesolu & Eze, 2011).

The question is what are the available tools and resources needed for building VR systems be it non-immersive VR systems, semi-immersive VR systems or immersive VR systems. There are a lot of companies that offer services in the field of VR and related areas. While some companies specialize in VR hardware, some specialize in VR software, be it 3D tools, 2D tools, or VR simulation tools. Some of these companies and software tools are provided in section 3 and section 5.

2. Virtual reality technology

VR technology enables users to immerse themselves in an artificial environment simulated by a computer, with the ability to navigate through the environment and interact with objects in it. Two keywords in the field of VR are presence and immersion. VR immerses the user in a simulation so that the user has a sense of being present in the virtual environment. The degree of immersion depends primarily on the computer hardware used whereas presence is achieved if the virtual environment causes the user to suspend disbelief and accept the computer-generated experience as real.

A computer system that generates an artificial world that tricks the user into feeling part of it would not be a complete definition of VR because it lacks the vital component of interactivity (Louka & Balducelli, 2001). VR is a highly interactive, computer-based multimedia environment in which the user becomes the participant in a computer-generated world (Kim et al., 2000; Onyesolu, 2009a; Onyesolu & Akpado, 2009). It is the simulation of a real or imagined environment that can be experienced visually in the three dimensions of width, height, and depth and that may additionally provide an interactive experience visually in full real-time motion with sound and possibly with tactile and other forms of feedback. VR is a way for humans to visualize, manipulate and interact with computers and extremely complex data (Isdale, 1998). It is an artificial environment created with computer hardware and software and presented to the user in such a way that it appears and feels like a real environment (Baieier, 1993). VR is a computer-synthesized, three-dimensional environment in which a plurality of human participants, appropriately interfaced, may engage and manipulate simulated physical elements in the environment and, in some forms, may engage and interact with representations of other humans, past, present or fictional, or with invented creatures. It is a computer-based technology for simulating visual auditory and other sensory aspects of complex environments (Onyesolu, 2009b). VR incorporates 3D technologies that give a real-life illusion. VR creates a simulation of real-life situation (Haag et al., 1998). VR is a three-dimensional user interface in which the user can perform actions and experience their consequences. It is a multidimensional real-time simulation rather than a linear animation with predefined camera movement.

This is what distinguishes VR from recorded, computer generated, images used in films and on television and from real-time computer animation where the user is a passive viewer (Louka & Balducelli, 2001). Unlike pre-rendered images of a 3D environment, the user of a VR system can usually move around freely in a virtual environment. The manner in which a user interacts with a virtual environment depends on the hardware and software used (Louka & Balducelli, 2001). In most cases, an off-the-shelf desktop computer with a 3D graphics acceleration and appropriate software are all that is necessary. This form of VR is often called desktop or fishtank VR (Louka & Balducelli, 2001, Onyeslu & Eze, 2011). In a desktop VR configuration, a 2D pointing device such as a mouse is typically used to select and manipulate objects, choose menu option, etc. Desktop VR is an effective, relatively cheap, option. The desktop VR experience can be taken a step further by using a projector and a large screen to display the virtual environment so that several users can work together in a meeting room or control centre, with one user controlling the computer. The 2D pointing device can also be replaced by a 3D input-device, which may improve usability.

Some 3D graphics cards and software support stereoscopic display, enabling users to view the virtual environment with an enhanced sense of depth using either a desktop display or a suitable projector. Stereoscopic displays typically require that users wear special glasses.

Some users find that stereoscopic viewing enhances their spatial understanding, however such display systems should only be used for brief viewing sessions (e.g. up to half an hour) to avoid simulator sickness (Louka & Balducelli, 2001).

For a greater sense of immersion, multi-screen projection systems or head-mounted displays can be used to place the viewer inside the model. While the hardware required to do this efficiently, with motion tracking and 3D input devices such as gloves, is relatively costly, immersive VR is particularly useful if a realistic view of a virtual environment is required. The user experiences the environment within the model as opposed to looking into it from the outside. VR systems based on immersive technology are relatively expensive, but can be justified when the benefits outweigh the cost (Louka & Balducelli, 2001).

In order to create usable virtual reality systems at a reasonable cost and with an appropriate level of performance, the application designer's understanding of the advantages and limitations of combinations of VR hardware and software is crucial (Louka & Balducelli, 2001).

3. Some VR technology resource companies

Some of the companies offering services in the field of VR and related areas are provided below (http://vresources.org/company_link_list).

3.1 3D Ace Studio

3D Ace Studio is a subsidiary of Program Ace LLC. 3D Ace studio delivers high quality graphics and programming services for high-end games, movies, etc. 3D Ace Studio's area of expertise includes creation of 2D concept art and design, GUI design, high-poly models for movies and games, 3D environments, low-poly and budget models, characters and creatures, animated next gen 3D movies, 3D SFX for feature and TV films, in-game cut scenes and intro reels, custom entire game development, CG, AI, tools and network programming (http://www.3dace.com).

3.2 3D Web (3DW) technologies

3DW technologies (3DW) provide a range of services based on interactive 3D computer graphics. 3DW Virtual Reality (VR) and Multimedia solutions provide innovative, dynamic and engaging solutions that improve communication and increase understanding. 3DW have spent so many years providing software and developing solutions in the fields of energy, regeneration and sport. 3DW technologies apply innovative, interactive graphics and software solutions to engage, communicate and entertain (http://www.3dwebtech.co.uk).

3.3 Virtual Heroes Inc. (VHI)

This is an "Advanced Learning Technology Company" that creates collaborative interactive learning solutions for Federal Systems, Healthcare and Corporate Training markets (http://www.virtualheroes.com/about.asp). VHI applications facilitate highly interactive, self-paced learning and instructor-led, distributed team training on its Advanced Learning Technology (ALT) platform. Major components of this platform include the Unreal® Engine 3 by Epic Games, and Dynamic Virtual Human Technology (DVHT). ALT leverages simulation learning and digital game-based learning paradigms to accelerate learning, increase proficiency and reduce costs. DVHT combines best-in-class electronic computer game technology with a digital human physiology engine, digital pharmacokinetic drug models, accurate biomechanical parameters and artificial intelligence subroutines for the most realistic virtual humans available anywhere.

3.4 5DT (Fifth Dimension Technologies)

5DT is a high technology company specializing in Virtual Reality (VR). 5DT develops, produces and distributes VR hardware, software and systems. 5DT's main focus is VR Training Simulators and VR Peripherals. 5DT products include VR hardware, Animation Software, Systems and Application Software (http://www.5dt.com).

3.5 Adacel Technologies Limited

Adacel Technologies Limited is a leading developer of advanced simulation and software applications and services for market segments such as aviation, defence, telecommunications, corporate and government (http://www.adacel.com).

3.6 CAE Electronic

CAE Electronic is a world leader in commercial flight simulation. CAE Electronic provides a wide range of flight simulation platforms for many commercial aircraft models (http://www.cae.ca/).

3.7 CMLabs Simulations, Inc.

CMLabs' Vortex team provides physics-based behaviour modeling solutions and services to companies and institutions throughout the real-time visual-simulation world. With a long history in the visual-simulation and gaming industries, the Vortex team produces feature-rich simulation tools that set the industry standard for interactive 3D dynamics and simulating mechanical equipment behaviour. Vortex expertise and technology put high-fidelity behaviour in motion in applications for training simulators, mission rehearsal, serious games, virtual prototyping and testing. Vortex customers include Honda, John Deere, L-3, Lockheed Martin, NASA, Carnegie Mellon University, and over 100 other leading companies and academic institutions (http://www.vxsim.com)

3.8 Digimation Defense

Digimation has developed the largest library of military and associated 3D models for use in simulations and training. Digimation currently has more than 1,500 models in industry standard OpenFlight format and more than 30,000 3D models in a wide range of 3D formats which can be used in anything from realtime applications to high-end product demonstrations. Some of Digimation military models at work in movies are seen in Black Hawk Down, The Rock, Independence Day, Lord of War and Air Force One among others (http://defense.digimation.com/).

3.9 EdgedSign Inc.

EdgedSign was founded in 2008 to provide professional 3D modeling services for the simulation, training and entertainment markets. Since its inception, EdgedSign unites the best human resources to provide highest quality of visual content. The leaders of the simulation industry trust EdgedSign to make their graphics (http://www.edgedsign.com)

3.10 On-Line Interactive Virtual Environment (OLIVE)

This is a product of Forterra Systems Inc. Forterra Systems Inc. builds distributed virtual world technology and turnkey applications for defense, homeland security, medical, corporate training, and entertainment industries (http://company.mmosite.com/forterra/index.shtml). Using the On-Line Interactive Virtual Environment (OLIVE) technology platform, customers can rapidly generate realistic three-dimensional virtual environments that easily scale from single user applications to large scale simulated environments supporting many thousands of concurrent users. Forterra's technology and services enable organizations to train, plan, rehearse, and collaborate in ways previously considered impossible or impractical.

OLIVE combines multimedia, scalable computing and network enabled connectivity to provide a complete IT-ready platform for developing and supporting truly collaborative, multiplayer interactive virtual environments. It is a 3D client-server virtual world platform using PC clients connected to a central server via a network. The architecture scales from a Windows based development environment to large scale Linux clusters. This architecture supports many thousands of concurrent, geographically distributed users (http://www.webbuyersguide.com/product/brief.aspx?src=rss&kc=rss&id=52841)

3.11 Icarus Studios Inc.

The company offers tools and products for creating massively multi-player online (MMO) environments, virtual worlds, and serious games for major entertainment, corporate, and government clients (Mousa, n.d). Icarus provides next generation technology, tools and production services enabling publishers and marketers to develop immersive environments to create new revenue streams and branding opportunities (http://www.icarusstudios.com/). Icarus Studios products include compatibility with industry standard tools such as 3D Max, Collada, and other 3D applications with simple editors.

4. The history of hardware components for VR application development

Hardware components for VR have evolved since the inception of VR. Hardware components for VR application development are computer workstation, sensory displays, process acceleration cards, tracking system and input devices. Other specialized types of hardware that have been developed or used for VR applications are navigation devices, interaction devices and tactile and force feedback among others (Isdale, 1998; Perry, Smith, & Yang, 2004).

4.1 Computer workstation

Computer workstation is used to control several sensory display devices to immerse you in 3D virtual environment (Onyesolu & Eze, 2011). A computer workstation is a microcomputer designed for technical or scientific applications. Intended primarily to be used by one person at a time, they are commonly connected to a local area network and run multi-user operating systems. The term workstation has also been used to refer to a mainframe computer terminal or a personal computer (PC) connected to a network. Workstations had offered higher performance than personal computers, especially with respect to CPU and graphics, memory capacity and multitasking capability. They are optimized for the visualization and manipulation of different types of complex data such as 3D mechanical design, engineering simulation animation and rendering of images, and mathematical plots. Workstations are the first segment of the computer market to present advanced accessories and collaboration tools. Presently, the workstation market is highly commoditized and is dominated by large PC vendors, such as Dell and HP, selling Microsoft Windows/Linux running on Intel Xeon/AMD Opteron. Alternative UNIX based platforms are provided by Apple Inc., Sun Microsystems, and Silicon Graphics International (SGI) (http://en.wikipedia.org/wiki/Workstation).

4.2 Sensory displays

Sensory displays are used to display the simulated virtual worlds to the user. The most common sensory displays are the computer visual display unit, the head-mounted display (HMD) for 3D visual and headphones for 3D audio.

4.2.1 Head mounted displays

Head mounted displays place a screen in front of each of the viewer's eyes at all times. The view, the segment of the virtual environment generated and displayed, is controlled by orientation sensors mounted on the "helmet". Head movement is recognized by the computer, and a new perspective of the scene is generated. In most cases, a set of optical lens and mirrors are used to enlarge the view to fill the field of view and to direct the scene to the eyes (Lane, 1993). Four types of Head Mounted Displays (HMDs) are: (a) Liquid Crystal Display (LCD) head mounted display; (b) Projected head mounted display; (c) Small CRT head mounted display; and (d) Single Column LED head mounted display.

LCD head mounted display uses LCD technology to display a scene. When a liquid crystal pixel is activated, it blocks the passage of light through it. Thousands of these pixels are arranged in a two dimensional matrix for each display. Since liquid crystals block the passage of light, to display a scene a light must be shone from behind the LCD matrix toward the eye to provide brightness for the scene (Aukstakalnis & Blatner, 1992). LCD head mounted display is lighter than most HMDs. As with most HMDs, it does provide an immersive effect, but the resolution and the contrast are low. The problem associated with low resolution is inability to identify objects and inability to locate the exact position of objects. Since the crystals are polarized to control the color of a pixel, the actual polarizing of the crystal creates a small delay while forming the image on the screen. Such a delay may cause the viewer to misjudge the position of objects (Bolas, 1994).

Projected head mounted display uses fiber optic cables to transmit a scene to the screen. The screen is similar to a cathode ray tube (CRT) except the phosphor is illuminated by the light transmitted through fiber optic cables. Ideally, each fiber would control one pixel. But due to the limitation in cost and manufacturing, each fiber controls a honeycomb section of pixels (Lane, 1993). Projected head mounted display provides better resolution and contrast than LCD displays. This HMD is also light weight. Higher resolution and contrast means that the viewer is able to see an image with greater detail. The downside of this type of HMD is that it is expensive and difficult to manufacture (Bolas, 1994).

Fig. 1. Visette 45 SXGA head mounted display (HMD)

Small CRT head mounted display uses two CRTs that are positioned on the side of the HMD. Mirrors are used to direct the scene to the viewers' eye. Unlike the projected HMD where the phosphor is illuminated by fiber optic cables, here the phosphor is illuminated by an electron gun as usual (Lane, 1993). CRT head mounted display is in many ways similar to the projected HMD. This type of HMD is heavier than most other types because of added electronic components (which also generate large amounts of heat). The user wearing this type of HMD may feel discomfort due to the heat and the weight of the HMD (Bolas, 1994).

Single Column LED head mounted display uses one column of 280 LEDs. A mirror rapidly oscillates opposite from the LEDs, reflecting the image to the user's eye. The LEDs are updated 720 times per oscillation of the mirror. As the LED column updates for each column of the virtual screen, the mirror redirects the light to the viewers' eye, one column at a time, to form the image of the entire virtual screen (Aukstakalnis & Blatner, 1992). Single Column LED HMDs allow the user to interact with a virtual world and the real world simultaneously. This type of display can be used to create a virtual screen that seems to float in the real world.

One of the common problems of HMDs is that the cable connecting the HMD and a computer restricts the mobility of the user. The user can only move as far as the cable allows. If the cable is not properly managed, the user could trip over it or become entangled in it. In addition, switching frequently between a virtual world and the real world is tedious and tiresome.

4.2.2 Binocular Omni-Orientation Monitor (BOOM)

The BOOM is mounted on a jointed mechanical arm with tracking sensors located at the joints. A counterbalance is used to stabilize the monitor, so that when the user releases the monitor, it remains in place. To view the virtual environment, the user must take hold of the monitor and put her face up to it. The computer will generate an appropriate scene based on the position and orientation of the joints on the mechanical arm (Aukstakalnis & Blatner, 1992).

Some of the problems associated with HMDs can be solved by using a BOOM display. The user does not have to wear a BOOM display as in the case of an HMD. This means that crossing the boundary between a virtual world and the real world is simply a matter of moving your eyes away from the BOOM.

Fig. 2. A binocular omni-orientation monitor (BOOM)

4.2.3 Visual Display Unit (VDU) or monitors

There are two types of computer visual display unit. The CRT monitors and the LCD monitors. The distinguishing characteristics of the two types are beyond the scope of this piece.

4.3 Process acceleration cards

Process acceleration card is an expansion card whose function is to generate output images to a display. Most video cards offer added functions, such as accelerated rendering of 3D scenes and 2D graphics, video capture, TV-tuner adapter, MPEG-2/MPEG-4 decoding, FireWire, light pen, TV output, or the ability to connect multiple monitors (multi-monitor). These cards help to update the display with new sensory information. Examples are 3D graphic cards and 3D sound cards. Other modern high performance video cards are used for more graphically demanding purposes, such as PC games (http://en.wikipedia.org/wiki/Video_card). Examples are 3D Nvidia Video Card and 3D ATI Video Card

4.4 Tracking system

This system tracks the position and orientation of a user in the virtual environment. The purpose of a tracking device is to determine the x, y, and z position, and the orientation (yaw, pitch, and roll) of some part of the user's body in reference to a fixed point. Most types of virtual reality interaction devices have a tracker on them. HMDs need a tracker so that the view can be updated for the current orientation of the user's head. Datagloves and flying joysticks usually have trackers so that the virtual "hand" icon will follow the position and orientation changes of the user's real hand. Full body datasuits will have several trackers on them so that virtual feet, waist, hands, and head are all slaved to the human user. This system is divided into: mechanical, electromagnetic, ultrasonic, infrared and inertial trackers.

Fig. 3. Patriot wireless electromagnetic tracker

Fig. 4. A.R.T. optical tracking system

A mechanical tracker is similar to a robot arm and consists of a jointed structure with rigid links, a supporting base, and an "active end" which is attached to the body part being tracked (Sowizral, 1995) often the hand. This type of tracker is fast, accurate, and is not susceptible to jitter. However, it also tends to encumber the movement of the user, has a restricted area of operation, and the technical problem of tracking the head and two hands at the same time is still difficult.

An electromagnetic tracker (EMT) allows several body parts to be tracked simultaneously and will function correctly if objects come between the source and the detector. In this type of tracker, the source produces three electromagnetic fields each of which is perpendicular to the others. The detector on the user's body then measures field attenuation (the strength and direction of the electromagnetic field) and sends this information back to a computer. The computer triangulates the distance and orientation of the three perpendicular axes in the detector relative to the three electromagnetic fields produced by the source (Baratoff & Blanksteen, 1993). Electromagnetic trackers are popular, but they are inaccurate. They suffer from latency problems, distortion of data, and they can be thrown off by large amounts of metal in the surrounding work area or by other electromagnetic fields, such as those from other pieces of large computer equipment. In addition, the detector must be within a restricted range from the source or it will not be able to send back accurate information (Sowizral, 1995), so the user has a limited working volume.

Ultrasonic tracking devices consist of three high frequency sound wave emitters in a rigid formation that form the source for three receivers that are also in a rigid arrangement on the user. There are two ways to calculate position and orientation using acoustic trackers. The first is called "phase coherence". Position and orientation is detected by computing the difference in the phases of the sound waves that reach the receivers from the emitters as compared to sound waves produced by the receiver. The second method is "time-of-flight", which measures the time for sound, emitted by the transmitters at known moments, to reach the sensors. Only one transmitter is needed to calculate position, but the calculation of orientation requires finding the differences between three sensors (Baratoff & Blanksteen, 1993). Unlike electromagnetic trackers that are affected by large amounts of metal, ultrasonic trackers do not suffer from this problem. However, ultrasonic trackers also have a restricted workspace volume and, worse, must have a direct line-of-sight from the emitter to the detector. Time-of-flight trackers usually have a low update rate, and phase-coherence trackers are subject to error accumulation over time (Baratoff & Blanksteen, 1993). Additionally, both types are affected by temperature and pressure changes (Sowizral, 1995), and the humidity level of the work environment (Baratoff & Blanksteen, 1993).

Infrared (optical) trackers utilize several emitters fixed in a rigid arrangement while cameras or "quad cells" receive the IR light. To fix the position of the tracker, a computer must triangulate a position based on the data from the cameras. This type of tracker is not affected by large amounts of metal, has a high update rate, and low latency (Baratoff & Blanksteen, 1993). However, the emitters must be directly in the line-of-sight of the cameras or quad cells. In addition, any other sources of infrared light, high-intensity light, or other glare will affect the correctness of the measurement (Sowizral, 1995).

Inertial trackers apply the principle of conservation of angular momentum (Baratoff & Blanksteen, 1993). Inertial trackers allow the user to move about in a comparatively large working space where there is no hardware or cabling between a computer and the tracker. Miniature gyroscopes can be attached to HMDs, but they tend to drift (up to 10 degrees per minute) and to be sensitive to vibration. Yaw, pitch, and roll are calculated by measuring the resistance of the gyroscope to a change in orientation. If tracking of position is desired, an additional type of tracker must be used (Baratoff & Blanksteen, 1993). Accelerometers are another option, but they also drift and their output is distorted by the gravity field (Sowizral, 1995).

4.5 Input (interaction) devices

They are used to interact with the virtual environment and objects within the virtual environment. Examples are joystick (wand), instrumented glove, keyboard, voice recognition etc.

For interaction with small objects in a virtual world, the user can use one of several gloves designed to give feedback on the characteristics of the object. This can be done with pneumatic pistons, which are mounted on the palm of the glove, as in the Rutgers Master II (Gomez, Burdea, & Langrana, 1995). Gloves are used for sensing the flexion of the fingers.

Dataglove is a neoprene fabric glove with two fiber optic loops on each finger. Each loop is dedicated to one knuckle and this can be a problem. If a user has extra large or small hands, the loops will not correspond very well to the actual knuckle position and the user will not be able to produce very accurate gestures. At one end of each loop is an LED and at the other end is a photosensor. The fiber optic cable has small cuts along its length. When the user bends a finger, light escapes from the fiber optic cable through these cuts. The amount of light reaching the photosensor is measured and converted into a measure of how much the finger is bent (Aukstakalnis & Blatner, 1992). Dataglove requires recalibration for each user (Hsu, 1993). Fatigue effects and recalibration during a session are problems associated with long term use of Dataglove (Wilson & Conway, 1991).

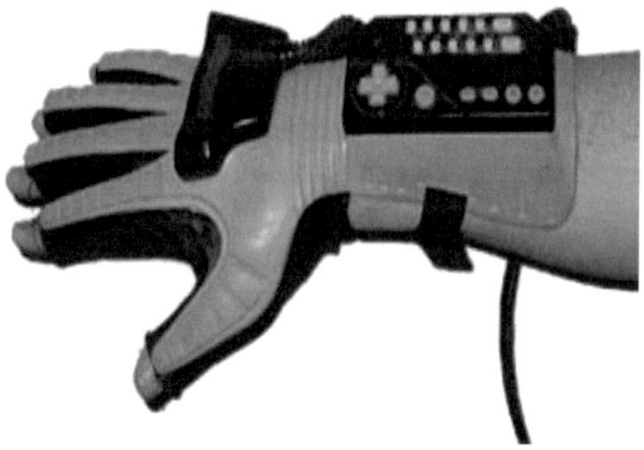

Fig. 5. An instrumented glove (Nintendo power glove)

Powerglove uses strain gauges to measure the flexion of each finger. A small strip of mylar plastic is coated with an electrically conductive ink and placed along the length of each finger. When the fingers are kept straight, a small electrical current passing through the ink remains stable. When a finger is bent, the computer can measure the change in the ink's electrical resistance (Aukstakalnis & Blatner, 1992). Powerglove is less accurate than the Dataglove, and also needs recalibration for each user, but is more rugged than the Dataglove.

The dexterous hand master (DHM) is not exactly a glove but an exoskeleton that attaches to the fingers with velcro straps. A mechanical sensor measures the flexion of the finger. Unlike the Dataglove and Powerglove, the DHM is able to detect and measure the side-to-side movement of a finger. The other gloves only measure finger flexion. The DHM is more accurate than either of the gloves and less sensitive to the user's hand size, but can be awkward to work with (Hsu, 1993).

The main strength of the various types of gloves is that they provide a more intuitive interaction device than a mouse or a joystick. This is because the gloves allow the computer to read and represent hand gestures. Objects in the environment can therefore be "grasped" and manipulated, the user can point in the direction of desired movement, windows can be dismissed, etc (Wilson & Conway, 1991). Wilson and Conway (1991) opined that more work is needed to expand glove's set of command gestures beyond the current simple mapping. Another area of improvement is feedback for the user to aid hand-eye coordination and proprioceptive feedback to let a user know when an object has been successfully grasped (Wilson & Conway, 1991).

The final category of interaction device is the wand or floating joystick. Basically, this device works exactly the same as a conventional joystick, but it is not attached to a base that sits on a tabletop. Instead, the joystick is equipped with an orientation tracker so the user simply holds it in their hand and tilts it. Most flying joysticks also have some buttons on the stick for "clicking" or selecting, similar to a mouse (Hsu, 1993).

4.6 Cave Automatic Virtual Environment

Cave Automatic Virtual Environment (CAVE) is an immersive virtual reality environment where projectors are directed to three, four, five or six of the walls of a room-sized cube (Fisher, 2003; http://en.wikipedia.org/wiki/Cave_Automatic_Virtual_Environment).

4.6.1 General characteristics of the cave

The CAVE is a large theatre that sits in a larger room measured of a varied size. The walls of the CAVE are made up of rear-projection screens, and the floor is made of a down-projection screen. High-resolution projectors display images on each of the screens by projecting the images onto mirrors which reflect the images onto the projection screens. The user will go inside of the CAVE wearing special glasses to allow for the 3D graphics that are generated by the CAVE to be seen. With these glasses, people using the CAVE can actually see objects floating in the air, and can walk around them, getting a proper view of what the object would look like when they walk around it. This is made possible with electromagnetic sensors. The frame of the CAVE is made out of non-magnetic stainless steel in order to interfere as little as possible with the electromagnetic sensors. When a person walks around in the CAVE, the person's movements are tracked with these sensors and the video adjusts accordingly. Computers control this aspect of the CAVE as well as the audio aspects. There are multiple speakers placed from multiple angles in the CAVE that give the user 3D audio (http://en.wikipedia.org/wiki/Cave_Automatic_Virtual_Environment).

4.6.2 The first CAVE

The first CAVE was developed in the Electronic Visualization Laboratory at the University of Illinois at Chicago. This was announced and demonstrated at the 1992 SIGGRAPH (Fisher, 2003). The CAVE was developed in response to a challenge from the SIGGRAPH 92 Showcase effort for scientists to create and show off a one-to-many visualization tool that utilized large projection screens. The CAVE answered that challenge, and became the third major physical form of immersive VR (after goggles 'n' gloves and vehicle simulators). Carolina Cruz-Neira, Thomas A. DeFanti and Daniel J. Sandin are credited with its invention. It has been used and developed in cooperation with the National Centre for Supercomputing Applications (NCSA), to conduct research in various virtual reality and scientific visualization fields. CAVE is a registered trademark of the University of Illinois Board of Regents (http://en.wikipedia.org/wiki/Cave_Automatic_Virtual_Environment).

4.6.3 How the CAVE works

A lifelike visual display is created by projectors positioned outside the CAVE and controlled by physical movements from a user inside the CAVE. Stereoscopic LCD shutter glasses convey a 3D image. The computers rapidly generate a pair of images, one for each of the user's eyes. The glasses are synchronized with the projectors so that each eye only sees the correct image. Since the projectors are positioned outside of the cube, mirrors often reduce the distance required from the projectors to the screens. One or more computers, often SGI workstations, drive the projectors. Clusters of desktop PCs are popular to run CAVEs, because they cost less and run faster (http://en.wikipedia.org/wiki/Cave_Automatic_Virtual_Environment).

4.6.4 Developments in CAVE research

The biggest issue that researchers are faced with when it comes to the CAVE is size and cost. Researchers have realized this and have come up with a derivative of the CAVE system, called ImmersaDesk. With the ImmersaDesk, the user looks at one projection screen instead of being completely blocked out from the outside world, as is the case with the original CAVE. The idea behind the ImmersaDesk is that it is a single screen placed on a 45-degree angle so that the person using the machine has the opportunity to look forward and downward. The screen is 4′ X 5′, so it is wide enough to give the user the width that they need to obtain the proper 3D experience. The 3D images come out by using the same glasses as were used in the CAVE. This system uses sonic hand tracking and head tracking, so the system still uses a computer to process the users' movements (http://en.wikipedia.org/wiki/Cave_Automatic_Virtual_Environment).

This system is much more affordable and practical than the original CAVE system for some obvious reasons. First, one does not need to create a "room inside of a room". That is to say that one does not need to place the ImmersaDesk inside of a pitch-black room that is large enough to accommodate it. One projector is needed instead of four and only one projection screen. One does not need a computer as expensive or with the same capabilities that are necessary with the original CAVE. Another thing that makes the ImmersaDesk attractive is the fact that since it was derived from the original CAVE, it is compatible with all of the CAVE's software packages and also with all of the CAVE's libraries and interfaces (http://en.wikipedia.org/wiki/Cave_Automatic_Virtual_Environment).

4.6.5 Applications of CAVE

The concept of the original CAVE has been reapplied and is currently being used in a variety of fields. Many universities own CAVE systems. CAVEs are used for many things. Many engineering companies use CAVEs to enhance product development. Prototypes of parts can be created and tested, interfaces can be developed, and factory layouts can be simulated, all before spending any money on physical parts. This gives engineers a better idea of how a part will behave in the entire product (http://en.wikipedia.org/wiki/Cave_Automatic_Virtual_Environment).

5. Software tools for VR application development

As interest in Virtual Reality technology has increased, so has the number of tools available to the developers of virtual worlds. Some of these are libraries and toolkits, while others are application frameworks, and still others are full development environments, integrating every aspect of the creation of a VR application - modeling, coding, and execution - into a single package (Bierbaum & Just, 1998). The software components are divided into 3D modeling software, 2D graphics software, digital sound editing software and VR simulation software.

5.1 3D modeling software

3D modeling software refers to programs used to create 3D computer-generated imagery (http://en.wikipedia.org/wiki/3D_computer_graphics_software). 3D modeling software is used in constructing the geometry of the objects in a virtual world and specifies the visual properties of these objects. Some 3D modeling tools are presented below.

5.1.1 Autodesk 3d Max (3D Studio MAX)

Autodesk 3d Max was originally called 3D Studio MAX. It is a modeling, animation and rendering package developed by Autodesk Media and entertainment. It is a comprehensive and versatile 3D application used in film, television, video games and architecture for Windows and Apple Macintosh. It can be extended and customized through its SDK or scripting using a Maxscript. 3d Max is the third most widely-used off the shelf 3D animation program by content creation professionals. It is also used for movie effects and movie pre-visualization.

5.1.2 AC3D

This is a 3D modeling application that began in the 90's on the Amiga platform. AC3D is an easy-to-use, powerful and affordable 3D modeling package. It is perfectly suited to creating in-game objects and characters. It is used in a number of industries. AC3D does not feature its own renderer. It supports many output/input formats including Renderman RIB, Povray, Milkshape, Lightwave LWO, Collada, Alias triangle and Wavefront OBJ among others (http://www.thegamecreators.com/?m=view_products&id=2092).

5.1.3 Acron 3D Modeller

The Acron 3D Modeller application is a powerful integrated 3D modeling tool for real time graphics. This application has been specifically engineered for the Modelling, Simulation and Gaming (MS&G) industry with support for industry standard 3D formats and modelling formats used in the entertainment industry such as Microsoft Flight Simulator ™. With Acron 3D Modeller, it is easier than ever to share models across synthetic environments, or create new models from the tens of thousands of freeware and shareware models available on the internet. It's easy to learn environment enables artists and modellers to quickly produce stunning quality models and environments in less time (http://www.acroneng.com/3D%20Modeller.htm)

5.1.4 Alibre Design

This is another 3D design software. Alibre Design is a parametric 3D CAD suite that provides 3D model creation and documentation capabilities for a variety of downstream applications such as CAM, Rendering or 3D Printing. The software consists of several integrated modules that allow the creation of parts, unfoldable sheet metal parts, assemblies, and 2D drawings, photo realistic rendering and CAM (http://www.alibre.com).

5.1.5 Cinema 4D

This is a light (Prime) to full featured (Studio) 3D package by MAXON Computer GmbH. Cinema 4D is used for creating advanced 3D graphics quickly and easily. Although used in film usually for 2.5D work, Cinema's largest user base is in the television motion graphics and design/visualisation arenas. Originally developed for the Amiga, it is also available for Mac OS X and Windows (http://www.maxon.net/products/cinema-4d-studio/who-should-use-it.html).

5.1.6 GL Studio

GL Studio creates interactive 3D graphics, instrumentation and user interfaces for training, simulation, and virtual prototyping. It generates portable C++ and OpenGL source code that can run standalone or be easily integrated into existing programs (http://www.simulation.com/products/glstudio/glstudio.html).

5.1.7 Cobalt

Cobalt is a parametric-based computer-aided design (CAD) and 3D modeling software for both the Macintosh and Microsoft Windows. It integrates wireframe, freeform surfacing, feature-based solid modeling, photo-realistic rendering, and animation (http://www.ashlar.com/3d-modeling/3d-modeling-cobalt.html).

5.1.8 Electric Image Animation System (EIAS)

EIAS is an eminent 3D animation and rendering package available on both Mac OS X and Windows. Mostly known for its rendering quality and rendering speed it does not include a built-in modeler. EIAS is extensively used in Hollywood, and by professional studios all over the globe to create world-class animations. The popular film *Pirates of the Caribbean* and the television series *Lost* used the software (http://www.eias3d.com/products/eias-overview).

5.1.9 Houdini

This is used for visual effects and character animation. It was used in Disney's feature film *The Wild*. Houdini uses a non-standard interface that it refers to as a "NODE system". It has a hybrid micropolygon-raytracer renderer, Mantra, but it also has built-in support for commercial renderers like Pixar's Renderman and mental ray (http://www.sidefx.com).

5.1.10 LightWave 3D

This software was first developed for the Amiga. It was originally bundled as part of the Video Toaster package and entered the market as a low cost way for TV production companies to create quality CGI for their programming. It first gained public attention with its use in the TV series *Babylon 5* and it is used in several contemporary TV series. Lightwave is also used in a variety of modern film productions. It is available for both Windows and Mac OS X. LightWave's tools are designed for fast productivity and easy, intuitive use (http://www.newtek.com/lightwave.html).

5.1.11 MASSIVE

This is a 3D animation system for generating crowd-related visual effects, targeted for use in film and television. It was originally developed for controlling the large-scale CGI battles in *The Lord of the Rings*. Massive has become an industry standard for digital crowd control in high end animation and has been used on several other big-budget films. It is available for various Unix and Linux platforms as well as Windows (http://en.wikipedia.org/wiki/MASSIVE_(software)).

5.1.12 Maya

Autodesk Maya 3D animation software delivers an end-to-end creative workflow with comprehensive tools for animation, modeling, simulation, visual effects, rendering, match moving, and compositing on a highly extensible production platform. This software is currently used in the film, television, and gaming industry. Maya has developed over the years into an application platform in and of itself through extendibility via its MEL programming language. It is available for Windows, Linux and Mac OS X (http://usa.autodesk.com/maya)

5.1.13 Poser

Poser is a 3D CGI rendering and animation software program optimized for models that depict the human and animal figures in three-dimensional form. Poser has a basic library of human, animal, robotic, and cartoon figures. Poser software package also include poses, hair pieces, props, textures, hand gestures and facial expression (http://en.wikipedia.org/wiki/Poser).

5.2 2D graphics software

2D graphics software is used to manipulate texture to be applied to the objects which enhance their visual details. 2D graphics software (also known 2D graphics editor or drawing program) is an application-level software for the creation of images, diagrams and illustrations by direct manipulation (through the mouse, graphics tablet, or similar device) of 2D computer graphics primitives. These editors generally provide geometric primitives as well as digital images; and some even support procedural models. The illustration is usually represented internally as a layered model, often with a hierarchical structure to make editing more convenient. These editors generally output graphics files where the layers and primitives are separately preserved in their original form. MacDraw, introduced in 1984 with the Macintosh line of computers, was an early example of this class; recent examples are the commercial products Adobe Illustrator and CorelDRAW (http://en.wikipedia.org/wiki/CorelDRAW), and the free editors such as **xfig** or **Inkscape**. There are also many 2D graphics editors specialized for certain types of drawings such as electrical, electronic and VLSI diagrams, topographic maps, computer fonts, etc.

5.3 VR simulation software

Simulation software brings the components of VR together. It is used to program how these objects behave and set the rules that the virtual world follows. Some examples are presented:

5.3.1 WITNESS VR

This simulation software incorporates 3D displays and is designed to be used where first class presentation of a key proposal is required. This is an established general purpose simulation tool used by thousands of organizations to support continuous process improvement activities. WITNESS VR comes complete with a world building and editing package called mantra4D. This enables objects to be created from simple primitives (spheres, cylinders, boxes, etc) or to be imported from a variety of CAD and solid modeling packages (3DS, WRL formats included). Complex CAD models can be simplified using tools in mantra4D to render them suitable for real time fly-around VR. Backdrops can be created easily using simple surfaces and applied digital images which can be taken with any typical digital camera (http://www.laner.com/en/media/witness/vr.cmf).

5.3.2 Flexsim DS

Flexsim DS incorporates the latest advances in 3D simulation software-from realistic VR environments to network collaboration. Flexsim DS can create custom installations and build distributed modeling environment (http://www.flexsim.com/products/ds/).

5.3.3 OpenSimulator (OpenSim)

OpenSimulator is a 3D application server. It can be used to create a virtual environment (world) which can be accessed through a variety of clients, on multiple protocols (Mousa, n.d). OpenSimulator allows you to develop your environment using technologies you feel work best (Onyesolu & Eze, 2011). OpenSimulator has numerous advantages which among other things are:

a. OpenSimulator is released under BSD license, making it both open source, and commercially friendly to embed in products.
b. It has many tools for developers to build various applications (chat application, buildings, and avatars among others).
c. OpenSimulator can be extended via modules to build completely custom configuration.
d. It is a world building tools for creating content real time in the environment.
e. Supports many programming languages for application development such as Linden Scripting Language / OpenSimulator Scripting Language (LSL/OSSL), C#, and/or Jscript and VB.NET
f. It incorporates rich and handy documentations and tutorials.

5.3.4 Croquet

Croquet is an open source 3D graphical platform that is used by experienced software developers to create and deploy deeply collaborative multi-user online virtual world applications on and across multiple operating systems and devices (http://www.opencroquet.org/index.php/Main_Page). Croquet is a next generation virtual operating system (OS) written in Squeak. Squeak is a modern variant of Smalltalk. Squeak runs mathematically identical on all machines. Croquet system features a peer-based messaging protocol that dramatically reduces the need for server infrastructures to support virtual world deployment and makes it easy for software developers to create deeply

Name	Creator	Linux	Mac OS X	Unix	Windows	Free Software
Acoustica	Acon Digital Media	No	No	No	Yes	No
Amadeus Pro	HairerSoft	No	Yes	No	No	No
Ardour	Paul Davis	Yes	Yes	Yes	No	Yes
Audacity	Dominic Mazzoni	Yes	Yes	Yes	Yes	Yes
Audiobook Cutter Free Edition		No	No	No	Yes	Yes
Audio Dementia	Holladay Audio	No	No	No	Yes	No
Audition	Adobe Systems	No	yes (in beta)	No	Yes	No
BIAS Peak	BIAS	No	Yes	No	No	No
Creative Wavestudio	Creative Technology	No	No	No	Yes	No
Diamond Cut DC7	Enhancedaudio.com, Inc.	No	No	No	Yes	No
Ecasound	Kai Vehmanen	Yes	Yes	Yes	No	Yes
Eko	Peter Semiletov	Yes	Yes	Yes	No	Yes
Freecycle		Yes	No		No	Yes
Fast Edit	Minnetonka audio	No	No	No	Yes	No
Fission	Rogue Amoeba	No	Yes	No	No	No
FlexiMusic Wave Editor	FlexiMusic	No	No	No	Yes	No
Goldwave	Goldwave Inc.	No	No	No	Yes	No
Jokosher	Jokosher community	Yes	No	Yes	Yes	Yes
LMMS	Tobias Doerffel	Yes	Yes	Yes	Yes	Yes
Logic Pro	Apple	No	Yes	No	No	No
MAGIX Music Maker	MAGIX	No	No	No	Yes	No
Media Digitalizer	Digitope	No	No	No	Yes	No
mp3DirectCut		Yes (WINE)	No		Yes	Yes
MP3 Stream Editor	3delite	No	No	No	Yes	No
MusE		Yes	No		No	Yes
n-Track Studio	FAsoft	No	No	No	Yes	No
NU-Tech	Leaff Engineering	No	No	No	Yes	No
Pro Tools	Avid	No	Yes	No	Yes	No

Table 1. Some digital sound editing software and compatible operating systems. Source: http://en.wikipedia.org/wiki/Digital_audio_editor

collaborative applications. Croquet provides rich tutorials, resources and videos as educational materials for developers (Onyesolu & Eze, 2011).

5.3.5 Ogoglio

Ogoglio is an open source 3D graphical platform like Croquet. The main goal of the Ogoglio is to build an online urban style space for creative collaboration. Ogoglio platform is built from the languages and protocols of the web. Therefore, it's scripting language is javascript; it's main data transfer protocol is hypertext transfer protocol (HTTP), it's 2D layout is hypertext markup language (HTML) and cascading style sheet (CSS), and it has lightwave object geometry format for its 3D (http://foo.secondlifeherald.com/slh/2007/01/interview_with_.html). Ogoglio is very different from the other virtual reality world development platforms because it uses Windows, Linux, Solaris operating system platforms and runs on web browsers such as Internet Explorer, Firefox, and Safari.

5.3.6 Syzygy

This is a cross-platform, distributed operating system for PC-cluster-based VR. Syzygy is a programming toolkit for writing virtual reality or other graphical applications. Syzygy applications can run on a single computer, but Syzygy is especially designed for the creation of applications to run on clusters of networked computers. Programs or instances of the same program running on different computers in the cluster communicate with one another and share data. The cluster as a whole effectively becomes a single computer with multiple screens and input devices. The rendering of your virtual world is synchronized on all of the computers (to within a few milliseconds), so different screens in the cluster give you different simultaneous views on the virtual world. Included utilities handle communication with 6DOF trackers and other input devices. Spatially-localized sound is supported using the FMOD libraries and non-localized text-to-speech on Windows (http://www.isl.uiuc.edu/syzygy.htm).

5.4 Digital sound editing software

Digital sound editing software is used to mix and edit sounds that objects make within the virtual environment. There are so many digital sound editors. Some are presented in table 1.

6. Conclusion

There are so many VR resources and tools from industry providers. Some companies specialize in providing hardware components for use in VR system such as accelerator cards, pointing and manipulation devices, helmets, shutter glasses, motion platforms, projection system and spatial position and detection systems. There some others companies that specialize in software tools such as 2D software tools, 3D software tools and VR simulation tools. There are a quite handful of companies and institutions that specialize in providing VR applications for manufacturing, education, simulation, design evaluation (virtual prototyping), architectural walk-through, ergonomic studies, simulation of assembly sequences and maintenance tasks, assistance for the handicapped, study and treatment of phobias, entertainment, rapid prototyping and much more.

The exciting field of VR has the potential to change our lives in many ways. There are many applications of VR presently and there will be many more in the future. Many VR applications have been developed. VR technology is now widely recognized as a major breakthrough in the technological advance of science. In Japan today, with the help of VR technology, a customer can walk into a department store, done a VR helmet (HMD) and glove, and proceed to design his own kitchen. The customer can walk around inside the virtual kitchen, open and close drawers; turn on the water, etc. Once the customer is satisfied, the plans are produced and the kitchen is made to order. The Japanese are further developing this system to include various aspects of lighting, noises, humidity, and drafts.

7. References

Aukstakalnis, S., & Blatner, D. (1992). *Silicon mirage: The art and science of virtual reality.* Berkeley, California: Peachpit Press Ltd.

Ausburn, L. J. & Ausburn, F. B. (2004). Desktop virtual reality: A powerful new technology for teaching and research in industrial teacher education. *Journal of Industrial Technical Education,* Vol. 41, No.4, [Online], Available:http://scholar.lib.vt.edu/ejournals/JITE/v41n4/ausburn.html

Ausburn, L. J., & Ausburn, F. B. (2003). A comparison of simultaneous vs. sequential presentation of images in a visual location task to learners with visual and non-visual perceptual styles: A study of supplantational instructional design. *Journal of the Oklahoma Association of Teacher Educators, 7,* 1-20.

Baratoff, G., & Blanksteen, S. (1993). Tracking devices. *Encyclopedia of Virtual Environments.* Retrieved July 30, 2007. Source: http://www.hitl.washington.edu/ scivw/EVE/I.D.1.b. TrackingDevices.html

Baieier, K.P. (1993). *Virtual reality: Short introduction.* [Online]. Available: http://www-vrl.umich.edu/intro.html/

Bierbaum, A. & Just, C. (1998). Software tools for virtual reality application development, http://citeseerx.ist.psu.edu/viewdoc/download?doi=10.1.1.25.8123&rep=rep1&type=pdf

Bolas, M. T. (1994). Human factors in the design of an immersive display. *IEEE Computer Graphics and Applications* January: 55-59.

Gomez, D., Burdea, G., & Langrana, N. (1995). Integration of the rutgers master II in a virtual reality simulation. In *IEEE: Proceedings of the Virtual Reality Annual International Symposium in Research* Triangle Park, NC, March 11-15, 1995, IEEE Computer Society Press. Washington: IEEE Computer Society Press, 198-202.

Haag, S.; Cummings, M., & Dawkins, J. (1998). *Management Information Systems for the Information Age.* Irwin/McGraw Hill, ISBN 0-07-025465-6, New York.

Hsu, J. (1993). Active Interaction. *Encyclopedia of Virtual Environments.* Retrieved July 30, 2007 Source: http://www.hitl.washington.edu/scivw/EVE/I.D.1.a.ActiveInteraction.html

Isdale, J. (1998). *What is virtual reality? A web-based introduction.* Retrieved December 12, 2005. Source: http://whatis.techtarget.com/definition/0.sid9_gci213303,00.html

Kim, J., Park, S., Yuk, K., Lee, H. and Lee, H. (2000). Virtual reality simulations in physics education. *Interactive Multimedia Electronic Journal of Computer-Enhanced Learning* [Online]. Available: http://imej.wfu.edu/articles/2001/2/02/index.asp

Lane, C. (1993). Display Technologies. *Encyclopedia of Virtual Environments*. Retrieved June 26, 2007. Source; http://www.hitl.washington.edu/scivw/EVE/I.A.1.Displays.html

Louka, M.N. & Balducelli, C. (2001). Virtual reality tools for emergency operation support and training, *Proceedings of TIEMS (The international emergency management society 2001*, ISBN: 8270173428. http://www2.hrp.no/vr/publications/tiems2001.pdf

Mousa, H. E. (n.d.). Alternative Virtual reality and virtual worlds development tools and Health care! [Online], Available: http://www.goomedic.com/alternative-virtual-reality-and-virtual-worlds-development-tools-and-health-care.html

Onyesolu, M.O. (January, 2011). Solving the Perennial Problems of Inadequate Physical Laboratories in Africa Through the Use of Virtual Reality Technology and Tools, *Computer Technology and Applications*, Vol. 2, No. 1. ISSN 1543-7332, USA. Available: http://www.cqvip.com/QK/71165X/201101/36756836.html

Onyesolu, M.O. & Eze, F.U. (2011). Understanding Virtual Reality Technology: Advances and Applications, in Schmidt, M. (ed.) *Advances in Computer Science and Engineering*, Rijeka, Croatia: InTech Open Access Publishers, ISBN 978-953-307-173-2. Available: http://www.intechopen.com/book/show/title/advances-in-computer-science-and-engineering

Onyesolu, M.O. (2009a). Virtual reality laboratories: The pedagogical effectiveness and use in obtaining cheap laboratories using the computer laboratory, *Journal of Science Engineering and Technology*, Vol. 16, No.1, (March 2009) 8679-8689, ISSN 1117-4196.

Onyesolu, M.O. (2009b). Virtual reality laboratories: An ideal solution to the problems facing laboratory setup and management, *Proceedings of world congress on engineering and computer science 2009*, pp. 291-295, ISBN: 978-988-17012-6-8, San Francisco, USA, October 2009, Newswood Limited, Hong Kong.

Onyesolu, M.O. & Akpado, K.A. (2009). Virtual reality simulations in computer engineering education. *International Journal of Electrical and Telecommunication Systems Research*, Vol. 3, No.3, (July 2009) 56-61, ISSN 0795-2260.

Onyesolu, M.O. (August, 2006). Virtual Reality: An Emerging Computer Technology of the 21st Century. *International Journal of Electrical & Telecommunication Systems Research*, Vol. 1, No. 1. 36-40. ISSN: 0795-2260. Available: http://www.electroscope-edu.org/vol1abstr7.php

Perry, L.D.S., Smith, C. M., & Yang, S. (2004). An investigation of current virtual reality interfaces. The Student ACM Magazine. Retrieved September 20, 2007. Source: http://www.acm.org/crossroads/xrds3-3/vrhci.html

Sowizral, H. (1995). Tutorial: An Introduction to Virtual Reality. *Virtual Reality Annual International Symposium*.

Wilson, M., & Conway, A. (1991). Enhanced Interaction Styles for User Interfaces. *IEEE Computer Graphics and Applications*, March: 79-89.

http://company.mmosite.com/forterra /index.shtml

http://defense.digimation.com/

http://en.wikipedia.org/wiki/3D_computer_graphics_software

http://en.wikipedia.org/wiki/Cave_Automatic_Virtual_Environment

http://en.wikipedia.org/wiki/CorelDRAW

http://en.wikipedia.org/wiki/Digital_audio_editor

http://en.wikipedia.org/wiki/MASSIVE_(software)).

http://en.wikipedia.org/wiki/Poser
http://en.wikipedia.org/wiki/Video_card
http://en.wikipedia.org/wiki/Workstation
http://usa.autodesk.com/maya
http://vresources.org/company_link_list
http://www.3dace.com
http://www.3dwebtech.co.uk
http://www.5dt.com
http://www.acroneng.com/3D%20Modeller.htm
http://www.adacel.com
http://www.alibre.com
http://www.ashlar.com/3d-modeling/3d-modeling-cobalt.html
http://www.cae.ca/
http://www.edgedsign.com
http://www.eias3d.com/products/eias-overview
http://www.flexsim.com/products/ds/
http://www.icarusstudios.com/
http://www.isl.uiuc.edu/syzygy.htm
http://www.laner.com/en/media/witness/vr.cmf
http://www.maxon.net/products/cinema-4d-studio/who-should-use-it.html
http://www.newtek.com/lightwave.html
http://www.sidefx.com
http://www.simulation.com/products/glstudio/glstudio.html
http://www.thegamecreators.com/?m=view_products&id=2092
http://www.virtualheroes.com/about.asp
http://www.vxsim.com

3

Training of Procedural Tasks Through the Use of Virtual Reality and Direct Aids

Jorge Rodríguez[1], Teresa Gutiérrez[2], Emilio J. Sánchez[1],
Sara Casado[2] and Iker Aguinaga[1]
[1]CEIT, Centro de Estudios e Investigaciones Técnicas de Gipuzkoa
[2]Tecnalia
Spain

1. Introduction

A high percentage of the human activities are based on *procedural tasks*, for example cooking a cake, driving a car, fixing a machine, etc. Reading an instruction book, watching a video or listening the explanation from an expert have been the *traditional methods* to learn procedural tasks. But, most researchers agree that procedural tasks are learnt gradually as a result of practice through repeating exposures to the task.

Nowadays, *Virtual Reality (VR) technologies* can be used to improve the learning of a procedural task and moreover to evaluate the performance of the trainee. For example, a Virtual Environment (VE) can allow the trainees to interact physically with the virtual scenario, integrating a haptic device with the computer vision system, so that trainees can interact and manipulate the virtual objects, feeling the collisions among them and, the most important, they can practice the task under the approach of *learning by doing*. In this way, trainees can practice in order to improve their abilities until they are proficient with the task.

This chapter introduces a **new Multimodal Training System (MTS)** that provides a **new interactive tool** for assisting the trainees during the **learning of a procedural task** in the assembly and disassembly operations. This MTS uses the haptic feedback to simulate the real behaviour of the task and special visual aids to provide information and help trainees to undertake the task. One of the main advantages of this platform is that trainees can learn and practice different procedural tasks without the necessity of having physical access to real tools, components and machines. For example, trainees can assemble/disassemble the different components from a virtual machine as it would be done in the real life. This system was designed and implemented as an activity in the context of the SKILLS project[1].

During the *learning of a task*, most of the times, **trainees need to receive aids with information about how to proceed** with the task. From the point of view of the authors, these aids can be divided into two groups according to the type of information that they provide and how this information is provided: ***direct aids and indirect aids.*** The difference between both types of aids is in the cognitive load requested by the trainees to interpret and understand the information provided by the aid. In this way, *indirect aids* require that trainees are active in

---

[1] IST FP6 ICT-IP-035005-2006

order to cognitively translate the information received to the actions that must be undertaken at that step, meanwhile using *direct aids*, the information is explicit that the cognitive load is almost null.

The *use of direct aids* is attractive for both trainers and trainees since they are easy to implement and they provide useful information to perform the task in an easy way. However, some research works such as Yuviler-Gavish et al. (Yuviler-Gavish et al. (2011)) suggest that the use of direct aids can have adverse effects on training since they prevent trainees from actively exploring the task. In addition, trainees can create dependences with the training system that impede the skills transfer in the real situation when these aids are no longer available. In this way, it would be useful to define **a strategy to provide direct aids that maintains the benefits of these aids but eliminates their negative effects.**

This chapter analyzes the **hypothesis** that if **direct aids are provided in a controlled way** during the training process, then **the transfer of knowledge will not be hindered.** This chapter describes the test conducted to compare the performances obtained with a training strategy based on controlled direct aids with a training strategy based on indirect aids.

This chapter is organized as follows. The rest of this section provides a brief introduction to theoretical concepts about procedural tasks and its learning. The section 2 describes the use of virtual reality technologies for training focusing mainly on multimodal systems and the section 3 presents a new Multimodal Training System for leaning assembly and disassembly procedural tasks. Section 4 describes the results of an experiment conducted to analyze the use of direct aids to train a procedural task. Lastly, section 5 provides the conclusions derived from this chapter and propose some future research challenges.

1.1 What is a procedural task

A *procedural task* involves the execution of an ordered sequence of operations/steps that need to be carried out to achieve a specific goal. In other words, this kind of activities require following a procedure and they are usually evaluated by the speed and accuracy of their performance. There are two main types of skills (abilities) that may be involved in each step:

1. Physical skill, called here *motor skill*, which entails the execution of physical movements, like unscrewing a nut.
2. Mental skill, called here *cognitive skill*, which entails the knowledge about how the task should be performed, like knowing what nut should be unscrewed in each step.

The cognitive skill has an important role in the process of learning a procedural task, it reflects the ability of the humans to *obtain a good mental representation of task organization*, and to knows *what* appropriate actions should be done, *when* to do them (appropriate time) and *how* to do them (appropriate method).

1.2 Learning of procedural tasks

From a dictionary, one can identify two primary meanings for the word learning. The first definition is the *active process* of acquiring information, knowledge, procedures and capabilities for performing operations and achieving goals to satisfy the requirements of a given task. The second one is *knowledge or ability* that is acquired by instruction or study. During the learning process, the learner selects and transforms information, constructs hypotheses, and makes decisions, relying on a cognitive structure (e.g. schemas and mental models) using their past/current knowledge and experiences (Dale (1969)).

There are many ways by which people can learn a new task. People can learn by reading instructions, by watching a video, by listening to an expert, and of course by practicing themselves. In the context of procedural tasks, the training involves the learning of the sequence of the needed steps to accomplish the goal of the task, as well as, the learning of new motor skills or the improvement of existing ones.

Edgar Dale (Dale (1969)) developed from his experience in teaching and his observations of learners the *cone of learning*. He demostrates that the least effective methods to learn and remember things are by means of reading a manual and hearing a presentation because after two weeks people remember the 10% of what they read and 20% of what they hear. In contrast, the most effective method involves direct learning experiences, such as doing the physical task and simulating the real task because people are able to remember the 90% of what they do. This approach is called *enactive learning* or *learning by doing*.

Learning by doing is the acquisition of knowledge or abilities through *direct experience of carrying out a task*, as a part of a training, and it is closely associated with the practical experience (McLaughlin & Rogers (2010)). The reason to focus on guided enactive training is that it is direct, intuitive, fast, embodied into common action-perception behaviours, and that it may be more efficient than other types of training methods for becoming an expert. Besides, if the learning by doing approach is supervised, trainees not only could practice the task, but they also could also receive feedback about their actions along the training sessions in order to avoid errors and improve their performance.

In this way, *direct practice* under the guidance of an expert seems to be the preferable approach for both acquiring procedural cognitive knowledge and motor skills associated with procedural tasks. However, this preferred situation is expensive and many times hard to achieve with the traditional training methods. Sometimes the practice on the real environment is impossible due to safety, cost and time constraints; other times the physical collocation of the trainee and expert is impossible. Consequently, new training tools are requested to improve the learning of procedural tasks. And here it is where the VR technologies can play an important role.

2. The use of VR technologies for training

Virtual environments are increasingly used for teaching and training in a range of domains including surgery (Albani & Lee (2007); Howell et al. (2008)), aviation (Blake (1996)), anesthesia (Gaba (1991); Gaba & DeAnda (1988)), rehabilitation (Holden (2005)), aeronautics assembly (Borro et al. (2004); Savall et al. (2004)) and driving (Godley et al. (2002); Lee et al. (1998)). These simulated and virtual worlds can be used for acquiring new abilities or improving existing ones (Derossis et al. (1998); Kneebone (2003); Weller (2004)). In general, VR technologies can provide new opportunities compared to traditional training methodologies to capture the essence of the abilities involved in the task to be learnt, allowing to store them and to transfer them efficiently. The speed, efficiency, and mainly transferability of training are three major requests in the process of design of new virtual training systems.

2.1 Advantages and risks of the VR technologies for training

The use of VR technologies for training provides a range of benefits with respect to traditional training systems, mainly:

- It allows teach a task under the approach of *learning by doing*, so the trainees can practice the task as many time as needed to achieve the level of proficiency requested.
- It eliminates the constraints for using the real environment mainly: availability, safety, time and costs constraints. For example, in medical domains there is no danger to the patients, and little need for valuable elements such as cadavers or animals. Similarly for aviation, there is no risk for the aircraft, nor fuel costs. In the case of maintenance tasks, VR systems can offer a risk free environment for damaging machines of technicians (Morgan et al. (2004); Sanderson et al. (2008)).
- It can provide extra cues, not available in the real world, and that can facilitate the learning of the task. These cues can be based on visual, audio or/and haptic feedback. A combination of these cues is called *multimodal feedback*[2]. For example, to provide information about the motion trajectory that users should follow, the system could provide: visual aids (for example displaying the target trajectory on the virtual scenario) or haptic aids (for example applying an extra force to constraint the motion of the user along the target trajectory) or audio aids (for example sending a sound when the user leaves the target trajectory).
- It allows simulating the task in a flexible way to adapt it to the need of trainees and the training goal, for example removing some constraints of the task in order to emphasize only key aspects.
- It can provide enjoyment, increasing the motivation of trainees (Scott (2005)).
- It allows logging the evolution of the trainees along the training process.

On the other hand, the greatest potential danger of the use of VR systems is that learners become increasingly dependent on features of the system which may inhibit the ability to perform the task in the absence of the features.

Developing dependence, or at least reliance, on VR features that do not exist in the real environment or are very different from their real world counterparts can result in negative transfer to the real world. If *fidelity* cannot be preserved or is hard to achieve, it is much better to avoid the use of the VR instantiation, or alternatively, particular care must be taken to develop a training program that identifies the VR-real world mismatch to the trainee and provides compensatory training mechanisms. It may also be necessary to manipulate the relational properties between feedbacks, i.e., the congruency between visual, audio, and haptic stimulations, in order to favor cross-modal attention.

The experiment described in this chapter demonstrates that the controlled use of multimodal feedback does not damage the trainee performance when the trainee changes from the VR system to the real world and therefore it eliminates the main disadvantage of the use of VR reported in the bibliography: the negative or no transfer.

2.2 Multimodal systems for training

Within the virtual reality systems we can find the multimodal systems. The term *multimodal* comes from the word multi that refers to *more than one* and the word modal that refers to *the human sense that is used to perceive the information*, the sensory modality (Mayes (1992)). Therefore, in this chapter a *multimodal system* is defined as a virtual reality system that supports communication with the trainees through more than one sensory modality (see Figure 1), mainly visual, haptic and auditory. In order to support this multimodal

[2] It refers to the use of different human sensory channels to provide information to users.

communication in a proper way, the multimodal sytems need high requiring hardware and software technologies. Nowadays, due to the last advances in computer technologies to increase their capabilities for processing and managing diverse information in parallel, the multimodal systems are increasing their use.

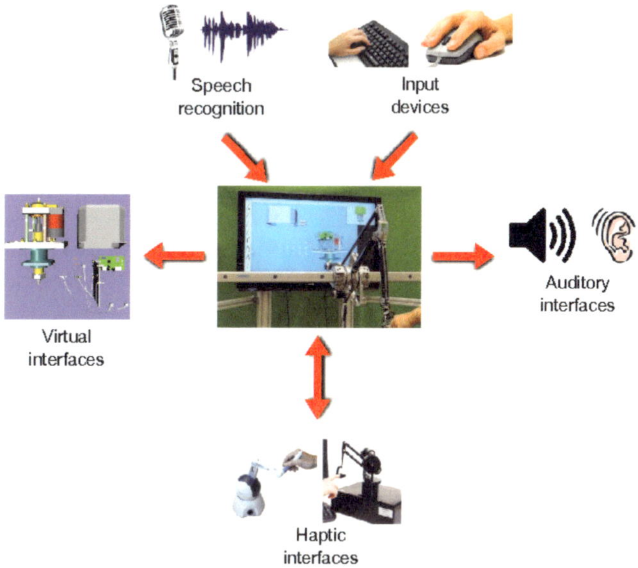

Fig. 1. Multimodal system is a virtual system where the user interacts with the virtual scene through more than one sensory modality.

According with Figure 1, a multimodal system can provide information to the user through different types of interfaces, mainly:

1. *Visual intefaces*: the primary interaction style of the multimodal interfaces is usually the visual interaction through computer display technology (such as, computer screens and 3D projections) to render the virtual scenario. In addition, these interfaces can be used to provide relevant information for the task through messages, animations and visual aids.
2. *Auditory interfaces*: traditionally, sound in computer systems has been used either to convey feedback to the users or alert them from a system event, for example, a beep to indicate an error. However, some research studies are looking at the use of more complex speech systems to provide richer non-visual information/interaction to the user. One example of the research work in auditory interfaces is the auditory icons (Gaver (1994)) which provide information about computer system events without the need to use any of the visual display space.
3. *Haptic interfaces*: the word haptic comes from the greek *haptikós* and refers to the *sense of touch*. The human touch system consists of various skin receptors, muscles and tendon receptors, nerve fibers that transmit the touch signals to the touch centre of the brain, as well as the control system for moving the body. In normal tactile exploration the receptors in the hairless skin play the dominant role but in haptic interaction the focus is shifted towards the proprioceptive and kinesthetic touch systems.There is usually a distinction made between: tactile interfaces and force (kinesthetic) feedback interfaces. The tactile interface is one that provides information more specifically for the skin receptors, and thus does not necessarily require movement in the same way as a kinesthetic interface

does. For simplicity, in this chapter, the haptic devices will denote the force feedback interfaces. Haptic devices are mechatronic input-output systems capable of tracking a physical movement of the users (input) and providing them force feedback (output). Therefore, haptic devices allow users to interact with a virtual scenario through the sense of touch. In other words, with these devices the users can touch and manipulate virtual objects inside of a 3D environment as if they were working in the real environment. These devices enable to simulate both unimanual tasks, which are performed with just one hand (for example grasping an object and insert it into another one), and bimanual tasks in which two hands are needed to manipulate an object or when two objects need to be dexterously manipulated at the same time (Garcia-Robledo et al. (2011)). Figure 2 shows some commercial haptic devices. Some relevant features of a haptic device are: its workspace, the number of degrees of freedom, the maximum level of force feedback and the number of contact points. The selection of a haptic device to be used in a MTS depends on several factors mainly, on the type of task to be learnt, the preferences/needs of trainees and cost constraints.

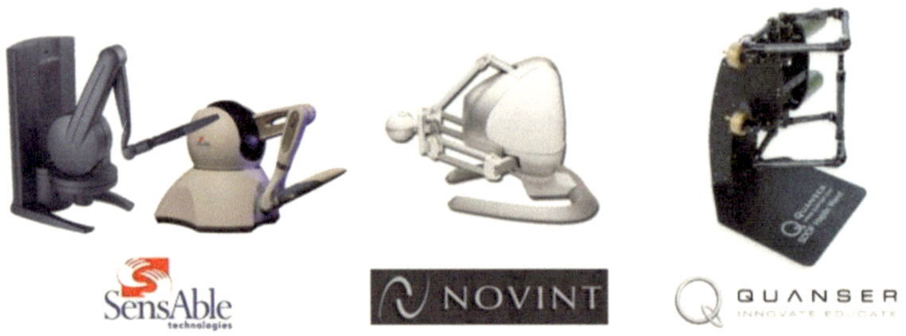

Fig. 2. Commercial haptic devices. On the left, PHANToM haptic devices with 6-DOF by SensAble. On the middle, the FALCON device with 3-DOF by NOVINT. On the right, the Quanser 5-DOF Haptic Wand, by Quanser

The sensorial richness of multimodal systems translates into a more complete and coherent experience of the virtual scenario and therefore the sense of being present inside of this VE is stronger (Held & Durlach (1992); Sheridan (1992); Witmer & Singer (1998)). The experience of being present is specially strong if the VE includes haptic (tactile and kinesthetic) sensations (Basdogan et al. (2000); Reiner (2004)).

In this chapter, a multimodal system combined with a set of suitable training strategies can be considered as a Multimodal Training System.

2.3 Multimodal feedback in Virtual Training Systems

The use of multimodal feedback can improve perception and enhance performance in a training process, for example, tasks trained over multiple feedbacks can be performed better than tasks completed within the same feedback (Wickens (2002)). Various studies have supported the multiple resource theory of attention.Wickens et al. (Wickens et al. (1983)) found that performance in a dual-task was better when feedback was manual and verbal than when feedback was manual only. Similarly, Oviatt et al. (Oviatt et al. (2004)) found that a flexible multimodal interface supported users in managing cognitive load.

Ernst and Bülthoff (Ernst & Bülthoff (2004)) suggested that no single sensory signal can provide reliable information about the structure of the environment in all circumstances.

Synergy[3], redundancy, and increased bandwidth of information transfer are proposed benefits of multimodal presentation (Sarter (2006)). If information is presented in redundant multiple modalities, then various concurrent forms and different aspects of the same process are presented. Concurrent information may coordinate activities in response to the ongoing processes.

Several studies have shown that using auditory and visual feedback together increase performance compared to using each of these feedbacks separately. For example, under noisy conditions, observing the movements of the lips and gestures of the speaker can compensate for the lost speech perception which can be equivalent to increasing the auditory signal-to-noise ratio (Sumby & Pollack (1954)). It was also demonstrated that reaction times for detecting a visual signal were slower in unimodal conditions, compared to a condition in which a sound was heard in close temporal synchrony to the visual signal (Doyle & Snowden (2001)). Handel and Buffardi (Handel & Buffardi (1969)) found that in a pattern judging task, performance was better using a combination of auditory and visual cues than either audition or vision alone.

On the other hand, adding haptic feedback to another modality was also found to improve performance compared to the use of each modality individually. Pairs of auditory and haptic signals delivered simultaneously were detected faster than when the same signals presented unimodally (Murray et al. (2005)). In a texture discrimination task, participants accuracy was improved (less errors) when they received bi-modal visual and haptic cues as compared to uni-modal conditions in which only the haptic or the visual cue was presented (Heller (1982)). Sarlegna et al. (Sarlegna et al. (2007)) demonstrated that feedback that was combined of different sensory modalities improved the performance in reaching task.

In general, the advantages of the use of multimodal feedback are summarized below:

1. Various forms and different aspects of the same task can be presented simultaneosly when information is presented using multimodal feedback.
2. The use of a second channel to provide information can compensate the lost of information of the first one.
3. When one sensorial channel is overloaded, other channel can be used to convey additional information.
4. The reaction times are slower and the performance is increased with the use of multimodal feedback.

But, in order to provide all these benefits it is essential to assure the coherence and consistence among the different stimuli. Conflicts among the information provided by the different channels can deteriorate the performance of trainees. In addition, it is important to identify the different components of the task to be learnt in order to select and employ the most suitable channel to provide useful information for each one.

2.4 State of the art on multimodal systems for procedural tasks

Some studies have tested and analyzed the use of the multimodal systems as a simulation tool or a training tool to teach and evaluate the knowledge of a trainee in procedural tasks. The review presented in this section is focused on procedural tasks related to the assembly and disassembly processes.

[3] The merging information from multiple aspects of the same task.

There are several multimodal systems that simulate assembly and disassembly tasks, although most of them are designed to analize and evaluate the assembly planning during the design process of new machines and only few of them provide additional training modules. Below there is a description of some of these systems:

- VEDA: Virtual Enviromnent for Design for Assembly (Gupta et al. (1997))

It is a desktop virtual environment in which the designers see a visual 2-D virtual representation of the objects and they are able to pick and place active objects, move them around, and feel the forces through haptic interface devices with force feedback. They also hear collision sounds when objects hit each other. The virtual models are 2-D in order to preserve interactive update rates. The simulation duplicated as well as possible the weight, shape, size, and frictional characteristics of the physical task. The system simulates simple tasks, such as peg-in-hole task.

- VADE: A Virtual Assembly Design Environment (Jayaram et al. (1999))

VADE was designed and implemented at the Washington State University. It is a VR-based engineering application that allows engineers to plan, evaluate, and verify the assembly of mechanical systems. Once the mechanical system is designed using a CAD system (such as Pro/Engineer), the system automatically exports the necessary data to VADE. The various parts and tools (screw driver, wrench, and so on) involved in the assembly process are presented to users in a VE. Users perform the assembly using their hands and the virtual assembly tools. VADE supports both one-handed and two-handed assembly. The virtual hand is based on an instrumented glove device, such as the CyberGlove, and a graphical model of a hand. VADE also provides audio feedback to assist novice users. The system lets users make decisions, make design changes, and perform a host of other engineering tasks. During this process, VADE maintains a link with the CAD system. At the end of the VADE session, users have generated design information that automatically becomes available in the CAD system.

- HIDRA: Haptic Integrated Dis/Reassembly Analysis. (McDermott & Bras (1999))

HIDRA is an application that integrates a haptic device into a disassembly/ assembly simulation environment. Two PHANToM haptic interfaces provide the user with a virtual index finger and thumb force feedback. The goal is to use HIDRA as a design tool, so designers must be able to use it in parallel with other CAD packages they may use throughout the design process. The V-clip library is used to perform collision detection between object inside the virtual scene. The system simulates simple scenarios, for example a simple shaft with a ring.

- MIVAS: A Multi-modal Immersive Virtual Assembly System (Wan et al. (2004))

MIVAS is a multi-modal immersive virtual assembly system developed at the State Key Lab of CAD&CG, Zhejiang University. This system provides an intuitive and natural way of assembly evaluation and planning using tracked devices for tracking both hands and head motions, dataglove with force feedback for simulating the realistic operation of human hand and providing force feedback, voice input for issuing commands, sound feedback for prompts, fully immersive 4-sided CAVE as working space. CrystalEyes shutter glasses and emitters are used to obtain stereoscopic view. Users can feel the size and shape of digital CAD models using the CyberGrasp haptic device (by Immersion Corporation). Since Haptic feedback was only provided in griping tasks, the application lacked in providing force information when parts collided. The system can simulate complex scenarios such as disassembling different components of an intelligent hydraulic excavator. To make the disassembly process easy the parts that can be currently disassembled are highlighted in blue color to help users make their selection.

- HAMMS: Haptic Assembly, Manufacturing and Machining System. (Ritchie et al. (2008))

HAMMS was developed by researchers at the Heriot-Watt University to explore the use of immersive technology and haptics in assembly planning. The hardware comprises a Phantom haptic device for interaction with the virtual environment, along with a pair of CrystalEyes® stereoscopic glasses for stereo viewing if required. Central to HAMMS is the physics engine, which enables rigid body simulations in real time. HAMMS logs data for each virtual object in the scene including devices that are used for interaction. The basic logged data comprises position, orientation, time stamps, velocity and an object index (or identifying number). By parsing through the logged data text files an assembly procedure can be automatically formulated.

- SHARP: Development of a Dual-handed haptic assembly system (Seth et al. (2008)).

SHARP is a dual-handed haptic interface for virtual assembly applications. The system allows users to simultaneously manipulate and orient CAD models to simulate assembly/disassembly operations. This interface provides both visual and haptic feedback, in this way, collision force feedback was provided to the user during assembly. Using VRJuggler as an application platform, the system could operate on different VR systems configurations including low-cost desktop configurations, Power Wall, four-sided and six-sided CAVE systems. Finally, different modules were created to address issues related to maintenance, training (record and play) and to facilitate collaboration (networked communication).

- HIIVR: A haptically enabled interactive virtual system for industrial assembly (Bhatti et al. (2008)).

This system is an interactive and immersive VR system designed to imitate the real physical training environments within the context of visualization and physical limitations. Head Mounted Displays are used for immersive visualization equipped with 6DOF trackers to keep the virtual view synchronized with the human vision, PHANTOM® devices are used to impose physical movement constraints. In addition, 5DT data gloves are used to provide human hand representation within the virtual world. The aim of the proposed system is to support the learning process of general assembly operators. Users can repeat their learning practices until they are proficient with the assembly task.

As it can be seen, most of the existing multimodal systems in the domain of assembly and disassembly tasks are focused mainly on their simulation without addressing explicitly their training. In the next Section, the authors present a new multimodal training system (combining visual, audio and haptic feedback) for training assembly and disassembly procedural tasks. Figure 3 shows a comparison among the previous systems and the new multimodal training system described in the next Section.

3. The new multimodal training system

This section presents a controlled multimodal training system, for learning assembly and disassembly procedural tasks. This platform supports the approach of *learning by doing* by means of an active multimodal interaction with the virtual scenario (visual, audio and haptic), eliminating the constraints of using the physical scenario (such as availability, time, cost, and

Systems	Use of tools	Bimanual operations	Force feedback	Sound feedback	Use of cues	Training module	Logging user data	User performance evaluation	Main goal
VEDA	no	no	yes	yes	no	no	no	no	Simulation of simple tasks.
HIDRA	no	no	yes	no	no	no	no	no	Simulation of simple tasks.
VADE	yes	yes	yes	yes	no	no	no	no	Assembly planning.
MIVAS	no	no	yes	yes	Visual	no	no	no	Assembly evaluation and assembly planning.
HAMMS	no	no	yes	no	no	no	yes	no	Assembly planning.
SHARP	no	yes	yes	no	no	yes (playback)	no	no	Simulation of assembly tasks.
HIIVR	no	no	yes	NIA*	yes	yes	yes	yes	Virtual training
New MTS	yes	yes	yes	yes	Visual and haptic	yes	yes	yes	Multimodal training.

Fig. 3. Comparison among the new multimodal training system and other systems. *NIA: no information available.

safety constraints). In this way, the trainees can interact and manipulate the components of the virtual scenario, sensing the collisions with the other components and simulating assembly and disassembly operations. In addition, the new system provides different multimodal aids and learning strategies that help and guide the trainees during their training process. One of the main features of this system is its flexibility to adapt itself to the task demands and to the trainees preferences and needs. In this way the sytem can be used with different types of haptic devices and allows undertaking mono-manual and bimanual operations in assembly and disassembly tasks with or without tools.

3.1 Set-up of the system

The new multimodal training system consists of a screen displaying a 3-D graphical scene, one haptic device and the training software, which simulates and teaches assembly and disassembly procedural tasks. As it will be discussed later, thanks to a special interface the platform is flexible enough to use different types of haptic devices with different features (large or small workspace, one or two contact points, different DoFs, etc.) depending on the task demands.

Figure 4 shows the training system in which trainees have to grasp the stylus of the haptic device with one hand to interact with the virtual pieces of the scene. Besides, trainees can use the keyboard to send commands to the application (e.g. grasp a piece, change the view, ...).

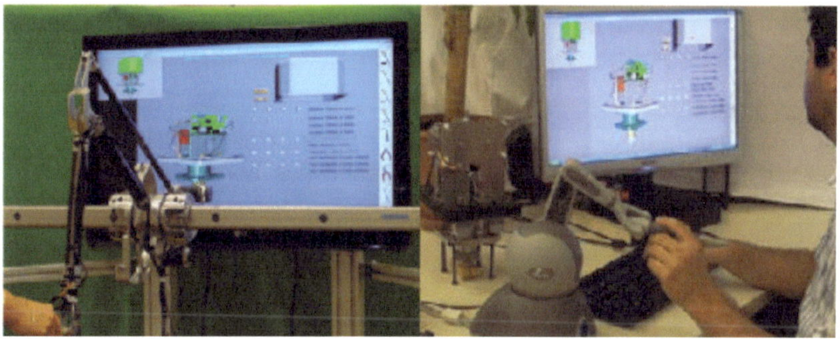

Fig. 4. Multimodal Training System. On the left, the system is configured to use a large workspace haptic device. On the right, the system is configured to use a desktop (small wokspace) haptic device.

The 3D-graphical scene is divided into two areas. The first area, the *repository*, is a back-wall, that contains the set of pieces to be assembled (in the case of an assembly task). The second area, *the working area*, is where trainees have to assemble/disassemble the machine or model. On the right part of the screen there is a *tools menu* with the virtual tools that can be chosen to accomplish the different operations of the task. When the user is closed to a tool icon, the user can "grasp" the corresponding tool and manipulate it. Figure 5 shows one example of a virtual assembly scene of the experimental task described in the next Section. Using the haptic device, the trainees must grasp the pieces from the repository (with or without tool) and move them to place them in its correct position in the model. Along the training session, the system provides different types of information about the task, such as: information about the "task progress", technical description of the components/tools and critical information of the operations. Critical information can also be sent through audio messages. When trainees make an error during the task, the system also displays a message with the type of error and plays a sound to indicate the fault.

Fig. 5. Virtual assembly scene. Trainees have to grasp the correct piece from the backwall and place it in its correct position in the model.

The platform also provides different utilities to configure the training process. For example, to start the training session at any step, to select the constraint in the order of the sequence of steps (the steps can be done in any flexible order or must follow a fixed order), to allow making steps automatically so the trainees can jump the easy steps and focus on the complex ones or even to "undo steps" to repeat difficult steps. The system logs information about the training sessions in order to analyze the performance of the trainee. Then, this information can be processed for extracting different performance measures. At the end of the session, the system provides a performance report containing information about:

- *Step performance*: time, information about how the step was performed (correct step, without errors but with aids, with errors but without aids, with errors and aids, not finished, performed automatically) and number of times that the help was needed to finish the step and number or errors.
- *Overall performance*: total time, description of the sequence done, total number of correct steps, total number of steps without errors but with aids, total number of steps with errors but without aids, total number of steps with errors and aids, total number of steps not finished, total number of steps performed automatically by the system, total number of times that the help was needed, total number or errors, and total number of consecutive steps done correctly.

3.2 Architecture and components

The multimodal interaction of the trainees with the virtual scene involves different activities, such as haptic interaction, collision detection, visual feedback, commands management, etc. All these activities must be synchronized and executed with the correct frequency in order to provide the trainees with a consistent and proper interaction. Therefore, a multi-threaded solution with 3 threads is employed (see Figure 6):

1. The *haptic thread* analyzes the user position, with the frequency requested by the haptic device (usually 1 Khz), in order to calculate the force that will be replicated to the trainee. It also manages the communication between the system and the haptic device through a special API (Application Programming Interface): the API–HAL (Haptic Abstract Library). This API makes the software application independent from the haptic device drivers and allows easily changing the system configuration, and using different haptic devices according to the task demands.

2. The *simulation thread* validates the motion requested by the trainee according to the task, for example: detecting collisions of the model in movement, simulating an operation or constraining the motion of trainees along a specific path, etc.
3. The *rendering thread* updates the graphical rendering of the virtual scene, sends the requested audio feedback at each time, processes the commands of the trainees (i.e. making a zoom in, rotating the view, etc.) entered by the keyboard or the switches of the haptic device and controls the training process.

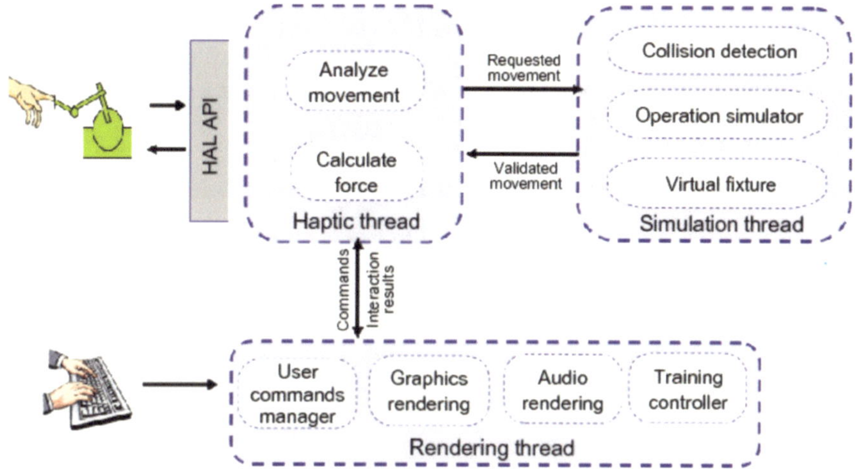

Fig. 6. Multi-thread solution implemented in the IMA-VR system.

The main components of the new training system are:

- *Graphics Rendering Module*: it loads and displays the virtual scenario from a VRML file. Each object is represented by a triangle mesh and a transformation matrix. This module also includes some features to simulate the visual deformation of flexible objects as cables.
- *Haptic Rendering Module:* it analysis the collisions between the user and the scene for exploration tasks and between the object in movement and the rest of the objects for manipulation tasks. This module also supports two haptic devices working simultaneously to simulate bi-manual operations.
- *Operation Simulator:* it simulates some of the most common operations of a assembly/disassembly task such as: insert/remove a component in/from another one, align two components along an axis, etc.
- *Virtual Fixtures Module*: the term *virtual fixture* is used to refer to a task dependent aid (visual, audio or haptic aid) that guides the motion and actions of users. This module provides both visual and haptic fixtures. Examples of *visual fixtures* are: changing the color of a virtual object, making a copy of an object and displaying it in a specific position, rendering auxiliary virtual elements such as arrows, trajectories, reference planes, points, etc. The output of the *haptic fixtures* is rendered in the form of forces dependent on the type of fixture: e.g. trainees can receive forces in order to constraint their hand-motion along a specific path or just attraction/repulsion forces with different levels of force and areas of influence (a surrounding area of a object or the whole-working space). This library of virtual fixtures is the basis of most of the training strategies provided by the system.

- *Training Controller Module*: this module provides several trainings strategies with different degree of interaction between the trainees and the system in order to perform the task. In one extreme it is the *observational learning* strategy, where the trainees do not have any interaction with the virtual scenario but they just receive information about how to undertake the task in order to develop a *mental model*[4] of the task. On the other hand, there are some strategies where the trainees have to perform the virtual task being able to receive different types of multimodal aids from the system (based on the fixtures explained before). In the next section, one of these training strategies is described in detail. Finally, it is the *learning test strategy* in which the trainees have to perform the virtual task by themselves without receiving any aid from the system. Usually, a training programme combines several of these strategies. The selection of the strategies will depend on the task complexity and the profile of the trainees.

4. Experiment: the use of direct aids to train a procedural task

During the learning of a task, trainees can need to receive information about how to proceed with the task. As commented in previous sections, the way of providing theses aids is essential to assure the effectiveness of the training. The *direct aids* provide the information to perform the task in an easy way, however, some research works suggest that their use can have adverse effects on training. This section describes the experiment conducted to analyze if the **controlled use of direct aids** to train a procedural task **does not damage the transfer** of the involved skills.

4.1 Experimental task

The selected experimental task was learning how to build a LEGO™ helicopter model composed of 75 bricks. Participants were trained in the task using the multimodal training system explained in the last section with the OMNI device by SensAble. In order to avoid the effect of the short-tem memory, the experiment was conducted in two consecutive days. In the first day, the participants had to learn the procedural task using the virtual training system. During the second day, they had to build the same model using the physical LEGO™ bricks, as it is shown in Figure 7.

4.2 Learning conditions

According to the goal of the experiment, two experimental groups were defined to compare the effectiveness of the controlled direct aids with respect to a classical aid as it is an instruction manual (indirect aids). The participants of both groups trained in the task using the same multimodal platform, so all participants were able to interact with the bricks of the virtual LEGO™ model, through the haptic device, and build the virtual helicopter. The difference between the groups was the way of providing the information about the task:

- *Group 1 - Indirect aids*: the participants did not receive any aid from the training platform; to get information about the immediate action to perform, they had to consult an instruction book and each consult was logged as one aid. This book contained step-by-step diagrams of the 75 steps of the task. Each diagram included a picture of the LEGO™ brick needed for the current step and the view of the model at the end of the step (see Figure 8). This

[4] They provide humans with information on how physical systems work. Scientists sometimes use the term *mental model* as a synonym for *mental representation, knowledge of the task or knowledge representation.*

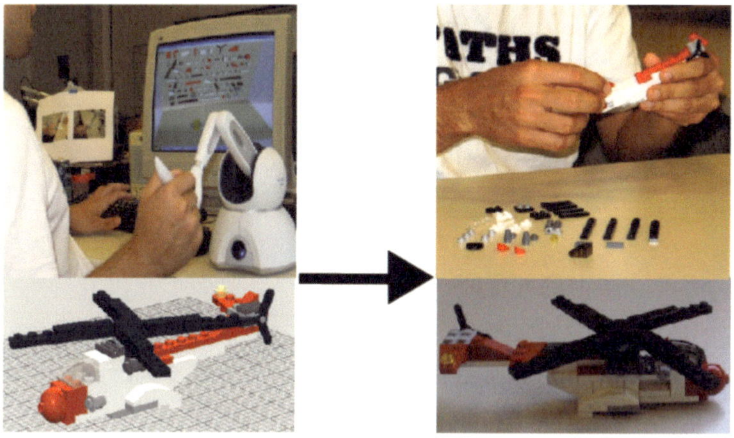

Fig. 7. Building a real LEGO™ helicopter after being trained in the task with a multimodal training system.

kind of aid was considered as an **indirect aid**, because the **participants** had to **translate in a cognitive way the information** of each diagram **to the actions** that had to be undertaken at that step.

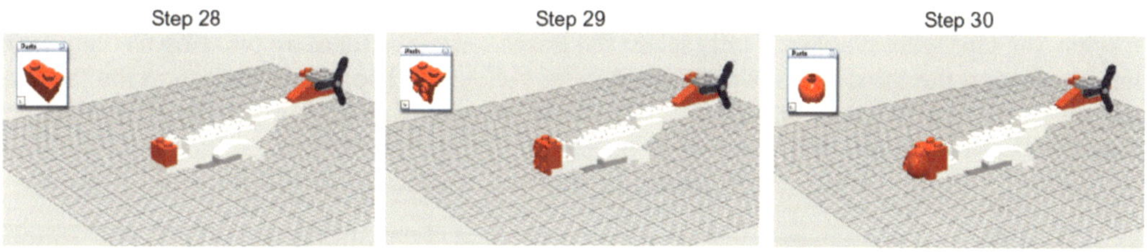

Fig. 8. Three pages of the instruction book, showing for each step the target brick and the final result of the step.

- *Group 2 - Direct aids:* the training platform provided **information about the immediate action** that **participants** had to **perform in a direct way** through visual and haptic aids. Each step consists of two main operations: select the correct brick and place the brick in its correct position on the model. For the first action, select the correct brick, the target brick was highlighted in yellow colour (visual aid) and the trainee received an attraction force to it (haptic aid), see Figure 9 on the top. For the second action, place the brick, a copy of the correct brick was rendered at its target position (visual aid) and an attraction force towards that position was applied as well (haptic aid), see Figure 9 on the bottom.

From the point of view of the authors, the main **disadvantage of the direct aids** is that their abuse of use can **inhibit an active exploration of the task** and the **trainees can become dependent on these aids**. This fact could impede the transfer of skills in the real situation, where these aids are no longer available. **To avoid this problem**, the authors proposed **a training strategy based on providing these direct aids in a controlled way** and reduce them along the training process. In this experiment, the training period consisted of four training sessions. Therefore, during the first training session, in order to have an overview of the task, the aids were displayed automatically by the system, i.e. after finishing an action the trainee received automatically information for the next action. After that, during the second training

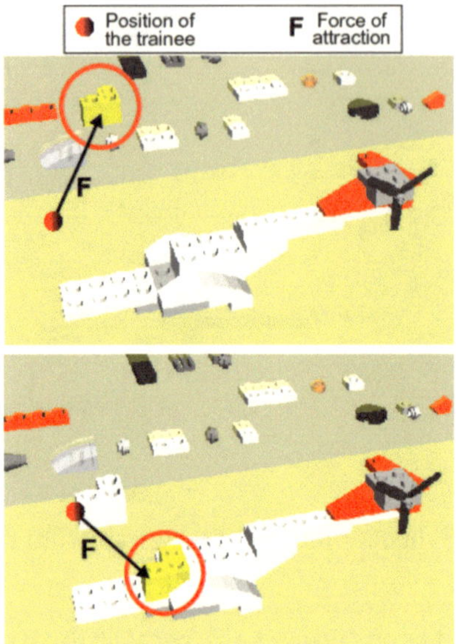

Fig. 9. Direct aids provided by the platform. On the top: aids to select the correct brick. On the bottom: aids to place the brick in its correct position.

session, the aids were displayed only when the trainees request them by pressing the help key. Finally, during the third and fourth sessions, the aids were displayed only when the trainee requested them as in the second one, but they had also made at least one attempt of selecting the correct brick, i.e. the trainees had to try selecting the correct brick by themselves before being able to receive the aid. Each requested help was automatically logged as one aid.

In both groups, when trainees selected an incorrect piece, the platform played a "beep" sound and displayed a message to indicate the mistake. To evaluate the performance of the trainee the system also logged the number of incorrect pieces selected. Additionally, the order of the steps was fixed and numbered from 1 to 75, therefore both strategies followed the same building order.

4.3 Participants

The experiment was undertaken with 40 undergraduate students and staff from CEIT, the University of Navarra and TECNALIA. Following a between-participants design, each participant was assigned to one of the two experimental groups (20 participants in each one). For the assignment of the participants to the groups, first they filled in a demographic questionnaire whose answers were used to distribute them along the two groups in an homogeneous way. In the direct aids group, 48% of participants were female, the average age was 33 with a range from 24 to 50, and only 32% of participants did not have any experience with LEGO™ models. Meanwhile, in the indirect aids group, 53% of participants were female, the average age was 36 with a range from 26 to 48 and only the 37% of participants did not have any experience with LEGO™ models. All participants reported normal sense of touch and vision and did not have experience in using haptic technologies.

Before starting the experiment, participants signed an informed consent agreement and they were informed that if they achieved the best performance of their group, they would receive a reward.

4.4 Procedure

The experiment was conducted in two consecutive days. The first day, the participants were familiarized with the MTS and the corresponding training condition. Later, they had to use the training system to learn how to build the virtual helicopter model during four training sessions (i.e. they built the virtual helicopter four times), with a short break between sessions to allow the examiner to restart the system. The initial position of the bricks was generated randomly, so it was different in each training session. The evaluator was in the room along with the participant and information about the task performance (number of aids, number of errors and the training time) was logged automatically by the system for further analysis of the data. At the end of the training, the participants of both groups were requested to fill in a questionnaire to evaluate their experience with the multimodal system.

The second day, the participants had to build the real LEGO™ helicopter model (the same one as in the training sessions). Each participant was instructed to complete the model as rapidly as possible, but without mistakes and missing bricks. At that time, the participants had the instruction book to consult it when they did not know how to continue with the task and this action was recorded as one "aid". The session was recorded in video for further analysis.

4.5 Performance measures

The measures to analyze the final performance of the trainee were: the training time, the real task performance (execution time, number of aids with the instruction book, number of non-solved errors and type of errors) and the evolution of the performance of the trainee along the training process and the transition from the training system to the real task. The subjective evaluation of the platform was also analyzed.

4.6 Results and discussion

Before starting to analyze the results, it would be note that although the experimental task is simple conceptually its correct execution is difficult due to the requested cognitive skills component. The task required memorizing the exact position of 75 bricks, most of them without any indication for functional or semantic meaning (just bricks with different size, color and number of pins) and some of the assembly procedure was totally arbitrary (different combinations of the bricks could generate the same shape of the helicopter model but only one specific combination was considered valid and the rest of options were considered as non-solved errors).

In general, there were not significant differences between the results obtained in both groups. Statistical analysis was performed with independent-samples t-tests, equal variances assumed.

Figure 10 shows that the mean real task execution time for the direct aids group, 18.6 minutes, dd not have significant difference with the mean time for the indirect group, 17.9 minutes ($t36=0.36$, $p=0.721$). Nevertheless, it is important to point out that during the building of the real LEGO™ model, the participants of the indirect aids group had some advantages respect to the others because they were used to consult the instruction book during the training period, and in this way they could get the information quicker than the others.

In order to analyze the real task performance obtained in each group, each step of the task (75 steps in total) was classified according to the following criteria:

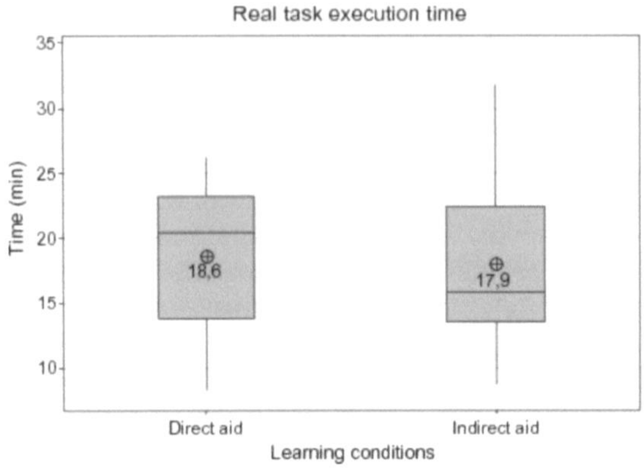

Fig. 10. Real task execution time.

- Correct step: the participants made the step correctly (without any non-solved error) and without the use of the instruction book.
- Step with aids: the participants made the step correctly (without any non-solved error), although they looked at the instruction book because they had some doubts about how to undertake the step, or they did not know how to continue or how to solve an error.
- Step with non-solved errors: the participants made some error in the step and they did not solve it because they did not know how to solve it or they were not aware of the error.

Taking into account this classification, Figure 11 shows that there were not significant differences between the real task performances obtained in each group. In both groups, the mean of correct steps (i.e. steps performed by the participants without the use of the instruction book and without non-solved errors) was around the 60% of the total steps, and the mean of steps with non-solved errors was very small, less than the 2% of the total steps. The typology of the non-solved errors was also similar in both groups. Most of the non-solved errors were related to the missing or wrong assembly of small pieces. Figure 12 shows some examples.

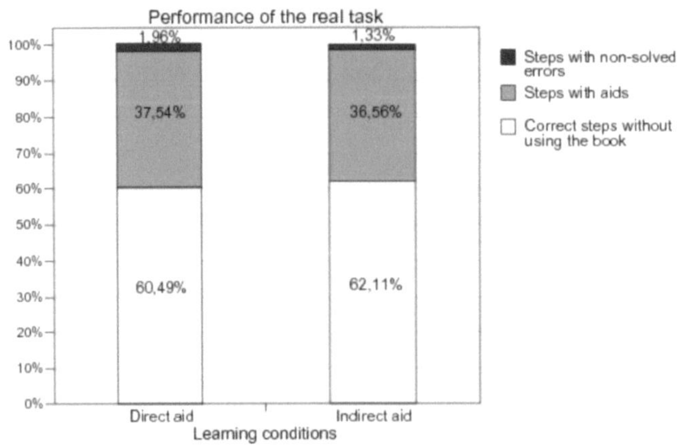

Fig. 11. Comparison of the real task performance between the two strategies.

In more detail, Figure 13 shows the mean number of consults to the instruction book during the real task, in which there were not significant differences between both groups

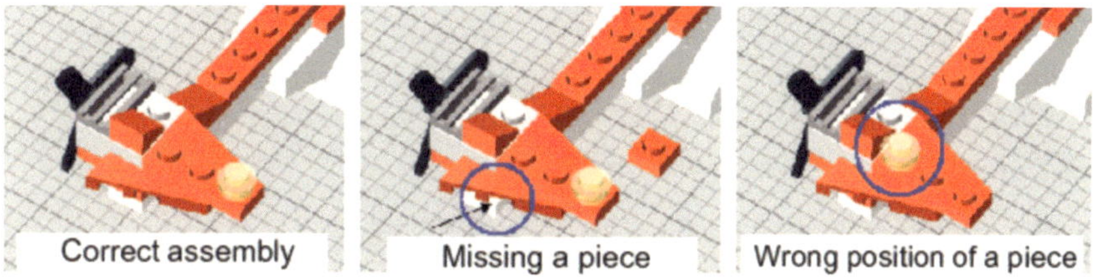

Fig. 12. Examples of a correct assembly, missing a piece and wrong position of a piece.

(t_{36}=0.14, p=0.889). Although no participant was able to build the real LEGO™ model without consulting the instruction book, the mean number of aids was less than 29 for both strategies. Additionally, the percentage of errors corrected by the participants without using the instruction book (see Figure 14) was larger in the direct aids group (28.6%) than in the indirect aids group (20.7%), so it seems the participants of the direct aids group could have created a better mental model of the task.

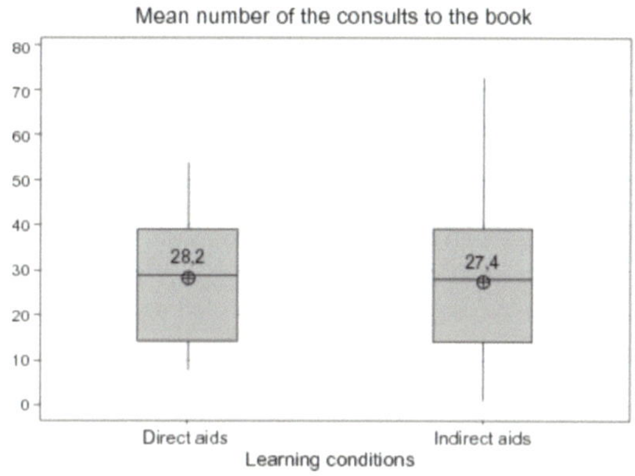

Fig. 13. Mean number of consults to the instruction book during the real task.

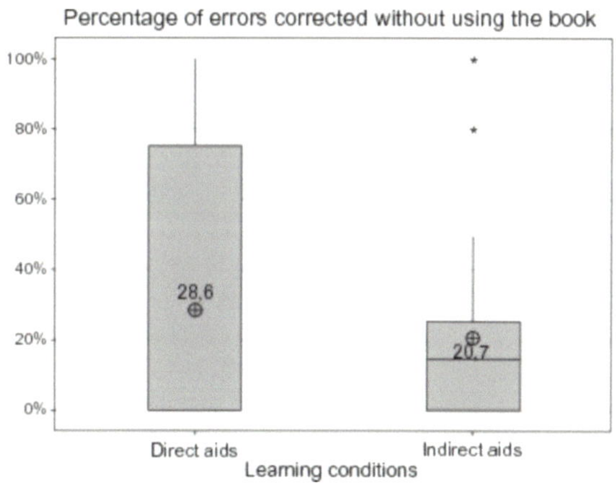

Fig. 14. Percentage of errors corrected by the trainees without using the book during the real task.

Regarding the analysis of the evolution of the performance of the trainees along the training process and the transition from the training platform to the real scenario, Figures 15 and

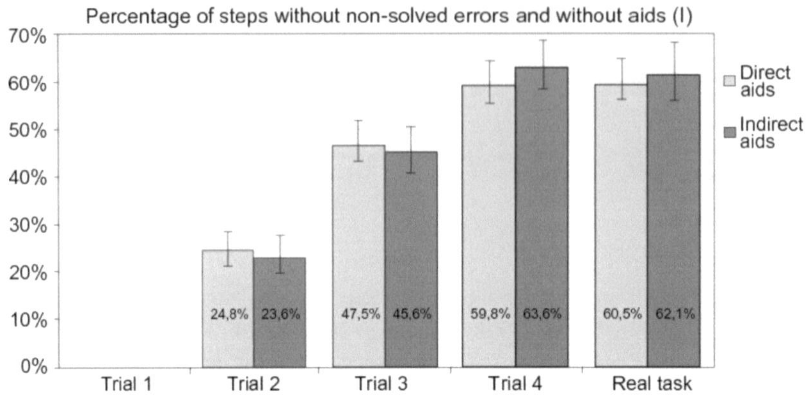

Fig. 15. Evolution of the performance of the trainees (percentage of steps without non-solved errors and without aids) in each group.

16 show that the percentage of correct steps (without non-solved errors and without aids) increased along the training trials. Moreover, in the direct aids group the performance obtained in the real task was a little better than in the last trial of the training process, even though the real task was performed the day after of the training sessions. Additionally, the statistical analysis demonstrates that there was not significant differences in the transition from the MTS to the real task between both groups ($t36=0.11$, $p=0.911$). This fact demonstrates that the controlled use of direct aids does not damage the trainees performance when they change from the training platform (virtual task) to the real world (physical task) and therefore it eliminates the main disadvantage of the use of direct aids reported in the bibliography (Yuviler-Gavish et al. (2011)). It means, the controlled direct aids did not impede the transfer of knowledge as it was hypothesised in this experiment.

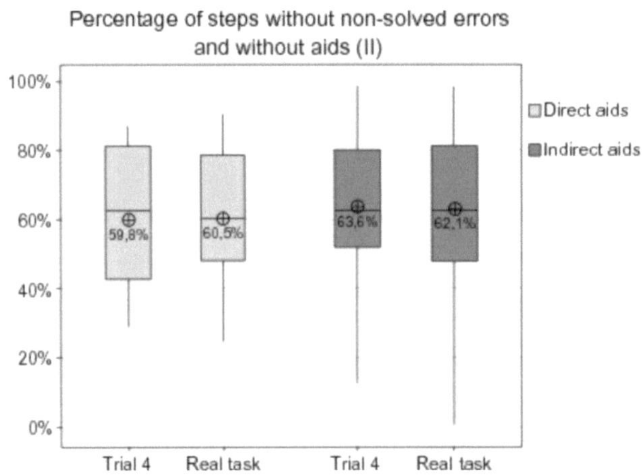

Fig. 16. Detailed information about the performance of the trainees (percentage of correct steps without non-solved errors and without aids) in the last training trial and in the real task.

In relation to the last performance measure, Figure 17 shows the mean total training time at each group where the statistical analysis demonstrates that there was not significant difference between both groups ($t36=-0.78$, $p=0.442$). But, it is also interesting to analyze the training time in each one of the training trials. Figure 18 shows that in the trial 1, in which the participants of both groups had just to use the information about the task in order to build the virtual model, the training time of the direct aids group was almost the half of the time of the indirect aids group (12.8 minutes in comparison with 22.5 minutes). And in the trials 3 and 4, although the participants of the direct aids group had the constraint of having to make an attempt of grasping the correct brick before being able to receive the aid, their training time was very similar to the time of the indirect aids group, in which the participants did not have this restriction. All these considerations indicate that a suitable use of direct aids can increase the efficiency of the training process since it could reduce the training time and maintain the same performance level.

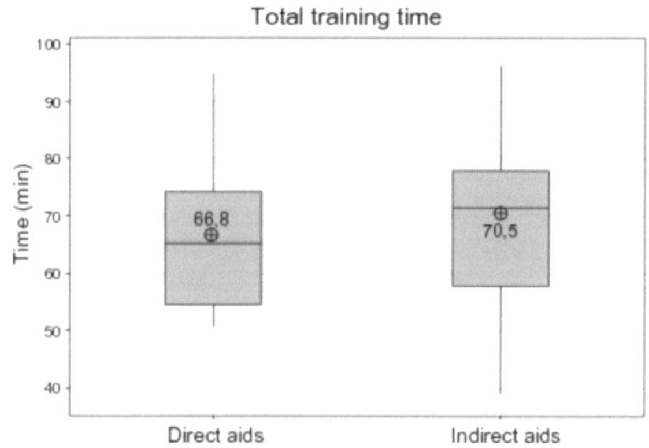

Fig. 17. Total training time at each experimental group.

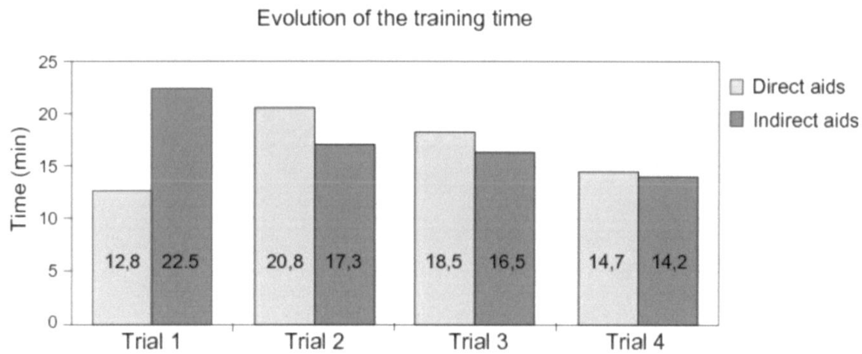

Fig. 18. Evolution of the time along the four training sessions

At the end of the training sessions all participants filled in a questionnaire, which was a reduced version of Witmer & Singer's Presence Questionnaire (Witmer & Singer (1998)). Since the haptic technologies provide a new interaction paradigm, this set of questions was useful to get extra information about the experience with the haptic training platform. The questionnaire consisted of 8 main semantic differential items, each giving a score in the scale from 1 (worst) to 7 (best).The questionnaire was elicited by the following questions:

- Q1. How natural was the mechanism which controlled movement through the environment? (Extremely artificial = 1, Natural = 7).

- Q2. How well could you concentrate on the assigned tasks or required activities rather than on the mechanisms used to perform those tasks or activities? (Not at all = 1, Completely = 7).
- Q3. How was the interaction with the virtual environment during the training session? (Difficult = 1, Easy = 7).
- Q4. During the training session how did you feel? (Nothing comfortable = 1, Strong comfortable = 7).
- Q5. During the training sessions, did you learn the task? (Nothing 0% = 1, All 100% = 7).
- Q6. Are you able to repeat the task with the real bricks? (No, I can't do it = 1, Yes, I can do it = 7).
- Q7. How consistent was you experience in the virtual environment with respect to the real scenario? (Nothing consistent =1, Strong consistent=7).
- Q8. What mark do you give to the Multimodal Training System as a training tool? (The worst = 1, The best = 7).

As it is shown in Figure 19 and 20, the results of the questionnaires did not have significant differences among the two groups. This fact seems logic since the interaction of the participants with the trianing system was similar in both groups; the difference was only the way in which the information about the task was provided. In general, the questionnaire results were quite positive.

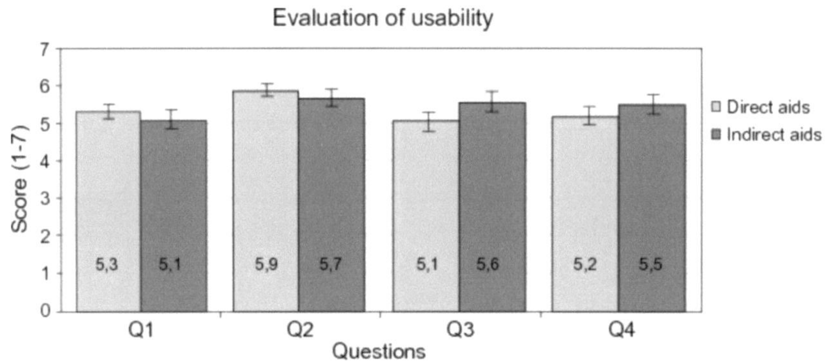

Fig. 19. Level of usability of the Multimodal Training System.

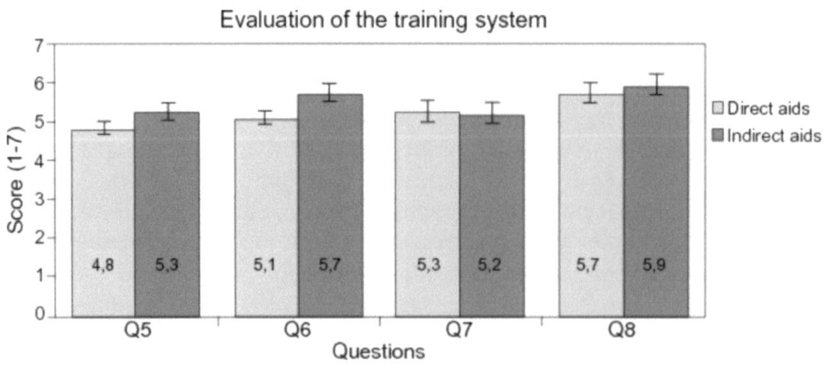

Fig. 20. Evaluation of the system as a tool to learn procedural tasks.

The questions 1 to 4 (see Figure 19) measured the usability of the training platform. The results of these questions indicate that participants concentrated quite well on the task and the platform was easy to use. Nevertheless, participants did not feel totally comfortable using the system. Some participants suggested eliminating the use of keyboard for sending commands to the application by adding more buttons in the stylus of the haptic device. Moreover, they suggested increasing the duration of the familiarisation session in order to increase the level of confidence using the training platform.

The questions from 5 to 8 evaluated the system as a training tool. As showed in Figure 20, participants were quite confident to perform the real task and rated the system with a score of 5.7 (in the direct aids group) and 5.9 (in the indirect aids groups) as a training tool. Some of the participants in the group of direct aids commented that they did not like to be forced to make an attempt of grasping the correct brick before being able to receive the aid.

5. Conclusions and future research

This chapter presents a new Multimodal Training System for assembly and disassembly procedural tasks. Some features of this system are:

- It supports the approach of *learning by doing* by means of an active multimodal interaction (visual, audio and haptic) with the virtual scenario, eliminating the constraints of using the physical (real) scenario: mainly availability, time, cost, and safety constraints. For example, providing training when the machine is still in the design phase or it is working and can not be stopped or when errors during the training can damage the machine or the trainee.
- It provides different multimodal aids, not available in the real world, that help and guide the trainees during the training process.
- Its flexibility to adapt itself to the demands of the task and to the preferences/needs of the trainees, for example: flexibility in the available training strategies, flexibility in the sensory channel used to provide feedback and flexibility in the supported haptic devices.

In this work the characteristics, advantages and dissavantages of the use of VR Technologies for training were also described. One of the main drawbacks in the use of Virtual Training Systems is that trainees become increasingly dependent on the features of these systems which may inhibit the ability to perform the task in the absence of them. This negative effect in the use of virtual aids was analyzed in the experiment described in this chapter and the findings suggest that the use of a strategy based on providing direct aids in a controlled way does not damage the knowledge transfer from the virtual system to the real world.

This outcome is in contrast with other research works that shows the negative effects of the use of direct aids. Moreover, from the point of view of the authors, the use of direct aids could reduce the training time and therefore increase the efficiency of the training process. In this way, further experiments should be run in order to analyze in which way the use of direct aids could decrease the training time without damaging the final performance of the trainees.

During the experiment described in this chapter, the authors detected three main behaviour patterns in the participants that can be useful to define some design recommendations for the design of the virtual aids:

1. Participants who like trying by themselves the next action but when they do not know how to continue they request help. In this case, it would not be necessary to add any constraint to be able to receive the aid, it would be enough that the aid was provided on demand.

2. Participants who prefer performing the next action by themselves although they do not know it, so they make a lot of attempts to guess the correct option. In most cases, these participants only spent more training time without making any improvement in their knowledge. It would be suitable to define a maximum number of attempts, so after achieving this limit the aid was provided automatically by the system. This maximum number of attempts should be configurable and could depend on the profile of the trainee or the target task.
3. Participants who want to have an easy access to the aid when they do not know how to continue. These participants were annoyed by being forced to make an attempt of grasping the correct brick before being able to receive the aid, and in addition the training time increased without any benefit. In this case, when the trainees do not know how to continue, it is important that they can receive the aid from the system easily.

Lastly, a final recommendation for the future implementation of virtual training systems is that the system should detect and evaluate the behaviour of trainees along the training session in order to display adequate information according with the evolution of their performance.

6. Acknowledgment

The authors would like to acknowledge the project SKILLS in the framework of European IST FP6 ICT-IP-035005-2006 and the "Ministerio de Ciencia e Innovación" (Spain).

7. References

Albani, J. & Lee, D. (2007). Virtual reality-assisted robotic surgery simulation, *Journal of Endourology* 21: 285–287.

Basdogan, C., Ho, C., Srinivasan, M. & Slater, M. (2000). An experimental study on the role of touch in shared virtual environments, *ACM Transactions on Computer-Human Interaction* 7: 443–460.

Bhatti, A., Khoo, Y., Bing, C., Douglas, A. J., Nahavandi, S. & Zhou, M. (2008). Haptically enabled interactive virtual reality prototype for general assembly., *Proceedings of the World Automation Congress WAC 08*, pp. 1–6.

Blake, M. (1996). The nasa advanced concepts flight simulator - a unique transport aircraft research environment., *The AIAA Flight Simulation Technologies Conference*.

Borro, D., Savall, J., Amundarain, A., Gil, J., García-Alonso, A. & Matey, L. (2004). A large haptic device for aircraft engine maintainability, *IEEE Computer Graphics and Applications*.

Dale, E. (1969). *Audio-Visual Methods in Teaching*, New York.

Derossis, A. M., Bothwell, J., Sigman, H. H. & Fried, G. M. (1998). The effect of practice on performance in a laparoscopic simulator., *Surgical Endoscopy* 12: 1117–1120.

Doyle, M. C. & Snowden, R. J. (2001). Identification of visual stimuli is improved by accompanying auditory stimuli: The role of eye movements and sound location., *Perception* 30: 795–810.

Ernst, M. O. & Bülthoff, H. H. (2004). Merging the senses into a robust percept., *Trends in Cognitive Science* 8: 162–169.

Gaba, D. M. (1991). Human performance issues in anesthesia patient safety., *Problems in Anesthesia* 5: 329–350.

Gaba, D. M. & DeAnda, A. (1988). A comprehensive anesthesia simulation environment: re-creating the operating room for research and training, *Anesthesiology* 69: 387–394.

Garcia-Robledo, P., Ortego, J., Ferre, M., Barrio, J. & Sanchez-Uran, M. (2011). Segmentation of bimanual virtual object manipulation tasks using multifinger haptic interfaces, *Instrumentation and Measurement, IEEE Transactions on* 60(1): 69 –80.
Gaver, W. W. (1994). *Using and creating auditory icons, in auditory displays: sonification, audification and auditory interfaces*, Addison Wesley.
Godley, S. T., Triggs, T. J. & Fildes, B. N. (2002). Driving simulator validation for speed research., *Accident Analysis & Prevention* 34: 589–600.
Gupta, R., Whitney, D. E. & Zeltzer, D. (1997). Prototyping and design for assembly analysis using multimodal virtual environments, *Computer-Aided Design* 29(8): 585–597.
Handel, S. & Buffardi, L. (1969). Using several modalities to perceive one temporal pattern., *Quarterly Journal of Experimental Psychology* 21: 256–266.
Held, R. & Durlach, N. (1992). Telepresence, *Presence: Teleoperators and Virtual Environments* 1: 109–112.
Heller, M. (1982). Visual and tactual texture perception: intersensory cooperation., *Perception & Psychophysics* 31: 339–344.
Holden, M. K. (2005). Virtual environments for motor rehabilitation: review., *CyberPsychology & Behavior* 8: 187–211.
Howell, J., Conatser, R., Williams, R., Burns, J. & Eland, D. (2008). The virtual haptic back: a simulation for training in palpatory diagnosis, *BMC Medical Education* .
Jayaram, S., Wang, Y., Jayaram, U., Lyons, K. & Hart, P. (1999). Vade: A virtual assembly design environment, *IEEE Computer Graphics and Applications* pp. 44–50.
Kneebone, R. (2003). Simulation in surgical training: educational issues and practical implications., *Medical Education* 37: 267–277.
Lee, W. S., Kim, J. H. & & Cho, J. H. (1998). A driving simulator as a virtual reality tool, *IEEE International Conference on Robotics and Automation*.
Mayes, T. (1992). *Multimedia Interface Design in Education*, Berlin: Springer-Verlag., chapter The M word: Multimedia interfaces and their role in interactive learning systems, pp. 1–22.
McDermott, S. D. & Bras, B. (1999). Development of a haptically enabled dis/re-assembly simulation environment, *Proceedings of DETC'99: ASME Design Engineering Technical Conferences*.
McLaughlin, A. C. & Rogers, W. A. (2010). Learning by doing: understanding skill acquisition through skill acquisition, *Human Factors and Ergonomics Society Annual Meeting Proceedings* pp. 657–661.
Morgan, P. J., Cleave-Hogg, D., DeSousa, S. & Tarshis, J. (2004). High-fidelity patient simulation: validation of performance checklists, *British Journal of Anaesthesia* 92: 388–392.
Murray, M. M., Molholm, S., Michel, C., Heslenfeld, D., Ritter, W., Javitt, D. C., Schroeder, C. & Foxe, J. J. (2005). Grabbing your ear: rapid auditory-somatosensory multisensory interactions in low-level sensory cortices are not constrained by stimulus alignment., *Cerebral Cortex* 15: 963–974.
Oviatt, S., Coulston, R. & Lunsford, R. (2004). When do we interact multimodally? cognitive load and multimodal communication patterns, *In Proc. of International Conference on Multimodal Interfaces*, ACM Press, pp. 129–136.
Reiner, M. (2004). The role of haptics in immersive telecommunication environments, *IEEE Transactions on Circuits and Systems for Video Technology* 14: 392–401.

Ritchie, J. M., Lim, T., Sung, R. S., Corney, J. R. & Rea, H. (2008). The analysis of design and manufacturing tasks using haptic and immersive vr: Some case studies, *Product Engineering* 5: 507–522.

Sanderson, P. M., Watson, M. O., Russell, W. J., Jenkins, S., Liu, D., Green, N., Llewelyn, K., Cole, P., Shek, V. & S., K. S. (2008). Advanced auditory displays and head-mounted displays: advantages and disadvantages for monitoring by the distracted anesthesiologist., *Anesthesia and Analgesia* .

Sarlegna, F. R., Gauthier, G. M. & Blouin, J. (2007). Influence of feedback modality on sensorimotor adaptation: Contribution of visual, kinesthetic, and verbal cues, *Journal of Motor Behavior* pp. 247–258.

Sarter, N. B. (2006). Multimodal information presentation: Design guidance and research challenges., *International Journal of Industrial Ergonomics* 36: 439–445.

Savall, J., Borro, D., Amundarain, A., Martin, J., Gil, J. & Matey, L. (2004). Lhifam - large haptic interface for aeronautics maintainability, *In Video Proceedings of the IEEE International Conference on Robotics and Automation (ICRA)*, New Orleans, Louisiana, USA.

Scott, O. (2005). Virtual environments for motor rehabilitation: review., *CyberPsychology & Behavior* 8: 215–216.

Seth, A., Su, H.-J. & Vance, J. M. (2008). Development of a dual-handed haptic assembly system: Sharp, *Journal of Computing and Information Science in Engineering* 8.

Sheridan, T. (1992). Musings on telepresence and virtual presence, *Presence: Teleoperators and Virtual Environments* 1: 120–125.

Sumby, W. & Pollack, I. (1954). Visual contribution to speech intelligibility in noise., *Journal of the Acoustical Society of America* 26: 212–215.

Wan, H., Gao, S., Peng, Q., Dai, G. & Zhang, F. (2004). Mivas: A multi-modal immersive virtual assembly system, *Proceedings of DETC'04: ASME Design Engineering Technical Conferences and Computers and Information in Engineering Conference*.

Weller, J. M. (2004). Simulation in undergraduate medical education: bridging the gap between theory and practice., *Medical Education* 38: 32–38.

Wickens, C. D. (2002). Multiple resources and performance predictions., *Theoretical Issues in Ergonomics Science* .

Wickens, C. D., Sandry, D. L. & Vidulich, M. (1983). Compatibility and resource competition between modalities of input, central processing, and output., *Human Factors* 25: 227–248.

Witmer, B. & Singer, M. (1998). Measuring presence in virtual environments: A presence questionnaire., *Presence: Teleoperators and Virtual Environments* 7: 225–240.

Yuviler-Gavish, N., Yechiam, E. & Kallai, A. (2011). Learning in multimodal training: Visual guidance can be both appealing and disadvantageous in spatial tasks., *Int. J. Hum.-Comput. Stud.* 69(3): 113–122.

4

The Users' Avatars Nonverbal Interaction in Collaborative Virtual Environments for Learning

Adriana Peña Pérez Negrón[1], Raúl A. Aguilar[2] and Luis A. Casillas[1]
[1]CUCEI-Universidad de Guadalajara
[2]Universidad Autónoma de Yucatán-Mathematics School
Mexico

1. Introduction

In a Collaborative Virtual Environment (CVE) for learning, an automatic analysis of collaborative interaction is helpful, either for a human or a virtual tutor, in a number of ways: to personalize or adapt the learning activity, to supervise the apprentices' progress, to scaffold learners or to track the students' involvement, among others. However, this monitoring task is a challenge that demands to understand and assess the interaction in a computational mode.

In real life, when people interact to carry out a collaborative goal, they tend to communicate exclusively in terms that facilitate the task achievement; this communication goes through verbal and nonverbal channels. In multiuser computer scenarios, the graphical representation of the user, his/her avatar, is his/her means to interact with others and it comprises the means to display nonverbal cues as gaze direction or pointing.

Particularly in a computer environment with visual feedback for interaction, collaborative interaction analysis should not be based only on dialogue, but also on the participants' nonverbal communication (NVC) where the interlocutor's answer can be an action or a gesture.

Human nonverbal behavior has been broadly studied, but as Knapp and Hall pointed out on their well-known book (2007): *"...the nonverbal cues sent in the form of computer-generated visuals will challenge the study of nonverbal communication in ways never envisioned"*.

Within this context, in a CVE each user action can be evaluated, in such a way that his/her nonverbal behavior represents a powerful resource for collaborative interaction analyses.

On the other hand, virtual tutors are mainly intended for guiding and/or supervising the training task, that is, they are task-oriented rather than oriented to facilitate collaboration.

With the aim to conduct automatic analyses intended to facilitate collaboration in small groups, the interpretation of the users' avatars nonverbal interaction during collaboration in CVEs for learning is here discussed. This scheme was formulated based on a NVC literature review in both, face-to-face and Virtual Environments (VE). In addition, an empirical study conducted to understand the potential of this monitoring type based on nonverbal behavior is presented.

1.1 Collaborative virtual environments for learning

Advances on technology, engineering, and instruction have enabled to diversify education and training support computer systems –see Table 1. Initially, the development of this kind of systems adopted the Computer Aided Instruction paradigm and was subsequently refined with Artificial Intelligence techniques implemented in the Computer Aided Intelligent Instruction paradigm. From the viewpoint of Artificial Intelligence, systems have been developed based on two rather divergent instructional approaches: Intelligent Tutoring Systems and Learning Environments (Aguilar, et al., 2010).

Computer Supported Collaborative Learning (CSCL) is probable the last of the paradigms emerged in the late nineteenth century. Koschmann (1996) referred to it as associated with instructional technology: "*This developing paradigm, for which the acronym CSCL has been coined, focuses on the use of technology as a mediational tool within collaborative methods of instruction*".

	Technology	Engineering	Instruction
T	Mainframes	Monolithic Programming	Behavioral Approach
I	Personal Computers	Structured Paradigm	Cognitive Approach
M	Networks & Peripheral Devices	Object Oriented Paradigm	Constructivist Approach
E	Virtual Reality	Agents Paradigm	Collaborative Learning Approach

Table 1. Advances on Technology, Engineering and Instruction

CSCL basis is the Socio-Constructivism theory, in which core idea is that human knowledge is constructed upon the foundation of previous learning and within the society. People, as social creatures, are highly influenced by the interaction with their socio-cultural environment, in such a way that this interaction contributes to the formation of the individuals.

CVEs for learning, the computer systems developed under the CSCL paradigm, can be described as a conceptual space in which a user contacts or interacts, in possibly different time and space conditions, with other users or their representation, or with elements of the environment such as data or objects. Thinking in CVEs in this way includes a conceptual asynchronous character that Churchill & Snowdon (1998) did not take into account.

According with the interface offered to the user, CVEs could be classified as:

- One-dimensional environments - based on text or text in combination with some symbols (e.g. emoticons).
- Two-dimensional environments - based on text and complemented with figures (e.g. comics).

- Three-dimensional (3D) environments - also known as Virtual Reality (VR) environments.

However, nowadays it is hard to imagine a multi-user VE without a graphical representation.

VR environments offer to their users different immersion degrees covering a wide range of possibilities that goes from the less immersive systems using only traditional desktop devices such as keyboard, mouse and monitor, to the highly immersive that use VR specific devices such as head-mounted displays (HMD), data gloves, or the CAVE™ .

The intend in using a CVE for instruction is to promote particular forms of interaction among the students inside the environment, by means of creating, encouraging, or enriching situations that would trigger learning mechanisms in the way Dillenbourg (1999) proposed.

CVEs provide the learner with a diversified set of computational features as well as a powerful context for learning in which time, scale and physics can be controlled; where participants can get new capabilities such as the ability to fly, or to observe the environment from different perspectives as an object or with any other virtual embodiment.

CVEs offer a space that brings remote people and remote objects together into a spatial and social proximity creating a natural interaction, which allows better communication awareness (Wolff et al., 2005) and where users are likely to be engaged in interaction with the virtual world and with other inhabitants through verbal and nonverbal channels. These characteristics make them a proper scenario for knowledge construction, concurrent with the socio-constructivist theory, as well as a proper tool for training in socio-technical tasks (e.g. in coordinated situation such as rescue operations or enterprise logistic).

For the multiuser condition, 3D CVEs represent a communication technology on their own right due to its highly visual and interactive interface character. They offer a learning context that may allow the trainees to practice skills and abilities, and to get knowledge in a situation that approximates the conditions under which they will be used in real life, but using a safe and flexible environment where materials do not break or wear out.

CVEs can be used to train one or more students in the execution of a certain task, mostly in situations in which training in the real environments is either impossible or undesirable because it is costly or dangerous.

1.2 Intelligent CVEs

In the Computer Aided Intelligent Instruction paradigm, there is a growing interest on the research aim of knowledge such as Intelligent Virtual Environments (IVE). VEs may incorporate in different degrees, characteristics of learning environments through an Intelligent Tutoring Systems (ITS). Where the intelligence skills generally fall into a Pedagogical Virtual Agent (PVA) to engage and motivate students along their learning process.

The traditional architecture for the ITS consists of four modules: the expert or domain module, containing the information to be taught; the student module, which maintains individualized information of the students; the tutoring module, which provides a model of the teaching process; and, the interactions with the learner controlled by the communication module. The ITS architecture adapted for an Intelligent Collaborative Virtual Environment (ICVE) (Aguilar et al., 2010) is shown in Figure 1.

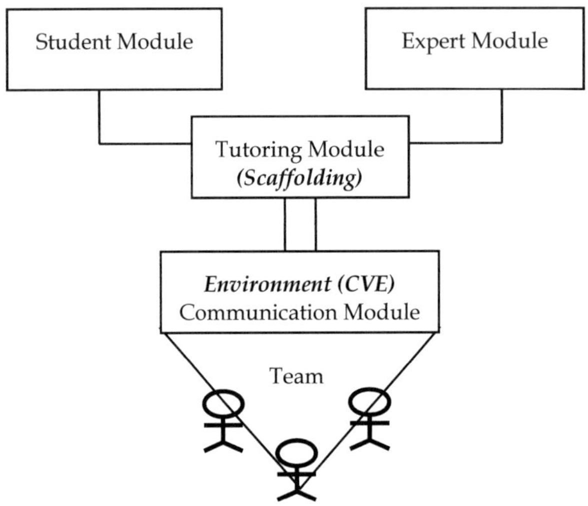

Fig. 1. ICVE Architecture

The systems for training developed to date may be classified depending on the issue they emphasize as: simulation processes, generation of believable environments, and collaboration processes; three aspects that can be integrated in a single system, an ICVE for learning.

The component in charge of the domain of the application has the capacity to execute the simulations of the task to be trained as they are executed in the present systems. VR technology allows recreating environments with believable features (Youngblut, 1998) offering the possibility of being trained in tasks that may be expensive, risky, or even impossible to reproduce in the reality.

Regarding the collaboration process, in an ICVE by including virtual agents to replace team members (Rickel, 2001), the trainees can have a team training experience when the complete human team is not available. It is also possible to integrate into the environment personified PVAs to offer them support, in the same way an instructor or a human peer would do.

Within VR technology, a PVA may assume a 3D representation similar to that used by a human in the environment; they can be embodied through an avatar. The PVAs personification seems to generate positive effects in the perception of the apprentices during their learning experiences (Lester et al., 1997), with two key advantages over earlier work: they increase the bandwidth of communication between students and computers; and they increase the computer's ability to engage and motivate students. Some early empirical results on PVAs embodied effectiveness are on the topics of (W. L. Johnson, Rickel, & Lester, 2000): interactive demonstrations, navigational guidance, gaze and gesture as attentional guides, nonverbal feedback, conversational signals, conveying and eliciting emotion, and virtual teammates.

A PVA can be defined as an intelligent agent that makes decisions about how to maximize the student learning process. PVAs as a result of its goal can function within the ICVE as tutors, mentors, assistances (Giraffa & Viccari, 1999), learning peers (Chou, Chan, & Lin, 2003) or as proposed in here, as a collaborative facilitator with the aim of enhancing the collaborative process; as mentioned, by the analysis of the nonverbal behavior of the users' avatars.

2. Nonverbal interaction in CVEs

Broadly defined, nonverbal behavior might include most of what we do; it even includes certain characteristics of verbal behavior by distinguishing the content, or meaning of speech, from paralinguistic cues such as loudness, tempo, pitch or intonation (Patterson, 1983). Moreover, the use of certain objects like our decided outfit, or the physical environment when used to communicate something, without saying it, has traditionally being considered as NVC. Nonverbal behavior can be used to substitute, complement, accent, regulate or even contradict the spoken message (Knapp & Hall, 2007).

In real life, nonverbal interaction involves three factors (Knapp & Hall, 2007): *environmental conditions*, *physical characteristics of the communicators*, and *behaviors of communicators*, all of them clearly restricted to the computer scenario conditions.

The *environmental conditions* that will probably affect the most during interaction in a computer scenario are given by the architecture and virtual objects around, what Hall (1968) defined as fixed-features, space organized by unmoving boundaries such as a room, and semi-fixed features, the arrangement of moveable objects such as a chair.

In a computerized environment, the *physical characteristics* of the interactants will be given by the users' avatar both appearance and body movements. While the appearance typically is given by a set of characteristics for the user to choose, like male or female avatar, and maybe a set of different cloths, skin or hair colors for example. As of body movements, Kujanpää & Manninen (2003) presented a considerable set of possible elements an avatar can include to manage the transmitting of NVC.

The avatar's body movements are usually restricted mainly due to their associated technology cost. Typically, in CVEs the users' avatars are naturalistic (Salem & Earle, 2000), with a low-level details approach and humanoid-like, they can display some basic humans' actions or expressions.

Other important consideration is that the means offered by the CVE to the user, in order to transmit NVC to his/her avatar, interfere with its spontaneity and therefore its revealing. The three different approaches to transmit nonverbal behavior from the users to his/her avatar in a VE (Capin et al., 1997) are:

1. directly controlled with sensors attached to the user;
2. user-guided, when the user guides the avatar defining tasks and movements; and
3. semi-autonomous, where the avatar has an internal state that depends on its goals and its environment, and this state is modified by the user. For example, when in a video game, the player achieves a goal and his/her avatar celebrates it.

The *behaviors of communicators* relay on the context that in a CVE will be given by its purpose. For example, in a video game, the users' interaction will be controlled by their intention on getting the goals of the game, while in a social CVE the participants interaction will be more likely to be directed to those they feel socially attracted –see Table 2.

Nonverbal interaction influential factors	Constrained in a CVE to	
Environmental conditions	• the fixed-features of the scenario • the semi-fixed features of the scenario	
Physical characteristics	the users' avatars	• appearance • body movements
Behaviors of communicators	according to the CVE purpose	

Table 2. Conditions of the nonverbal interaction factors in a CVE

Specifically *for a CVE for learning*, the *environmental conditions* will most likely to be constrained by the domain to be taught and the selected pedagogical strategy. The pedagogical strategy will determine the session configuration, like a theme of discussion, solving a problem or accomplishing a task.

Consistent with Collaborative Learning theories the participants' interaction should be implied in the CVE, and recommendable for learning purposes can be to solve a problem through the accomplishment of a task; considering that one of their main advantages is the spacial space with shared objects they offer. Within the CVE, the entities on it with the faculty of being manipulated by the users, the semi-fixed features, will take part of their verbal and nonverbal interchange on being the means to the accomplishment of the task.

As mentioned, the *physical characteristics* of the communicators in a computer-generated environment are determined by his/her avatar's stipulations. The avatar appearance in a learning scenario may represent the apprentices' role. For example, if a firefighter will be trained, his/her avatar will be most likely to use the firefighter's uniform to distinguish him/her from other users.

In order to accomplish the learning purpose in the CVE, the apprentices will control their avatars to communicate, navigate and modify the environment. For that, the mainly related areas of NVC are:

Paralinguistics that comprises all non-linguistic characteristics related to speech like the selected language, the tone of voice, or the voice inflexions, among others.

Proxemics, the analyses of the chosen body distance and angle during interaction (Guye-Vuillème et al., 1998).

And **Kinesics,** the study of what is called "body language", all body movements except physical contact, which includes gestures, postural shifts and movements of some parts of the body like hands, head or trunk (Argyle, 1990).

As of the *behaviors of communicators* in a virtual learning scenario, of special interest should be those related to collaborative interaction, that is, those behaviors that transmit something about how the group members collaborate in order to achieve the common goal; and they will be consistent with the nonverbal behavior carried out for the service-task function (Patterson, 1983).

The nonverbal behavior in collaborative interaction is expected to be mainly intended for the accomplishment of the task. Following the Miles L. Patterson (1983) Sequential Functional Model for nonverbal exchange, people's interaction behavior is the consequence of a sequence of related events. At the foundation of this model is the distinction made between the interaction behavior on itself and the functions served by them. Distinguishing the function served by the interaction behavior means to recognize that the same behavioral patterns can serve very different functions in an interaction.

In the service-task function proposed by Patterson (1983), the service component refers to interaction determined by a service relationship between individuals, for example, a physician-patient interaction. While the task function, influential for a CVE for learning, identifies focused or unfocused interactions that require people to relate others through a particular task or activity.

According to Patterson (1983), the necessity for variable involvement in task-oriented focused interactions, such as when people collaborate to accomplish a task, seems relatively straightforward. Understanding this type of nonverbal interaction keeps the interpretation of nonverbal behavior to an acceptable extent from cultural and personality influences, since the service-task function identifies determinants of nonverbal involvement that are generally independent of the quality of interpersonal relationships. Accordingly, the nonverbal interaction conditions for a CVE for learning are presented in Table 3.

Nonverbal interaction influential factors	**Their conditions in CVEs for learning**
Environmental conditions	• an scenario according to the domain to be taught • operable objects for the learning purpose
Physical characteristics	the users' avatars • appearance • allowed body movements
Behaviors of communicators	consistent with the service-task function

Table 3. Conditions of the nonverbal interaction factors in CVEs for learning

In order to make use of a nonverbal communication cue to monitor collaboration, it needs to have the faculty of being transmittable to the CVE and recognizable by the computer system. With this in mind, the nonverbal communication cues suggested for the interaction analysis as described in Peña & de Antonio (2010) are:

Talking turns - the paralinguistic branch that studies, not what or how people talk but amounts and patterns of talk and that have been use for the comprehension of interaction in different ways as in (Bales, 1970; Jaffe & Feldstein, 1970).

Proxemics – to understand the users' position within the environment and related to others.

Facial expressions – in real life, they might be difficult for interpretation, but when transmitted to a VE not directly controlled by the user, their intention is usually predefined by the system as in the case of the emoticons.

Artifacts manipulation – when they are part of the collaborative interaction.

Body movements - such as gaze direction, deictic gestures, head movements and some body postures.

In the next section the analysis of nonverbal behavior from the participants in a collaborative task within a CVE are discussed. Afterwards, a model for an intelligent tutor based on nonverbal behavior with the intent to facilitate collaborative sessions is presented.

3. Case of study

Working together to accomplish a task does not necessarily mean that the outcome is due to collaboration. It could be, for example, the result of splitting the task and then putting the parts together, or the task could be accomplished by some participants giving orders while others just follow them. In consequence, if Collaborative Learning is expected some factors have to be observed like the maintained focus on the task, the creation of shared ground, division of labor, and the Plan-Implement-Evaluate cycle.

A collaborative learning session usually begins with an initial introductory social phase, especially if the members of the group do not know each other; students tend to socialize before initiating collaboration in the strict sense (Heldal, 2007). This social conduct can be repeated in the session to maintain a balance between the social and the task aspects of the meeting. Nevertheless, even the fact that this social behavior is necessary for the proper function of a work group, it is also important that it is kept in due proportions, and *focus on the task* has to be maintained.

In order to achieve collaboratively a task, participants have to share information or common ground, that is, mutual knowledge, mutual beliefs, and mutual assumptions; and this *shared ground* has to be updated moment-by-moment (Clark & Brennan, 1991). This mechanism is the individual attempt to be understood, at least to an extent that the task can be accomplished.

Division of labor may appear during the whole session or in parts of it; the kind of task will determine its convenience.

In addition, whereas a maintained balance between dialogue and action is desirable, it is also expected an appropriate approach to problem solving, based on the *Plan-Implement-Evaluate* cycle (Jermann, 2004).

The study was conducted with the purpose of understanding the participation of the members of a group, in both dialogue and implementation; and the group process phases: Planning, Implementation, and Evaluation, by identifying patterns derived from selected NVC cues extracted from the group behavior during a session while they carry out a task in a CVE.

3.1 Observing NVC cues

In trying to understand the use of some NVC cues, an experimental application was developed. The VICTOR (VIrtual Collaborative Task- Oriented) application allows three users net-connected to work in a collaborative task, in which the three users' avatars are placed around a table, their workspace.

The NVC cues available in the environment were narrowed to those observed in a study conducted in a real life situation where three people seated around a shared workspace were asked to place a set of drawn furniture on an apartment sketch -see (Peña & de Antonio, 2009) for further details.

These NVC cues are talking turns, objects manipulation, gazes to the workspace and to peers, and pointing to objects, next described for collaborative interaction:

Talking turns and amount of talk. The idea of taking the time that group members speak to understand group process is not new. In 1949, Eliot Chapple created the chronograph interaction; a device to measure persons' amount of talk with the intention of analyzing talk-turns structure (Chapple, 1949). Since then, frequency and duration of speech have been useful tools for the analysis of group interaction in a number of ways, for example to create regulatory tools for meetings as in (Bergstrom & Karahalios, 2007). The students' rates of speech will help to determine if they are participating during discussion periods and to what extent.

Artifacts manipulation and implementation. When the group's common goal implies implementation, it is desirable a maintained balance between dialogue and action (Jermann, 2004). Artifacts manipulation is an object form of nonverbal behavior, as it can be part of the answer to an expression. The amount of work a student realizes, aside of its quality, is a good indicative of that student's interest and participation on the task.

Gazes. The eyes direction is a reliable indicative of a persons' focus of attention (Bailenson et al., 2003). Via the students' gazes, it can be determined to what they are paying attention.

Deictic Gestures. Deictic terms such as "here, there, that", are interpreted resulting from the communication context, and when the conversation is focused on objects and their identities, they are crucial to identify them quickly and securely (Clark & Brennan, 1991). Consequently, deictic gestures directed to the shared objects or the workspace should be useful to determine whether students are talking about the task.

In the application, the user does not see his/her own avatar −see Figure 2. The users' avatars do not have a natural behavior; they are just seated representations of the user that need a metaphorical representation of their actions in the environment.

The significant entities associated to the avatars actions are: colored arrows coupled to their hair color (yellow, red, or brown) that take the place of their hands, and can be used to point the objects or grab them to be moved; by a mouse click, the arrow is activated. To move the objects once they have being selected, the WASD keys can be used to direct them.

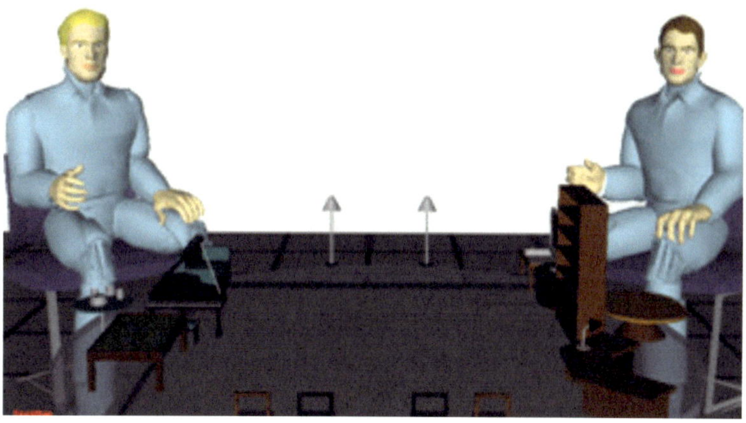

Fig. 2. Experimental application

The avatars' head is another entity that can take four positions to change the user field of view; to the front where the other two peers can be seen, to the right or left to see directly one of the peers, or down to see the workspace -see Figure 3, for that the arrow keys are used.

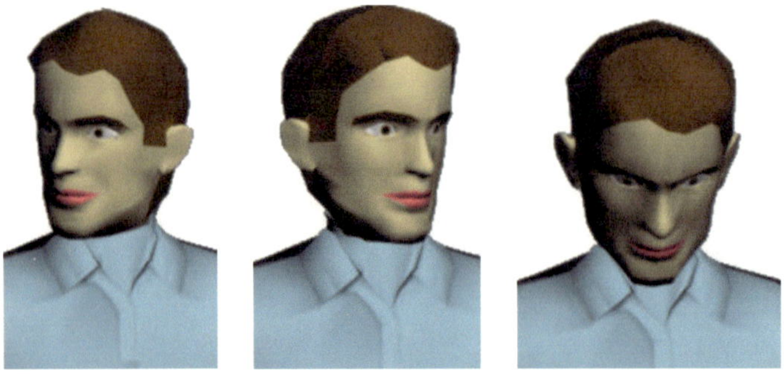

Fig. 3. The avatar head movements

And, when the user is speaking a dialogue globe appears near his/her right hand as showed in Figure 4., when the user wants to speak he/she needs to press the spacebar key.

This first trial was conducted with the aim of modeling a virtual tutor to facilitate collaboration. In the next session, the tutor implementation is discussed.

Fig. 4. The dialogue globe

3.1.1 Method

Subjects. Fifteen undergraduate students, 14 males and 1 female from the Informatics School at the Universidad de Guadalajara were invited to participate. Five groups of triads were formed voluntarily.

Materials and Task. The task consisted on the re-arrange of furniture on an apartment sketch to make room for a billiard or a ping-pong table; the group decided which one of them.

Procedure. A number of rules with punctuation were given regarding on how to place furniture such as the required space for the playing table, spaces between furniture and restriction on the number of times they could move each piece of furniture. The instructions were given both verbally and in written form.

Participants were allowed to try the application for a while before starting the task in order to get comfortable with its functionality. The time to accomplish the task was restricted to 15 minutes. Sessions were audio recorded.

Data. Every student intervention within the environment was recorded in a text log file. The logs content is the user identification; the type of action , i.e. move furniture, point furniture, a change in the point of view of the environment, when speaking to others; and the time the intervention was made in minutes and seconds. Data was manipulated to identify discussion periods and the session stages.

Discussion periods

Discussion periods are important in a collaborative session because when they occur, planes, evaluation and agreements are settled. A number of talking-turns involving most of the group members seems to be an appropriate method for distinguishing them from situations like a simple question-answer interchange, or the statements people working in a group produce alongside their action directed to no one in particular (Heath et al., 1995).

A talking turn, as defined by Jaffe and Feldstein (1970), begins when a person starts to speak alone, and it is kept while nobody else interrupts him/her. For practical effects, in a computer environment with written text communication, the talking turn can be understood as a posted message, and in oral communication as a vocalization.

Discussion periods for these trials were established as when each one of the three group members had at least one talking-turn. Because for automatic speech recognition the end of an utterance is usually measured when a silence pause occurs in the range of 500 to 2000 ms (Brdiczka, Maisonnasse, & Reignier, 2005), and the answer to a question usually goes in a smaller range, around 500 ms (A. Johnson & Leigh, 2001); to determine the end of a discussion period, pauses of silences were considered in the range of three seconds.

Initial-Planning-Implementation-Reviewing stages

The collaborative stages can be established by nonverbal cues in different ways, although it also has to relay on the specifications of the task and the instructor strategy for the session. For example, the initial phase could be the introduction to the problem within the environment.

In this case, because the task was explained in person, instruction were delivered to participants in written paper and they had an initial session to try the application, the initial stage was expected to be brief, more likely to be used to get the initiative to start. Then, the Planning stage was expected to start almost immediately; to identify it, the first discussion period was used.

The restrictions posted for the objects manipulation makes to expect that participants will not move objects if they have no implementation intention; therefore, the initiation of the stage was determined with the first movement of an object.

Once the group starts to implement, the discussions periods should mean that they are making new plans or changing them, because there is no way to differentiate new plans from reviewing those already made through the available nonverbal communication, the discussion periods within the Implementation stage were considered as Reviewing stages.

By the end of the Implementation, a final Reviewing stage to agree on the final details of the task was expected. The collaborative stages were then determined based on data logs as follows:

- *Initial stage* - starts with the session and ends when the Planning stage starts.
- *Planning stage* - starts with the first discussion period and ends when the Implementation stage starts.
- *Implementation stage* - starts when participants move the first piece of furniture.
- *Reviewing stage* - when discussion periods occur during the Implementation stage, and at the end of it.

3.1.2 Results

At a first glance to the data it could be overseen that the pointing mechanism was barely used; the speech content revealed that the users' had to make oral references to areas where there were no furniture because they could not point them. Due to this misconception in the design of the environment, pointing gestures were left out.

The changes in gazes were expected to be used to manage talking-turns. The number of times subjects directed their gaze to their peers while they were talking or listening, was relatively small compared to the number of times they were gazing to the workspace as shown in Table 4. A first attempt to understand gazes was to identify possible problems for the participants not using the mechanism as expected.

The possible identified problems in the experimental application were that when the user was viewing the workspace area, he/she did not receive enough awareness about the other users' gazes −see Figure 5. Users had sometimes to specify verbally whom they were addressing if not to both members. Also, sometimes even if they knew their peers names, they did not know which of the two avatars represented each of them.

An external person was asked to determine through the audio recorders, for each talking-turns interchange whether the students were having an episode in which they were taking decisions, making plans or reviewing one of those, that is, discussion periods. Only two interchanges involving two of the three members had these characteristics and the rest of them included the 43 discussion periods identified following the specifications. That is, almost 96% of the talking-turn interchanges with the three members involved were discussion periods.

Gazes	**While Talking**		**While Listening**	
Group	Workspace	Peers	Workspace	Peers
1	93	29	172	89
2	270	19	474	36
3	108	4	217	10
5	188	45	369	68

Table 4. Number of gazes to the workspace or peers while talking or listening

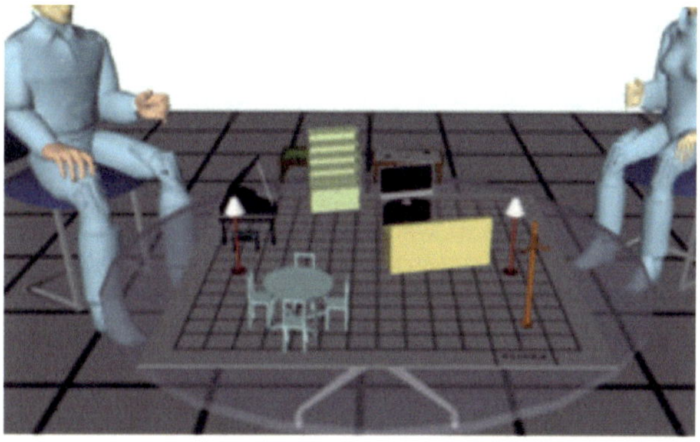

Fig. 5. Seeing down to the workspace

The team got points when its participants followed the given instructions, but if they did not, their punctuation was decremented. Other way to measure the group effectiveness was by comparing the number of movements required to get each piece of furniture where it was last placed, against the number of movements the team actually made; the more effective use of movements is then represented by a 0 difference. The game table was not taken into account for this effectiveness score because a group could not get to that point. In Table 5, the first and second rows show the score given for correctly following instructions as "Instructions Score", and the effectiveness in moving furniture as "Movements score".

The percentage of time each group spent in each session stage is also presented in Table 5, the row that follows the stage is the discussion time the group spent in that specific stage, and the final row presents the total percentage of time they used for discussion periods.

Regarding a collaborative intelligent tutor, a clear opportunity to intervene is the fourth team presented in Table 5. This team started almost immediately -after 2 seconds, with the implementation and then they had very short discussion periods; through the data, it seems that they worked almost in silence. In the audio tape at some point they commented "-remember that we are not supposed to talk" with apparently no reason and they worked to the end of the task in silence. However, they faked talking, that is, they pressed the talking-turn key probably to bring the others attention.

Stages / Group	1	2	3	4	5
Instructions score	39	93	22	-15	-17
Movements score	112	61	33	747	49
Initial	0.012	0.009	0.039	0.002	0.009
Planning	0.227	0.119	0.048	-	0.084
Discussion	0.194	0.115	0.025	-	0.071
Implementation	0.553	0.776	0.854	0.998	0.676
Discussion	0.366	0.574	0.277	0.043	0.178
Reviewing	0.209	0.097	0.058	0.002	0.231
Discussion	0.092	0.097	-	-	0.110
Total Discussion	0.651	0.786	0.303	0.043	0.360

Table 5. Percentage of time elapsed in session stages

This is a very small sample of data, and then it was decided not to treat it statistically. Even though it is worth mentioning, that the best scored groups in following the instructions, were those with the highest percentage of time in discussion periods.

The group 5 low score in following instructions was due to a misunderstanding about the task, they tried to put both gaming tables. With a PVA regarding the task during the session, it is probable that the collaborative process could be more attached to the task results.

This trial was meant to understand, the users' nonverbal behavior in order to model a PVA to facilitate collaboration. In the next session, how the tutor was modeled in this same application is presented.

3.2 Modeling the virtual tutor

The PVA model here propose, as already mentioned, aims to facilitate in time, understanding facilitation as guiding the group process, a collaborative 3D virtual session of a small group of participants. While they synchronously accomplish a task with an open-ended solution that implies the manipulation of objects, through monitoring their users' avatars NVC cues displayed during their collaborative interaction.

The experimental CVE was modified to implement the PVA and to correct some identified problems (see section 3.1.2). To solve the abovementioned misconception about the pointing mechanism, in this version, the arrow can be placed at some parts of the table, see Figure 6.

Then, to solve the awareness of others change of view when the user was viewing to the workspace, the avatars were shrunk in order to show a biggest part of their faces. For the participants to know whom to address verbally when talking, the name of the participant is now displayed in blue letters near his/her avatar - see Figure 6. Finally, the log files now include milliseconds in the timing.

Fig. 6. Experimental application, pointing to the table

Modeling the facilitator

The virtual facilitator has no graphical representation within the environment. Because the PVA is not meant to give feedback but in the collaborative process, it was considered that it might not need a body. The PVA advices are delivered via text messages posted at the bottom of the screen in black letters -see Figure 7.

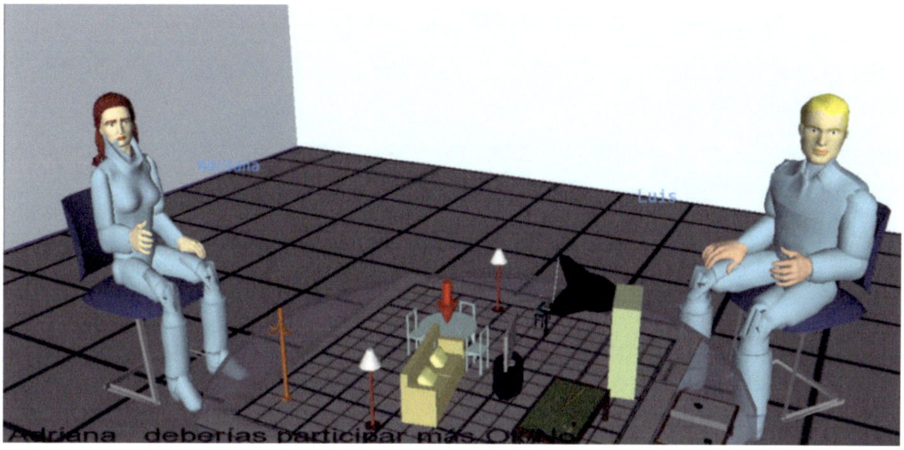

Fig. 7. A message from the IVA

Based on the participants' nonverbal behavior, the tutor makes recommendations regarding their participation and the expected stage sequence (i.e. Initial-Planning-Implement-Reviewing). The "F" key was activated, and when the participants end the session, one of them has to press it. The PVA messages regarding the stages are five and they are triggered under the circumstances described in Table 6.

The facilitator also displays other six messages regarding participation, two for each group member. The PVA verifies the percentage of participation from each member compared to the whole group participation, and applies a formula that implies a tolerance range to an exact equal participation.

Stage	Number / Message	Triggered when
Initial	0. "First step should be to talk about what to do"	Elapsed time *A* (3000 ms) from the beginning of the session in which participants do not initiate either a discussion period or implementation
Initial	1. "You should discuss before starting the implementation"	If they start implementation without having at least one discussion period, which implies they did not make a plan
Implement	2. "A review of what you have until now is advisable"	Elapsed time *B* (3000 ms) without a discussion period
Implement	3. "You should try to work as a team"	When the three of them were doing implementation at the same time
Implement	4. "Before leaving the session you should review your outcome"	Participants finish the session without having at least one discussion period after they finished the implementation.

Table 6. Messages from the facilitator to foster collaboration

The applied formulas were extracted from a real life situation (Peña & de Antonio, 2009) by a regression model. When the participants are in the Planning or a Reviewing stage the formula is based only on the subject talking time as follows:

1. subject's participation = −0.711 + (7.990 * percentage of talking time)

When the group is at the Implementation stage the applied formula includes the subject implementation as follows:

2. subject's participation = −1.759 + (6.742 * percentage of talking time) + (4.392 * percentage of manipulation time)

If the participant has an under participation (according to the formulas 1 or 2), that is when the result is under 1, this message encouraging him/her to increase his/her participation is sent: "<<participantName>>, you should try to increase your participation".

If the participant has an over participation, when the formula result is more than 3, the sent message is: "<<participantName>>, you should try to involve more your peers".

Message No	addressed to	with the intention to
5/6/7	SS / SA / SB	encourage his/her participation
8/9/10	SS / SAB/ SB	diminish his/her participation

Table 7. Messages from the facilitator regarding participation

The number of the triggered message corresponds to the user to be encouraged for participation or to diminish it as shown in Table 7; the three users were denominated SS, SA and SB. All the messages, although they have a participant target, are sent to the three group members.

When a message appears on the screen, the group members can agree or disagree with it by pressing the keys "O" for OK to agree or "N" for NO to disagree. Although users are not forced to answer the messages, when they do, a number of actions are taken: the message disappears from the screen; the chronograph of elapsed times is set to 0; the participant times are also set to 0; the participants' answers are included in the log file; and, if at least two of the three participants disagree with the message, it is deactivated, that means it will not appear again.

The log file has now information regarding the facilitator as another actor in the scenario, when the PVA sends a message and which one is sent by its number. There is an 11th message just to say "Good bye".

This second trial followed the same method as the first one, with the next differences:

Subjects. Twelve undergraduate students, 13 males from the Informatics School and a female from the Chemistry School at the Universidad de Guadalajara participated. Four groups of triads were formed voluntarily.

Procedure. Participants filled out a questionnaire at the end of the session.

Data. The starting time is now considered when the three computers are connected and not when the first action takes place as in the first trial.

Discussion periods were identified same as in the first trial, when the three group members have had at least one talking-turn, but now the pauses were considered in the range of 2000 ms since the system registers now the milliseconds.

3.2.1 Results

About pointing, in Table 8 is presented the number of times the group pointed a piece of furniture or to the table during each stage, the third row correspond to the Reviewing periods during the Implementation stage. Groups 2 and 3, same with the better performance in both collaborative process and the scores about the task, used the pointing mechanism during the Planning and the Reviewing stages, but Group 2, the highest score, pointed during Implementations most of the time during Reviewing periods.

Group	**1**	**2**	**3**	**4**
Planning	0	6	2	0
Implementation	13	8	10	13
Reviewing	2	14	0	0
Reviewing	0	2	1	0

Table 8. Pointing to the furniture and the workspace.

Gazes were now observed under a different perspective. It was detected that the change of view mechanism was being used, although as mentioned not while the user was talking or speaking, the users usually change their viewpoint repeatedly before doing something else, an average of 4.02 movements.

Because in real life people change the direction of gaze in a regular fashion notably associated with utterances (Kendon, 1990), it was decide to observe what the users were doing after they changed their viewpoint. For that, only the groups that went through the four stages were included. Results are shown in Table 9 for Groups 1 and 2 of the first trial; Table 10 for Groups 3 and 4 of the first trial; and Table 11 for Groups 2 and 3 of the second trial.

Group 1 without IVA										Group 2 without IVA									
Plan			Implement				Review			Plan			Implement				Review		
#	NA	GT	#	NA	GT	DP	#	NA	GT	#	NA	GT	#	NA	GT	DP	#	NA	GT
4	T	P	6	T	W					4	T	W	17	T	W		1	T	P
1	T	P	5	T	W	D							6	T	W	D	9	T	P
			5	M									18	T	W	D	12	T	P
			2	M									1	T	W	D	6	T	P
8	T	P	7	T	W	D	1	T	P				1	M		D	11	T	P
4	T	P											1	T	W		14	T	P
3	T	P								7	T	W	3	T	W	D	7	T	p
2	T	P								1	T	W	5	T	W		19	-	
5	T	W											2	T	W	D			
11	T	P	2	T	W	D	13	-					1	T	P	D			
4	T	P	2	M		D							4	T	W	D			
1	T	W											2	T	W	D			
2	T	W											3	T	W	D			
1	T	P																	
1	K	W																	

Table 9. Groups 1 and 2, of the first trial, gazes and the followed action

Group 3 without IVA										Group 4 without IVA									
Plan			Impement				Review			Plan			Impement				Review		
#	NA	GT	#	NA	GT	DP	#	NA	GT	#	NA	GT	#	NA	GT	DP	#	NA	GT
1	T	W	20	K	W	D	14	-		2	T	W					3	T	p
15	T	P	6	T	W		16	T	W								25	T	p
8	T	w	3	M	P												3	T	W
			4	T	W												1	-	
20	T	W								1	T	W	1	T	P	D	6	T	P
1	T	W											1	T	W		2	T	P
													1	T	P	D	1	T	W
													1	T	W	D	3	T	P
													7	T	W		1	T	P
										1	T	W	1	M	W		2	T	P
													2	M	P		2	T	P
													1	M	W	D	6	T	P
													3	T	W		1	T	P
													4	T	W		5	T	P
													4	T	W		3	T	P
																	4	T	P
																	8	T	P
																	4	T	W
																	6	T	P
																	10	T	P
																	4	-	

Table 10. Groups 3 and 4, of the first trial, gazes and the followed action

Group 2 with IVA										Group 3 with IVA									
Plan			Impement				Review			Plan			Impement				Review		
#	NA	GT	#	NA	GT	DP	#	NA	GT	#	NA	GT	#	NA	GT	DP	#	NA	GT
8	T	W	2	M	W								3	T	w		2	-	
1	T	P	2	K	W								3	T	w				
1	T	W	2	T	W								2	T	W				
			3	M	W								2	T	W	D			
			2	K	W	D				1	T	W	3	M	W				
			4	K	W	D							3	M	W				
			2	K	W	D							2	M	w	D			
13	T	P	2	T	P					3	T	W	1	M	P				
2	T	W	3	K									1	T	W	D			
1	T	P											2	M	W				
3	T	P											1	T	p	D			
2	T	W											1	T	w	D			
2	T	P																	
2	T	P																	
3	T	W																	
2	T	W	3	M	w		2	T	W										
3	T	P	3	M	w														
1	T	W																	

Table 11. Groups 2 and 3, of the second trial, gazes and the followed action

In these Tables (9, 10 and 11), for each group the first, second and third columns correspond to the Planning stage, columns 4, 5, 6 and 7th are for the Implementation stage, and the last three columns (8 to 10) are for the Reviewing stage. The first columns (#) of each group correspond to the number of times the user changed his/her point of view. The second column represents the next action (NA) after the viewpoint was changed as follows: "T" for talking, "K" for taking and "M" for moving a piece of furniture. In the third column is the final gaze target (GT) with a "P" when it was a peer and a "W" when it was the workspace. The same description can be applied for the 4, 5 and 6th columns, but the 7th column (DP) contains a "D" when the viewpoint changes were made during a discussion period. In the Reviewing stage, when the next action (NA) is a dash, it means that the user did nothing else afterwards. Each user has a different tone of gray.

Table 12 shows the messages sent by the PVA during the four group sessions. The number identifying the message is in the first column of each group. In the second column, the elapsed time of the session when it was sent, then the stage of the session in which it was sent. Columns 3, 4 and 5th contain the answer of the participant (SS, SA and SB). In the 6th column the tutor assumption regarding to the sent message, if two participants agreed with

Group 1

Msg	Elapsed Time	stg	SS	SA	SB	participants
1	01:24.428	Imp	OK	OK	NO	accepted
8	02:00.292	Imp	OK	OK	OK	accepted
8	03:04.611	Imp	-	OK	-	not answered
8	04:05.592	Imp	OK	OK	-	not answered
8	05:14.902	Imp	OK	OK	-	not answered
8	06:00.018	Imp	OK	OK	-	not answered
8	07:03.245	Imp	OK	OK	-	not answered
8	08:01.651	Imp	OK	OK	-	not answered
8	09:03.039	Imp	OK	OK	-	not answered
8	10:02.895	Imp	OK	OK	-	not answered
8	11:00.661	Imp	OK	OK	-	not answered
8	12:00.051	Imp	OK	OK	-	not answered
8	13:00.719	Imp	OK	OK	-	not answered
8	14:00.299	Imp	OK	OK	-	not answered

Group 2

Msg	Elapsed Time	stg	SS	SA	SB	participants
5	01:00.075	Pl	OK	NO	OK	accepted
5	03:11.334	Imp	OK	NO	OK	accepted
6	04:06.059	Imp	-	OK	OK	not answered
6	05:01.626	Imp	-	NO	OK	not answered
6	06:02.076	Imp	OK	OK	OK	accepted
9	07:04.133	Imp	-	OK	OK	not answered
9	08:04.147	Imp	OK	OK	OK	accepted
5	09:08.122	Imp	-	OK	OK	not answered
5	10:01.707	Imp	OK	OK	OK	accepted

Group 3

Msg	Elapsed Time	stg	SS	SA	SB	participants
9	01:00.824	Pl	OK	OK	OK	accepted
8	03:33.946	Imp	OK	OK	-	not answered
5	05:08.022	Imp	OK	-	-	not answered
5	05:17.445	Imp	-	-	-	not answered
5	05:24.917	Imp	-	OK	-	not answered
6	06:04.775	Imp	-	OK	-	not answered
5	07:00.779	Imp	-	-	-	not answered
5	08:00.091	Imp	-	-	-	not answered
6	09:01.539	Imp	-	OK	-	not answered
6	10:02.972	Imp	-	-	-	not answered
5	11:23.765	Imp	OK	NO	OK	accepted
5	12:00.893	Imp	NO	OK	-	not answered
5	13:05.846	Imp	OK	-	-	not answered
6	14:00.467	Imp	OK	OK	OK	accepted

Group 4

Msg	Elapsed Time	stg	SS	SA	SB	participants
0	01:19.576	Ini	OK	OK	-	not answered
0	03:17.621	Ini	OK	OK	OK	accepted
1	03:48.618	Imp	OK	OK	OK	accepted
5	05:02.890	Imp	OK	OK	-	not answered
5	06:20.266	Imp	-	-	-	not answered
9	07:00.936	Imp	OK	-	NO	not answered
8	08:03.414	Imp	OK	OK	OK	accepted
7	10:00.648	Imp	OK	OK	NO	accepted
5	11:02.028	Imp	OK	OK	OK	accepted
5	12:05.268	Imp	OK	OK	OK	accepted
5	13:04.828	Imp	OK	-	-	not answered
9	14:02.870	Imp	OK	OK	NO	accepted

Table 12. Facilitator messages sent during the sessions

it, the message is considered as "accepted". When one of the three members did not answer a message, it was considered as "not answered".

The resending of the same message responds, at some extent, to the fact that if the participants did not answer the message, the numbers were not cleared. None message was rejected, but there were many messages that were not answered by the whole group, and some participants ignored most of them.

Table 13 shows the scores each group got for following the instructions, the effectiveness in their furniture movements and the time each group elapsed in the stages.

Two of the four groups did no go through a Planning stage, Group 1 and 4. As can be seen in Table 13, the Group 4 had a very small amount of discussion time; this group did not finish the task.

Stages / Group	1	2	3	4
Score	-47	97	41	-18
Effectiveness	288	160	55	100
Initial	0.098	0.066	0.065	0.254
Planning	-	0.219	0.126	-
Discussion	-	0.090	0.081	-
Implementation	0.872	0.630	0.753	0.746
Discussion	0.064	0.282	0.230	0.077
Reviewing	0.030	0.085	0.056	-
Discussion	0.002	0.064	0.056	-
Total Discussion	0.066	0.397	0.367	0.077

Table 13. Percentage of time elapsed in session stages with the facilitator

3.2.2 Discussion

Most of the messages from the facilitator were to try to balance participation, 45 of 49 as can be seen in Table 12. From the 135 expected answers, almost a third (28.8%) did not arrive.

In Group 1, participant SB accepted the first two messages and then ignored the rest of them, but they were all the same message addressed to SS asking to diminish his participation. A similar condition can be found in Group 3 where participant SB ignored 11 messages, 7 of them addressed to encourage SS participation and 3 to encourage SA for participation, while in this same Group 3, SS ignored 7 messages from which 4 were addressed to him.

In summary, and although the answer to the specific question about the PVA that was "How proper do you consider the posted messages were?" in a scale of 1 to 4 got a 2.57 average score, there is not a clear perception from the participants of the PVA.

Did the facilitator affect the collaborative process?

Related to a balanced participation some observations can be done. Based in the personal messages responded by the target member, some members corrected their participation rate. For example, in Group 2, SA received three messages encouraging his participation, one of them was rejected, and then he received two messages asking him to involve more his peers, a clear change in his rate of participation. This type of change can be also observed, in Groups 3 and 4. Unfortunately, not all members corrected their participation rate, in that same Group 2, SS received two messages encouraging his participation and by the end received other two with the same advice.

A more concerning part could be regarding to the stages. Only four messages were sent, one to Group 1 and three to Group 4. The Group 1 received a message suggesting them to settle a plan before starting the implementation, members SS and SA agreed, but member SB who was the one who started the implementation, disagreed with the message and continued with it.

Group 4 received two messages suggesting to agree on decisions as a starting point. The group answered until the second one and agreed with it, but instead of having a discussion period as expected, they started the implementation. Thus, the facilitator sent a third message encouraging them to get an agreement before implementing, and even that the group agreed with the message, they kept moving furniture instead of having a discussion period as expected.

3.2.3 Learned lessons

As mentioned, the pointing mechanism can be used to monitor whether participants are talking about the task, to understand their involvement on it. In this case, the participants were video recorded and physically observed while they were carrying out the sessions; therefore, they were involved in the task no doubt. In these trials, the intention was its observation in order to incorporate data coming from it to the facilitator in the future, same as gazes.

In the accomplishment of a task like the one presented here, a mechanism to point objects or some areas is an advantage to identify them quickly; deictic gestures during collaboration in real life are more likely to appear during Planning and Reviewing phases. Although, we are completely aware that this is a very small data sample, in Table 13 can be observed that the Group 2 used it the most during these stages, and it is the one with the better scores regarding the task accomplishment and a more proper use of the collaborative stages. A first thought is to suggest its use during the collaborative session, especially during the Planning and Reviewing stages.

The change of gaze direction was used in a very particular way, see Tables 9, 10 and 11, a number of them (4.02 in average) usually preceded a talking turn, 81% of the times. This behavior may correspond to the fact that people try to get feedback from facial expressions when speaking or listening, but the avatars in the environment do not have them, then the users' change of gazes seem to be as an "announcement" that they were about to speak.

In the Planning stage, only one time the action following to the gaze changes was pointing. The final gaze target during the Planning stage to the peers was 43%, in the Implementation stage only 15%, and in the Reviewing stage, it was the 71 %. In the Reviewing stage, the followed action to the changes in the viewpoint, in 5 of the 34 times was the end of the session, this is consistent with a last look to verify what had been done. The change of gaze that ended in a moving action may be because of the user trying to see the workspace from other perspectives. Curiously, Group 2 from the first trial without facilitator, used these changes of gaze by the end of the session during the Reviewing stage, which imply head movements on their avatars, to say yes or not to the others.

In reserve of confirming these observations with a biggest sample of data, they may represent an adaptation of the users' nonverbal behavior facilities in a CVE, as awareness of their interaction with others.

Regarding the facilitator, it seems that the messages were sent very frequently, see column 2 in Table 12, it might be better to spread them, especially those regarding participation rates; also, statistics should be cleaned once a message is triggered regardless the users' answer to avoid repetitions. This, as an attempt of improving the number of answered messages, without forcing the participants to do so.

Other method to make the facilitator advices more acceptable could be to present them in a more attractive way like changing the color of the letters, or maybe in an imperative form, to give them via voice, or to give the facilitator a body.

Finally, following the logs files a kind of story can be tell about what is going on in the environment, the next lines were composed based on them and it correspond to a SS user:

Results from Loading: keyStrokeLog - 1.txt
SS(1)

Look at Both at 9:40:29
Look at Nobody at 9:40:29
Look at SB at 9:40:30
Look at SA at 9:40:31
Talk to SA at 9:40:31
Look at SB at 9:40:32
Talk to SB at 9:40:32
Talk to SB at 9:40:35
Talk to SB at 9:40:42
...
Take Dining Table at 9:44:14
Talk to SB at 9:44:32
Move Dining Table at 9:44:43
Move Dining Table at 9:44:44
Move Dining Table at 9:44:45
Move Dining Table at 9:44:46
...
Talk to SB at 9:44:52
Talk to SB at 9:44:58...

This information could be used in a number of ways such as to establish nets of communication or to oversee some participants' collaborative characteristics such as being implementers or leaders. For example, it has been found that talkative group members are more likely to be task leaders (Stein & Heller, 1979), and to receive more gazes and send less than their peers (Peña & de Antonio, 2009).

4. Conclusions and future work

Base on the nonverbal behavior of the users' avatars in a CVE for learning, an IVA was modeled within an experimental application with the intent to scaffold the collaborative process. The model used only two NVC cues, talking turns and artifacts manipulation, to give two types of advices: one regarding a balance in the group members' participation rates in both talk and implementation; and, the other regarding an expected sequence in the Plan-Implement-Review stages.

Two trials were presented, the first without the facilitator or IVA and the second one with it. In the second trial, the observation of other two NVC cues was conducted, deictic gestures and gazes, while some indications on this regard were pointed out.

Although in this chapter only nonverbal behavior took part in the facilitator modeling, our final intention is to incorporate the scheme to a verbal analysis, an example, can be found in (Peña, Aguilar, & de Antonio, 2010). In trying to avoid a restricted interface like the Sentence Opener approach, the analysis in (Casillas & Daradoumis, 2009) will be adapted to the model.

How people nonverbally behave in graphical environment through their avatars and how they will adapt the CVE facilitations for that, are big open issues. The analysis in here was narrowed to collaborative interaction during the accomplishment of a task in a small group through only a few nonverbal communication cues, barely a small brushstroke of what is suggested as a complete area for research.

5. References

Aguilar, R., Gómez, G., Moo, F., Uicab, R., & Tuyub, R. (2010). A model based on intelligent virtual environment to assist the learning of the programming and mathematics. Proceedings of the International Conference on Education and New Learning Technologies (Edulearn 2010). Barcelona, Spain. Gómez, L., Martí, D. & Cande, I. (Eds.). pp. 2564-2571.

Argyle, M. (1990). *Bodily communication* (2nd ed.). Madison, Conn.: International Universities Press.

Bailenson, J. N., Blascovich, J., Beall, A. C., & Loomis, J. (2003). Interpersonal distance in immersive virtual environments. *Personality and Social Psychology, 29*, 819-833.

Bales, R. F. (1970). *Personality and interpersonal behavior*. New York: Holt.

Bergstrom, T., & Karahalios, K. (2007). Conversation clock: Visualizing audio patterns in co-located groups. *HICSS*, 78.

Brdiczka, O., Maisonnasse, J., & Reignier, P. (2005). Automatic detection of interaction groups. *ICMI*, Trento, Italy.

Capin, T. K., Pandzic, I. S., Thalmann, N. M., & Thalmann, D. (1997). Realistic avatars and autonomous virtual humans in VLNET networked virtual environments. *From Desktop to Webtop: Virtual Environments on the Internet, WWW and Networks, International Conference*, Bradford, UK.

Casillas, L., & Daradoumis, T. (2009). Knowledge extraction and representation of collaborative activity through ontology-based and social network analysis technologies. *International Journal of Business and Data Mining*, 4(2), 141-158.

Chapple, E. D. (1949). The interaction chronograph: Its evolution and present application. *Personel, 25*, 295-307.

Chou, C., Chan, T., & Lin, C. (2003). Redefining the learning companion: The past, present and future of educational agents. *Computer & Education*, (40), 255-269.

Churchill, E. F., & Snowdon, D. (1998). Collaborative virtual environments: An introductory review of issues and systems. *Virtual Reality: Research, Development and Applications, 3*, 3-15.

Clark, H. H., & Brennan, S. E. (1991). Grounding in communication. In L. B. Resnick, J. M. Levine & S. D. Teasley (Eds.), *Perspectives on socially shared cognition* (pp. 127–149). Hyattsville, MD: American Psychological Association.

Dillenbourg, P. (1999). What do you mean by collaborative learning? In P. Dillenbourg (Ed.), *Collaborative-learning: Cognitive and computational approaches* (pp. 1-19). Oxford: Elsevier.

Giraffa, L., & Viccari, R. (1999). Intelligent tutoring systems built using agents techniques. *Intelligent Tutoring Systems Built using Agents Techniques*, 4(1), 23-40.

Guye-Vuillème, A., Capin, T. K., Pandzic, I. S., Thalmann, N. M., & Thalmann, D. (1998). Nonverbal communication interface for collaborative virtual environments. *Collaborative Virtual Environments*, University of Manchester. 105-112.

Hall, E. (1968). Proxemics. *Current Anthropology, 9*, 83-108.

Heath, C., Jirotka, M., Luff, P., & Hindmarsh, J. (1995). Unpacking collaboration: The interactional organisation of trading in a city dealing room. *Computer Supported Cooperative Work, 3*(2), 147-165.

Heldal, I. (2007). The impact of social interaction on usability for distributed virtual environments. *The International Journal of Virtual Reality, 6*(3), 45-54.

Jaffe, J., & Feldstein, S. (1970). *Rhythms of dialogue*. New York, NY: Academic.

Jermann, P. (2004). *Computer support for interaction regulation in collaborative problem-solving.* Unpublished University of Genéva, Genéva, Switzerland.

Jermann, P., Soller, A., & Lesgold, A. (2004). Computer software support for collaborative learning. *What we know about CSCL in higher education* (pp. 141-166). Amsterdam: Kluwer.

Johnson, A., & Leigh, J. (2001). *Tele-immersive collaboration in the CAVE research network.* London: Springer-Verlag.

Johnson, W. L., Rickel, J. W., & Lester, J. C. (2000). Animated pedagogical agents: Face-to-face interaction in interactive learning environments. *International Journal of Artificial Intelligence in Education, 11*, 47-78.

Kendon, A. (1990). *Conducting interaction: Patterns of behavior in focused encounters*. Cambridge: Cambridge University Press.

Knapp, M., & Hall, J. (2007). *Nonverbal communication in human interaction* (7 th ed.). Belmont, CA: Thomson Wadsworth.

Koschmann, T. (1996). Paradigm shifts and instructional technology: An introduction. In T. Koschmann (Ed.), *CSCL: Theory and practice of an emerging paradigm* (pp. 1-23). Mahwah, NJ: Lawrence Erlbaum Associates.

Kujanpää, T., & Manninen, T. (2003). Supporting visual elements of non-verbal communication in computer game avatars. *Level Up - Digital Games Research Conference*, Universiteit Utrecht. 220-233.

Lester, J. C., Converse, S. A., Kahler, S. E., Barlow, S. T., Stone, B. A., & Bhogal, R. S. (1997). The persona effect: Affective impact of animated pedagogical agents. *CHI '97*, 359-366.

Patterson, M. L. (1983). *Nonverbal behavior: A functional perspective*. New York: Springer-Verlang.

Peña, A., Aguilar, R. A., & de Antonio, A. (2010). Collaborative interaction analysis in virtual environments based on verbal and nonverbal indicators. Proceedings of the Ninth Mexican International Conference on Artificial Intelligence, pp.129 - 133.

Peña, A., & de Antonio, A. (2009). Nonverbal communication as a means to support collaborative interaction assessment in 3D virtual environments for learning. In A. A. Juan, T. Daradoumis, F. Xhafa, S. Caballe & J. Faulin (Eds.), *Monitoring and assessment in online collaborative environments: Emergent computational technologies for E-learning support* (pp. 172-197). Hershey, PA: IGI- Global.

Peña, A., & de Antonio, A. (2010). Inferring interaction to support collaborative learning in 3D virtual environments through the User's avatar nonverbal communication. *International Journal of Technology Enhanced Learning, 2*(1/2), 75-90.

Rickel, J. W. (2001). Intelligent virtual agents for education and training: Opportunities and challenges. *Third International Workshop, Intelligent Virtual Agents*, Madrid, Spain. 15-22.

Salem, B., & Earle, N. (2000). Designing a non-verbal language for expressive avatars. *Collaborative Virtual Environments*, San Francisco, CA, USA. 93-101.

Stein, R. T., & Heller, T. (1979). An empirical analysis of the correlations between leadership status and participation rates reported in the literature. *Journal of Personality and Social Psychology, 37*, 1993-2002.

Wolff, R., Roberts, D., Steed, A., & Otto, O. (2005). A review of tele-collaboration technologies with respect to closely coupled collaboration. *International Journal of Computer Applications in Technology,*

Youngblut, C. (1998). *Educational uses of virtual reality technology* No. Technical Report No. IDA Document D-2128). Institute for Defense Analyses.

5

ROTATOR Model: A Framework for Building Collaborative Virtual Workspaces

Charles J. Lesko Jr, Christine R. Russell and Yolanda A. Hollingsworth
East Carolina University, East Carolina University, Middlesex College
USA

1. Introduction

The impacts of virtual world technologies are beginning to resonate on a global scale. The recent developments and use of virtual world technologies in the form of virtual workspaces has demonstrated distinct characteristics and outcomes that can be used to plan and gauge levels of development and incorporation within a given business process framework. In supporting business processes, virtual workspaces can provide collaborative and immersive environments to better enable core business processes over a specified period of time. Virtual workspaces are particularly valuable today because they can provide workers with an online collaboration suite with varying levels of functionality that allow groups of workers to communicate in a highly interactive, self-contained collaborative workspace.

Recent uses of virtual workspaces have begun to identify some distinct characteristics and outcomes related to their integration in live working environments. Collectively, these characteristics and outcomes can be articulated through the identification of various functional stages that businesses realize to establish and maintain a distinct level of virtual world collaborative capability. However, to date there is no effective strategic model for evaluating and planning implementation of virtual workspaces in a business setting. To frame a discussion on implementation and planning processes for virtual workspaces the authors are proposing a new systematic model in this paper. This proposed model provides a staged breakdown outlining the characteristics and functionalities businesses can currently expect to encounter when implementing virtual workspaces. This proposed model is referred to herein as the ROTATOR Model.

In a broad sense, the concept of rotation involves having a clear central point that stays fixed, in this case that fixed point is the process of virtual workplace collaborations and like any palindrome it can be viewed from either end having movement from real to virtual with varying degrees of reality and virtualization processes and capabilities enmeshed in between.

This chapter presents the ROTATOR Model as a proposed framework for managing the development and implementation of virtual workspaces. The purpose of the ROTATOR model is to: (1) provide a pragmatic approach for describing various levels of virtual world application used for implementing virtual workspaces; (2) assist in identifying what level of virtual world implementation is needed to achieve desired business outcomes; and (3) create a practical framework that represents the varying levels of both functionality and capability for establishing and maintaining virtual workspaces. In this chapter the authors propose the ROTATOR model to establish a series of incremental stages that form the foundation for a virtual workspace framework.

As a foundation for this analysis, the concepts, history and use of the terms virtual collaboration and virtual workspaces are also discussed in this article to clarify their import and use in industry. These discussions include a description of the recent evolution of virtual collaborative environments with a focus on the most important online global workforce drivers. The impact of other key technologies with respect to the ROTATOR Model within the virtual workspace arena including cloud computing, semantic web, and web 3-D are also discussed.

2. Defining the collaborative virtual workspace landscape

Over the past few decades, computing sciences has grappled with different approaches to presenting digitally generated content. In recent years the field of virtual reality (VR) has become one of the most intriguing technologies in the area of content presentation. Although most people tend to relate virtual reality to its use in more common entertainment arenas like gaming, the real impacts are in the broader areas of the, "arts, business, communication, design, education, engineering, medicine and many other fields" (Briggs, 1996). Over the last 15 years, John Brigg's prediction has proven to be correct--the biggest impacts of virtual reality technology use are now being felt especially in the business, communication and medical fields (Briggs, 1996). While the virtual world technology is still evolving and developing, it has finally matured to a level where we are routinely implementing it in whole or part in educational and business settings. The issue for businesses seems to be less one of will they implement VR technology in workspaces, but rather more one of how it will be done and in what sequence investment in the requisite technology will be made. This includes considering not just current VR technology but also requires understanding the likely evolution and trajectory of the technology development in the future. Additionally, savvy users should ask themselves now what other technologies are being or might be co-implemented to supplement the virtual environments along the way.

Appropriate planning and scaling of implementation of VR technologies based on knowing your industry goals, your company's historical and future growth patterns, your immediate real needs and your tolerance for risk are all crucial to planning implementation of VR platforms and workspaces. Poor planning for implementation of VR workspaces or any new technology may result in unnecessary risk exposure, cost overruns and simple ineffective use of costly infrastructure that is both unnecessary and/or inefficient. While there are many studies of the implementation of virtual, mixed and augmented reality spaces most or many of those have been focused on education and medical uses (Caudell & Mizell, 1992)(Steuer, 1992) (Barfield & Caudell, 2001) (van Krevelen & Poelman, 2010). Before considering the available studies and their place in the ROTATOR model though it's important to understand exactly what virtual reality is and how it is affected by other technologies like augmented reality. Additionally as cloud computing becomes more widely used in industry we will consider how that storage process along with some other most common storage processes may affect the implementation plan for VR workspaces in a business setting. Often people mix up virtual reality and augmented reality so let's begin first with clear definitions of those concepts as used in this chapter and for purposes the ROTATOR model of virtual reality and augmented reality implementation.

One expert defines virtual reality as a "three-dimensional, computer generated simulation in which one can navigate around, interact with and be immersed in another environment" (Briggs, 1996). While this definition has been expanded over time to include spaces that are less real in terms of mimicking the real world for business purposes, these business spaces almost always mirror closely in some way a real world setting. Virtual reality, (Milgram & Kishino, 1994) takes a computer-generated world and begins to immerse the user through varying levels of "real" content (Hampshire, Seichter, Grasset, & Billinghurst, 2006) (Haller, Billinghurst, & Thomas, 2007) (Ritsos, Ritsos, & Gougoulis, 2011).

As for augmented reality, various technologies have and continue to be developed that seek to enhance a user's current perception of real world reality in varying degrees. Where virtual reality attempts to replace the entire real world perception with a simulated one the concept of augmented reality takes the user's unmodified or actual reality and begins to infuse computer-generated elements into that real world reality (Alem & Huang, 2011). The computer-generated elements in this environment then in effect 'augment' what the user senses in their real world environment (Kroeker, 2010). So, for example someone working in a design environment and as a support the person might see computer-generated materials that are overlaid by computer projection into the client's landscape environment so the client can see what it would look like if there were palm trees in the west corner of the garden. The most common example of simple augmentation in fact is in TV sports casting where the viewer of an American football game might see lines and graphics depicting the ball placement or movement overlaid on the live TV feed from the game.

As computer graphics and generations become more sophisticated these augmentations are becoming more and more sophisticated as well and are drifting closer to merging with the virtual reality environment in a natural way. For example, as applications become mobile there are new and more challenging options for the use of augmented reality. Some recent examples of mobile applications that augment one's reality include Layar, a 'reality browser' that retrieves point-of-interest data on the basis of GPS, compass, and camera view (Alem & Huang, 2011). GraffittiGeo is another augmented reality application that lets users read and write virtual Twitter-style comments on the walls of restaurants, movies and cafes (Kroeker, 2010). There are additional advanced uses of augmented reality being employed in design and urban renewal work as well; allowing designers to literally sit together at a table and manipulate and overlay computer generated materials and design drawings on say a real world table in front of them using programs like ARUDesigner (Wang, 2009).

Additionally, the concepts of augmentation coincide with real-time presentation that is in semantic context with the real world. So if we had a sliding scale viewpoint of these concepts, we would see the real world reality on one end of the continuum—say to the left with full immersive virtual reality worlds (we have not yet reached the capability to use practically fully immersive virtual reality technologies) on the far other end of the scale—say to the far right. Augmented reality would of course fall on that scale somewhere in between but close to real world reality and relatively far away from the virtual reality side of the scale at the other end. However, as augmentation develops it trends closer and closer to the VR side of the equation. One challenge for planning implementation of VR worlds and/or augmented reality use then is to better understand the characteristics between the two extremes of 3D virtual reality and real world reality with augmented reality spanning the spectrum in between.

2.1 Virtual verses real environments

Milgram's Reality-Virtuality Continuum defined in 1994 describes a continuum that spans space from the real environment into a pure virtual environment. In between those end points there are spaces of augmented reality that are closer to the real environment and /or augmented virtuality that are closer to the fully virtual environment (Milgram & Kishino, 1994). From the virtual reality perspective an environment is presented to the end user that can either contain totally virtual (computer-generated) content or be somewhere in between thereby containing relative levels of realism or actual existent artefacts not computer generated.

There is a natural merging (see Figure 1) of the two concepts where the purely virtual environment meets the natural or real environment. In essence, virtual reality evolves from systematically-generated environmental content that is presented to the end-user and gradually adds real world content while augmented reality (from an opposing perspective) evolves from the real world and gradually infuses digital content into the end-users presentation.

Fig. 1. Converging Realities: Real vs. Virtual

In a real environment we might have a live meeting with all the participants in the room in the same place at the same time to discuss or work on some kind of business problem. Of course this has become more and more impractical as people are geographically farther and farther apart because of workforce globalization and decentralization. To respond to the need to communicate across geographic boundaries we saw the introduction of technologies like Skype, live meetings online, instant message usage or even some kinds of social networking that involved either synchronous or asynchronous communications. The use of these tools has now become ubiquitous in the workplace as businesses find one or more combinations of these communications tools, which can be used to smooth and speed up communication and business processes.

We have rapidly developed beyond even these latest technologies now and are seeing rapidly evolving; newer ones emerge that include virtual reality and augmentation tools. While these new virtual reality and augmentation tools, allow for more depth and expression in communication thereby facilitating increasingly effective communication processes like training programs and client communications, users are finding that they are often costly to implement and fraught with more risk factors than the earlier technologies like Skype and instant messaging (IM). For example, there is a steeper learning curve for use in VR technologies and there are risks associated with storage of information that may be considered meeting or business communications required by law to be housed and accessible. Additionally there may be significant upfront costs for software development or implementation that businesses don't anticipate. This does not mean that use of VR technologies should be avoided by businesses as effective implementation can have far more advantages then disadvantages when they are properly planned and implemented.

We are now beginning to see more extensive adoption by Universities, hospitals and medical companies as well as industry of these VR environments and augmented reality technologies. However, there seems to be little consideration given to the actual choice and implementation of the technologies with regard to their place on the continuum, their long-term viability and evolution, and the requisite return on investment (ROI) of implementation and use. By placing technologies on the proposed ROTATOR continuum and evaluating the goals and needs of an organization, companies can better plan and more efficiently use limited resources for implementation and adoption of VR and augmented technologies in business applications. Additionally, use of the ROTATOR model should aid in illuminating any potential risks associated with their implementation depending on the company and application. Use of the ROTATOR model can also shed light on possible risks associated with use and maintenance of VR and should help minimize risks based on planned and appropriate implementation policies and procedures.

2.2 Collaborative virtual workspaces: What they are and why we use them

Collaboration itself is a recursive process where two or more co-workers, groups or organizations bring their knowledge and experience together by interacting toward a common goal in the best interests of their customers and to improve their organization's success (Martinez-Moyano, 2006) (Wagner, 2005). A virtual synchronous collaboration involves interaction within a virtual space wherein all colleagues, without respect to time or geographic separation, are able to negotiate, discuss, brainstorm, share knowledge, and generally work together to carry out a given work task. These environments aim to provide technology-based solutions where participants can cooperatively work as a group to construct and share knowledge (Ghaoui, 2003).

Virtual collaborative workspaces provide a common working environment where employees can not only collaborate systematically with corporate computing resources but also communicate with other co-workers and customers. Many of the virtual collaborative environments are 3D virtual environments that allow for multiple users. Recent evolution of virtual collaborative environments has focused heavily on online digital solutions, with these solutions providing for:

1. **Shifts in training and instruction for business and academia**. Business organizations have begun to shift their training practices using distributed teams in blended approaches (Alavi & Gallupe, 2003) (Simeon, 2003) with the use of online and web-based networking contributing to a boost in what is often referred to as e-Learning. The

increase in distance programs at higher educational institutions has also been cause for the development of more group-oriented learning modalities for its remote participants (Harasim, 2000). Educational institutions are moving more agressively into 3-D virtual environments in order to create more social environments and to teach community involvment, creative thinking and social interaction skills (Ritzema & Harris, 2008) (Parsons, Stockdale, Bowles, & Kamble, 2008) (Bainbridge, 2007).

2. **Introduction of social context and peer influence into goal-setting**. Technology guides the movement from a "sense of belonging to a sense of purpose" helping to orchestrate "communities of knowledgeable" among peers (Gerben, 2009). This collaboration of peers is viewed as relevant in discourse, evaluation and community building and follows directly in line with a ripple-effect when circular organizational system values function (Watts, 2007) (Browning, Saetre, Stephens, & Sornes, 2008).
3. **Recognition of ownership and authority for decision-making**. Organizational structures tend to be flattened and decentralized in virtual collaborative settings such that all partners within a virtual team look to be included within the decision-making or else the technology can be perceived negatively (Cascio, August 2000). Ownership and trust need to be based on a shared understanding for effective decision-making to occur. It has also been noted that the flexibility and demands for more employee empowerment can place the owners of these types of collaborative toolsets as the enabler (Peters, 2007)(Fain, Kline, Vukasinovic, & Duhovnik, 2010).
4. **Method of Cost Containment**. Less overhead for companies to use teleworkers and a growing movement towards environmentally green ventures (less travel/gas consumption) has aided in the exponential growth in the use of virtual collaborative spaces. The advantages of this type of collaboration are more often clear offsets to such factors as maintenance and setup costs, trust and cultural differences, and the dynamic nature of virtual teams/organizations (Goel & Prokopec, March 2009) (Avats, 2010).
5. **Knowledge and Creativity Capitalization.** Increased interactions between departments and subunits otherwise unconnected could share information more freely in a virtual environment. A non-linear activity of information sharing across multiple departments , units and subunits sparks new ideas and initatives. This process will provide an heightening of overall knowledge access, management and organizational creativity (Bergiel, Bergiel, & Balsmeier, 2008)(Fain, Kline, Vukasinovic, & Duhovnik, 2010). Regardless of specialization, lateral unit activity increases knowledge and creativity which can optimize assessments with regard to user needs or customer satisfaction. Particularly in new product development (NPD), this capitalization serves to implement successfully innovative ideas going fromembeddedto embodied knowledge (Madhaven & Grover, 1998)(Badrinarayanan, 2008) as well as shifting that creativity to situated knowledge where dispersed teams share (Sole & Edmunson, 2002).

Behind the growth in the use of virtual collaborative environments are drivers such as the global distribution of both human and computing resources. Recent approaches to outsourcing, a distinct focus shift from time to results, and a mobile to global movement are all business forces that are fueling an increased interest in and use of these virtual workspaces.

1. **Approaches to outsourcing**. In this current era of outsourcing, the core ideology centers on "finding core competencies and outsource the rest" (known as the Bill Gates philosophy)(Crossman & Lee-Kelley, 2004)(Vashistha & Vashistha, 2006). Necessary

skills are not found in-house and local networks must tap external resources. Between the need for non-local resources and cost containment issues this causes organizations to go global where unique or specific skills are less costly (Crossman & Lee-Kelley, 2004)(Rowley & Jackson, 2009)(Howells, 1999) (Watkins, 1995).

2. **Focus Shift from Time to Results**. Managers are needing to focus more on results rather than time.This is aligned with themanagement by objective approach when time and competency matters little if results are not adequately evaluated and or determined as satisfactory (Shillabeer, Buss, & Rousseau, 2011). Further, managers need to be results-oriented instead of task or time-oriented (Amigoni & Gurvis, 2009).
3. **Mobile and Global**. As stakeholders and organizations become more mobile so too will the local and global networks. As these networks become more mobile so does the demand for more mobile technologies or those technologies that can eliminate natural and real barriers of geography, time zones and simultaneous communications (anytime/anywhere). These global and mobile teams or networks are viewed as complex for work and management (Ruohomaki, 2010). Once these elements or factors have the proper evaluation of tools and practices implemented the groundwork for accepting and cultivating virtual partnerships in virtual workspaces is laid (Vartiainen & Hyrkkänen, 2010)(Ruohomaki, 2010).

2.3 A virtual working space

Virtual world technologies provide computer-mediated three-dimensional (3D) interactive environments through which end users control one or more avatars (computer-generated proxies) in a persistent-state. Unlike other computer-mediated entertainment or simulation environments, virtual worlds typically retain a strongly temporal character where there is a persistent record of interaction from session to session. With respect to business processes, virtual workspaces utilize virtual world technologies to provide business users with a collaborative and immersion environment designed to better enable core business processes over a specified period of time (Cherbakov, Brunner, Lu, & Smart, 2009).

Virtual workspaces typically provide workers with, "a complete online communication/collaboration package that allows workgroups to share files and applications, use an online whiteboard, and communicate via chat or instant messaging"(Toolbox for IT, 2007). A virtual workspace is a workplace that is not located in any one physical space. That is, virtual workspaces consist of several workplaces that are technologically connected (typically via the Internet) without any regard for specific geographic boundaries. Workers are able to work and communicate interactively with one another in a collaborative environment regardless of their actual geographical location. There are a variety of advantages related tot he use of virtual workspaces for businesses and education.

For example, some advantages of implementing virtual workspaces are:

- Affecting a decrease in unnecessary costs by integrating technology processes, people processes, and online processes.
- Enabling employees to work from anyplace at any time supporting both the needs of the employees and an ever increasing global customer-base.
- Streamlining systems from multiple facets of work into a single unified unit easily accessible by both the consumer and the employee.

- Making it easier for employees because of business traveling, consolidates services, and assists in the communication processes.
- Increasing productivity because employees' are more focused with business related projects with only a single system to interact in.
- Making collaborations with team members easier with a singular virtual workplace.
- Allowing a company to reach more of its employees via meeting workspaces and virtual training sessions (Shafia, Ebrahim, Ahmed, & Taha, 2009)(Hertel, Geister, & Konradt, 2005) (Demster, 2005).

Some challenges to integrating virtual workspaces still exist. For example, some challenges of implementation of virtual workplaces are:

- Failure to leverage the technology that supports virtual workplaces resulting in decrease in productivity.
- Lack of human contact effecting team motivation, trust and productivity.
- Increased sensitivity to communication, interpersonal and cultural factors.
- Increased number and use of various formal and informal communications channels with the constantly-expanding use of social networking sites (Greenlee, 2003) (Powell, Piccoli, & Ives, 2004).

3. The need for a virtual collaborative workspace framework

The exponential growth of the World Wide Web (WWW) over the past two decades has driven both technological innovation and increased senstivity to immediacy in communication and collaborative business functions. As the web has evolved so too has our desire to become more involved with the process of content-sharing and content-creation. Now new web-based semantic technologies are providing smarter, more meaningful content and virtual world technologies are presenting that content with a new level of depth and interactivity (Lesko & Hollingsworth, 2010). Additionally, we do this all faster and with less willingness to wait for the process to evolve. As an interface, today's virtual collaborative technologies provide users with some unique capabilities including:

- Shared Space: the world allows multiple users to participate at once.
- Graphical User Interface: the world depicts space visually.
- Immediacy: interaction takes place in real time.
- Interactivity: the world allows users to alter, develop, build, or submit customized content.
- Persistence: the world's existence continues regardless of whether individual users are logged in.
- Socialization/Community: the world allows and encourages the formation of in-world social groups (Book, 2008).

As a collaborative medium virtual workspace integration within any business requires some basic understanding of four key components. Those four key components are as follows:

1. Business Environment - this component recognizes both the internal and external factors that may impact the process of use of the collaborative medium. Factors such as geographical location, corporate policies and procedures, and collaborations with

external organizations can all influence the effectiveness of the virtual collaborative process (Duncan, 1972) (Mescon, Albert, & Khedouri, 1988).

2. Collaborative Tasks - this component highlights key activities in the collaborative process. Collaboration is a means of producing something joined and new, from the interactions of people or organizations, their knowledge and resources. These interactions are facilitated by relationships—the personal bonds or 'connections'—that are established and maintained by the people and organizations participating in the collaboration. Relationships give collaboration strength, allowing it to form and function effectively. The quality of those relationships is determined by three primary factors: trust, reciprocity and mutuality (Miller & Ahmad, 1981) (Davis, Murphy, Owens, Khazanchi, & Zigurs, 2009) (Schmeil & Eppler, 2010).
3. End-Users - this component focuses on modeling user needs, values, skills, perceived challenges and their capabilities in decision making. End users are those who directly interact with the virtual collaborative workspace. Other users or stakeholders may also require consideration including those who are not directly involved in the use but whose inputs and decisions may have influence on the features of use. Other stakeholders may include those involved in the development of the workspace and/or those whose participation and input are needed for the development of the workspace. (Geumacs, 2009) (Koehne, Redmiles, & Fischer, 2011).
4. Encompassing Technologies - this component outlines the collaborative media that are required to support virtual collaborative processes. The media consists of communication tools, shared business intelligence data, and shared virtual workspaces. These media allow the end-users to explore both synchronous and asynchronous collaborative experience across a common solution (Lim & Khalid, 2003) (Robidoux & Andersen, 2011) (Montoya, Massey, & Lockwood, 2011).

The characteristics of each of these components is unique to the level of virtual workspace integration within a given business scenerio. These four components can be used to more clearly understand the technological level of functionality experienced by businesses that integrate collaborative medium virtual workspaces with in their business processes.

4. Proposing a collaborative virtual workspace framework

The ROTATOR model describes seven stages of virtualization/augmentation that do or will characterize virtual workdspaces at varying different stages of development and capability. The model presumes fluidity and that actual business use may swing back and forth between different stages much the way a pendulum glides back and forth depending on the outside forces impacting the particular business need or use at any given time. The focus of the ROTATOR model is to provide businesses with a common framework for analyzing their needs for and processes related to implementing collaborative virtual workspaces. The purpose of the ROTATOR model is to:

- Provide a practical model for describing various levels of virtual verses real presentation end-users might have immersed in any given virtual workspace solution.
- Assist in identifying what level of virtual world/augmentation implementation is needed to achieve the business's described, desired business outcomes.
- Create a practical framework that represents the varying levels of both functionality and capability for planning, establishing and maintaining virtual workspaces.

The ROTATOR model has seven distinct stages that extend from a purely virtual world communicative environment to a real world presentation with no augmentation or virtual world presentation. The operative characterisitcs of each stage of this model are divided into four areas: 1) Business Environment, 2) collaborative tasks, 3) end-users, and 4) other encompassing technologies. These areas are designed and described because they are the ones most likely to affect and represent the business needs, uses, and outcomes available. The ROTATOR framework is specifically designed to be used as a situational, needs analysis based tool for business and other industries to use to guage the best investment of their time and money if they choose to begin using virtual reailty or augmented reality environments. The use of the term ROTATOR is indicative of the fact that business can approach the integration of virtual workspaces from either end of the model. In its broadest sense, the concept of rotation involves having a clear central point that stays fixed and in this context that fixed point is the process of virtual workplace collaborations and like any palindrome it can be approached from either end. In the case of virtual workspace collaborations that movement is between the two extremes of real and virtual environments, with varying degrees of reality and virtualized processes and capabilities enmeshed in between.

ROTATOR MODEL

STAGE		DESCRIPTION
I_{ar}	**R**eenforcing	Initial infusion of business content into real world presentation for individual user.
II_{ar}	**O**bverse	Integration of social content and sharing within visual presentation for multiple users.
III_{ar}	**T**ransversal	Limited ability to build and manupulate environment with extensive use of user proxy.
IV	**A**ttainment	Full 3D immersion and representation of business content with sense of personal presence for all collaborators.
III_{vr}	**T**ransactional	Interaction between virtual workspaces and external content with multi-sensory input/output.
II_{vr}	**O**rganization	In-world grouping, collaboration & social interaction.
I_{vr}	**R**endering	Visually appealing, immersive, systematically-generated spaces.

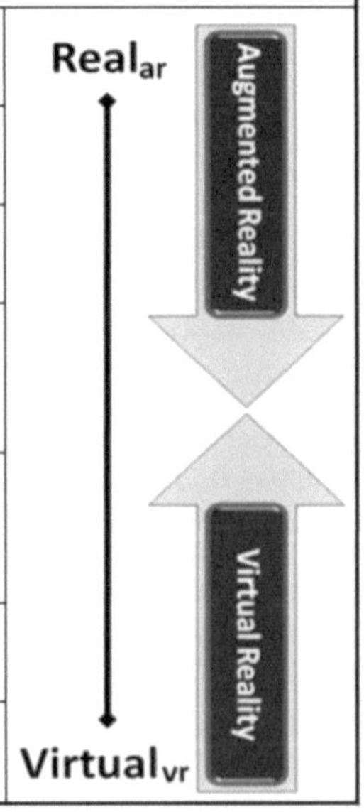

Fig. 2. Stages in the ROTATOR Model

Stage numbering begins at boths ends as well using roman numerals I through IV with Stage IV being at the center point. Beginning from the real end of the spectrum, the first three stages are designated Stage I_{ar}, Stage II_{ar}, and Stage III_{ar}. Beginning from the virtual end of the spectrum, the first three stages are designated Stage I_{vr}, Stage II_{vr}, and Stage III_{vr}. Note the the center has no subscript denoting a blend of both virtual reality and augmented reality at the center.

4.1 Stage I_{ar} – Reinforcing Stage

The Reinforcing Stage (Stage $I_{ar)}$ represents the initial infusion of digital content into a real world end-user presentation. The concept of augmenting reality involves superimposing digital graphics, audio and other sensory enhancements onto realtime environments. An evolving field in an of itself, augmented reality goes beyond the static graphics technology of television where the graphics imposed do not change with the perspective (Tech-Faq, 2011). At the Reinforcing Stage, the augmenting content is presented to a broad user base. For virtual workspaces at this stage the focus is on presenting business content to a broad audience with minimal end-user interaction. The following characteristics are anticipated from virtual workspaces at the Reinforcing Stage (Stage $I_{ar)}$ of the model:

1. *Business Environment* - The environment created by virtual workspaces at Reinforcing Stage of the model is characterized by its ease of use. There is minimal to no persistence and most content would be static or streamed in real-time. Management structured environment. Management may use environment for activity and time tracking. Document share and exposure a focus.
2. *Collaborative Tasks* - Basic collaborative tasks would include centralized distribution of preselected and relatively static content to a broad user base. Collaboration would be limited to central or corporate entity and end-user.
3. *End-users* - At this stage, end-users at looking for basic business content and minimal to no direct collaboration with other end users. As this stage, presentation is to singular end-users. Interaction with mostly non-verbal content such as email, circulars, team/corporate correspondence and documentation, and websites.
4. *Encompassing Technologies* - At this stage, technologies beyond the basic use of televised augmented content would include smart phone applications that combine the use of global positioning data with online data with video streams. Management structured and presented content for individual use.

4.2 Stage II_{ar} – Obverse

The Obverse Stage (Stage II_{ar}) infers a turning toward or facing to the end-user. At this stage, of the model virtual collaborative workspaces look to incorporate end-user input in the end-users presentation. Multiple end-users are expected at this level with an increasing degree of social interaction. The following characteristics are anticipated from virtual workspaces at the Obverse Stage (Stage II_{ar}) of the model:

1. *Business Environment* - The environment created by virtual workspaces at Obverse Stage of the model is characterized by an influx of end-user content and ability of end-user to manipulate pre-defined environment. Auto-environment construction based on systematically negotiated rules is expected.
2. *Collaborative Tasks* - Basic collaborative tasks would include group collaborations, presentation of multiple end-users in a singular presentation and interaction with presented business content are all a focus at this stage. Interactions include virtual meetings and various levels of digital socializing.
3. *End-users* - At this stage, end-users are looking for collaborative media to interact with others. Virtual teaming and the ability to create and manage specific groups and present content specific to that group is a focus here.

4. *Encompassing Technologies* - At this stage, technologies should include incorporation of various virtual meeting and presentation/demo capabilities. Although management structured and presented content is predominating, some end-user space definition and creation is included.

4.3 Stage III_{ar} – Transversal Stage

The Transversal Stage (Stage III_{ar}) involves a deliberate incorporation of business intelligence into presentation. It is at this level that we evaluate virtual working relationships, compare process needs and create virtual business communities. The following characteristics are anticipated from virtual workspaces at the Transversal Stage (Stage III_{ar}) of the model:

1. *Business Environment* - The environment created by virtual workspaces at Transversal Stage of the model is characterized by ability of end-users to interact and construct "intuitively" with the virtual environment. Automated workflow and content presentation are also anticipated.
2. *Collaborative Tasks* – Basic collaborative tasks include ability to team and structure flow if work from within the environment. Transversal Stage also infers activity across multiple virtual workspaces.
3. *End-users* - Although the focus would be on real world presentation of end-users, avatar/digital proxies are available.
4. *Encompassing Technologies* - At this stage, technologies would include automated workflow and content generation. A virtual work environment that allows for both auto-generated and end-user construction.

4.4 Stage IV – Attainment Stage

The Attainment Stage IV describes the intersection of real world spatial imagery ultimately forming a paraverse. From a more visual perspective, the ability to interact with data in-world and then present that data in 3-D is also a virtual workspace building consideration. Up to this point, most of the content has been presented via various 2D common formats found in our daily interactions with browsers, application sharing software, document viewers, videos, etc. To maximize the use of virtual workspace requires moving into the realm of 3D content presentation and interaction.

At this point it is important to incorporate the concepts of interreality physics and how they play a distinct role in the middle stages of this model. Interreality physics takes a systematic viewpoint of Milgrams virtuality continuum (Milgram & Kishino, 1994). An interreality system refers to the coupling of virtual reality systems with their real-world counterparts comprising a real physical pendulum coupled to a pendulum that only exists in virtual reality. According to Gintautas and Hübler (2007) an interreality system has two stable states of motion: a "Dual Reality" state where the motion of the two pendula are uncorrelated and a "Mixed Reality" state where the pendula exhibit stable phase-locked motion which is highly correlated (Gintautas & Hübler, 2007). The following characteristics are anticipated from of virtual workspaces at the Attainment Stage (Stage IV) of the model:

1. *Business Environment* - The environment created by virtual workspaces at Attainment Stage of the model is characterized by the fluidity of the environment and its ability to

intermesh and shift content and presentation between real and virtual. Both synchronous and asynchronous collaborations are available and the virtual workspace is able to support both persistence as well as well as streaming real-time flow of content and environment structure.

2. *Collaborative Tasks* - From a virtual collaborative perspective this tends to substantiate the movement notion of the ROTATOR model and a movement that flows between virtual and real. Automated teaming and workflow events are constructed to meet predetermined business requirements.
3. *End-users* - End-users are fully immersed within the environment with multiple sensory inputs and outputs. End-users are able to select and real or proxy presentation (avatar) within this virtual workspace.
4. *Encompassing Technologies* - At this stage, technologies would maximize the use and scalability of virtual machine and cloud technologies.

4.5 Stage III_{vr} – Transactional Stage

At the Transational State (Stage III_{vr}) of the model, where the user content comes from is a critical component to the business implementation and operation. There is an increasing demand for rich data resources found across the web so access to resouces external to the corporate environment capabilities with the virtual workspace is becoming critical. The following characteristics are anticipated from of virtual workspaces at stage III of the model:

1. *Business Environment* - At this stage the process of housing generated content and information becomes more critical and should be considered by the business attempting to integrate virtual world environmental collaborations at this level. Additionally, businesses may be more concerned than with security of auto-generated materials, risk involved with interactions with client, customers or professional clients for example for doctors or lawyers with professional requirements for protection of communications and data.
2. *Collaborative Tasks* - Building a virtual workspace capable of automating the content collection process and generating unique content for academic or business delivery is another way business manages these environments. An example of this might be similar to the way many online newspapers are being auto-generated today. Team projects or course assignments generate rules for collection and assignment bots perform the tasks of locating and presenting the content for users to manage and disseminate in the appropriate way or form.
3. *End-users* - Integration with team members, especially from outside the corporate infrastructure are expected. Sharing of corporate knowledge-based from within the virtual workspace becomes critical. Extensive use of digital proxy/avatar with infusion of real presentation of end-user.
4. *Encompassing Technologies* - At this stage, technologies focus on auto-generation of virtual workspace content and structure. There is a sense of both time and persistence within the environment.

4.6 Stage II_{vr} – Involvement Stage

The Involvement Stage (Stage II_{vr}) describes the basic collaborative functionalities utilized in virtual online sessions. Text chat, image depictions, including static slide presentations, document viewers, and whiteboards are common collaborative tools incorporated early in virtual workspace developments. It should be noted here, that these tools are replications of 2-D tools used in real world (RL) applications. Additionally, the content from these tools is housed within the virtual world solution itself and is not generally pulled from external resources or over the Internet. Content for slide presentations and document viewings are often uploaded directly to the virtual world environment for viewing. The following characteristics are anticipated from of virtual workspaces at the Involvement Stage (Stage II_{vr}) of the model:

1. *Business Environment* - The environment created by virtual workspaces at Involvement Stage of the model is characterized by manually management established workflows and auto construction of the virtual workspace. Teaming is controlled at the management level as well. Management ability to track resource time and activity, and provide automated task assignment.
2. *Collaborative Tasks* – Basic collaborative tasks would include: enhanced communication from avatar including use of non-verbal cues such as avatar position, movement and gestures. The Involvement Stage also describes the inclusion of audio and video collaborative features incorporated beyond basic in-world collaboration functionalities. These may include use of voice chat, avatar body gesturing (i.e. pointing, raising hand, laughing, etc.) and use of video streams. As with basic in-world collaborations discussed previously, the content from background audio is housed within the virtual world solution itself and is not generally pulled from external resources. Content from voice chats and basic avatar action and gesturing is logged and maintained internally within the virtual world solution.
3. *End-users* – Although most of the virtual workspace is pre-created for the end-user, there is some capability for workspace definition by the end-users. End-users are involved in formal and informal socializing, virtual meetings, conference calls, and webinar type sessions.
4. *Encompassing Technologies* – At this stage, technologies would include built-in voice/text chat capabilities. Access to social sites and user interaction. Extensive use of digital proxy/avatar within the virtual workspace. Sharing of corporate/private correspondence, document collaboration, and virtual social gatherings are supported.

4.7 Stage I_{vr} – Rendering Stage

The focus at the Rendering Stage (Stage I_{vr}) is on creation of a shared presence and experience with the user. The virtual workspace are designed with specific processes in mind that are temporal or lasting for a finite period of time. The physical laws of the real world are applicable aiding in familiarity and assimilation with spaces and business processessupported. At this beginning stage, businesses will have encorporated visually appealing, immersive and and systematically-generated virtual workspaces. The following characteristics are anticipated from virtual workspaces at the Rendering Stage (Stage I_{vr}) of the model:

1. *Business Environment* - The environment created by virtual workspaces at Rendering Stage of the model is characterized by displays and exhibits, architectural design and modeling, virtual tourism, and marketing. Predefined virtual workspaces. Most content is static and persistent with minimal fluidity to the content of the environment. Management has full control of virtual workspace design.

2. *Collaborative Tasks* - Basic collaborative tasks would include a limited exchange with system data internal to the virtual environments infrastructure. This stage is focused on the management collaborating with individual end-users.
3. *End-users* - Other than general interaction within the virtual environment itself, end-users would have minimal to no object creation or manipulation. There may or may not be an avatar proxy for end-user visualization and use. The emotional realism you might experience with your avatar or digital proxy would be limited to non-existent. It should be noted here that use of a digital proxy or avatar can have a certain degree of anonymity to it that can encourage more personal exploration; where shy users are more likely to participate (Lesko & Pickard, 2011).
4. *Encompassing Technologies* - At this stage, technologies would be limited to manual creation of virtual spaces. Spaces at this level have a degree of visual familiarity with layout and objects within the space for the end-users. When applicable, the liberation from the physical laws of the real world can make possible the creation of innovative and imaginative spaces, activities and experiences.

5. Conclusions

So the ROTATOR model is a proposed staged theoretical model that moves from reality and augmented reality towards collaborative virtualized environments or from purely virtual environments towards reality in four like steps. The model is set up to allow organizations to effectively understand and then evaluate their collaborative virtual workspace goals and objectives in order to create a long term plan for implementation and deployment of those workspaces. This model is just the first step in a larger framework the authors intend to develop based on case study analysis of past and projected implementations to help companies find the proper fit for their needs when using virtual spaces and like technology options for company communication and work.

The ROTATOR model is built on the premise that businesses may be starting from either a fully reality-based setting that does not yet use any virtualized communication mediums and move towards more aggressive forms of virtual medium use by adding augmented spaces to their systems. As the model moves towards the center space-labeled Section IV in the model—businesses can evaluate the delivery of each stage of the virtualized medium before reaching the fuller virtual reality space and/or plan for movement based on uses, needs and goals of the organization.

On the far right of the ROTATOR model a business might begin to see ways to continue it's movement into the more complex arenas of fully immersive virtual reality as these capabilities become more plausible for the organization to manage. It is anticipated that along with the more aggressive stages, nearer to the center Stage IV of the model, there will be greater risks for businesses to consider and a more difficult process of maintaining business content that may increase cost and some exposure for these businesses. However, this should not preclude some businesses from investing in the newest emergent options of virtual reality tools.

The impetus behind the ROTATOR model is to provide a structured first step in assisting businesses in evaluating and planning ahead for these kinds of implementations—be they aggressive use of newer immersion techniques for business collaborations or more stable use of the mature, foundational collaborative toolsets. Further research will focus incorporated use of the ROTATOR Model and its ability to more clearly articulate the virtual workspace functionals needs and requirements.

6. References

Distance Education by Postsecondary Faculty: Indicator 47 . (2006). Retrieved July 11, 2009, from National Center for Education Statistics: http://nces.ed.gov/programs/coe/2006/section5/indicator47.asp

Virtual Worlds Platforms and User Numbers. (2007, October 1). Retrieved July 11, 2009, from Virtual Worlds News: http://www.virtualworldsnews.com/2007/10/virtual-worlds-.html

Metaverse Roadmap Forecasts - Part A. (2009). Retrieved October 12, 2009, from Metaverse Roadmap: http://www.metaverseroadmap.org/inputs2A.html#trends

North America Internet Usage Statistics, Population and Telecommunications Reports. (2009). Retrieved July 11, 2009, from Internet World Stats: http://www.internetworldstats.com/stats14.htm

What is a Virtual World? (2009). Retrieved Sept 10, 2009, from Virtual Worlds Review: http://www.virtualworldsreview.com/info/whatis.shtml

Agarwal, A. (2009, May 30). *Web 3.0 Concepts Explained in Plain English.* Retrieved Sept 7, 2009, from Digital Inspiration: http://www.labnol.org/internet/web-3-concepts-explained/8908/

Aker, B. (2009, July 6). *The Race to Shape the Semantic Web.* Retrieved July 9, 2009, from AltSearchEngines: http://www.altsearchengines.com/2009/07/06/the-race-to-shape-the-semantic-web---score-one-microsoft/

Alavi, M., & Gallupe, R. B. (2003). Using Information Technology in Learning: Case Studies in Business and Management Education Programs. *Academy of Management Learning and Education*, 139-152.

Alem, L., & Huang, W. (2011). *Recent Trends of Mobile Collaborative Augmented Reality Systems.* New York, NY: Springer Science and Business Media.

Amigoni, M., & Gurvis, S. (2009). *Managing the Telecommuting Employee: Set Goals, Monitor Progress, and Maximize Profit and Productivity.* Avon, MA: Admas Media.

Amoako-Gyampah, K. (2004). An extension of the technology acceptance model in an ERP implementation environment. *Information & Management Volume 41, Issue 6*, 731-745.

Avats, R. (2010, March 18). *The Importance of Work-Life Balance: Aligning Staff Preferences and Business Need to Achieve Business Success.* Retrieved October 16, 2010, from Corpmagazine.com: http://www.corpmagazine.com/management/human-resources/itemid/1369/the-importance-of-worklife-balance-aligning-staf

Azuma, R. (1997). A Survey of Augmented Reality. *Presence: Teleoperators and Virtual Environments*, 355-385.

Badrinarayanan, V. (2008). Effective virtual new product development teams: an integrated framework. *Journal of Business & Industrial Marketing, Vol. 23, Issue 4*, 242-248.

Bainbridge, W. (2007). The Scientific Research Potential of Virtual Worlds. *Science, vol. 31]*, 472-476.

Barfield, W., & Caudell, T. (2001). *Fundamentals of wearable computers and augumented reality.* Mahwah, NJ: Lawrence Erlbaum Associates, Inc., Publishers.

Bergiel, B. J., Bergiel, E. B., & Balsmeier, P. W. (2008). Nature of virtual teams: a summary of their advantages and disadvantages. *Management Research Review*, 99-110.

Berners-Lee, T. (1998, September). *Semantic Web Roadmap*. Retrieved July 10, 2009, from www.w3.org: http://www.w3.org/DesignIssues/Semantic.html

Book, B. (2008). *Virtual Worlds Review: What is a Virtual World?* Retrieved September 13, 2011, from Virtual Worlds Review: http://www.virtualworldsreview.com/info/whatis.shtml

Briggs, J. C. (1996). The promise of Virtual Reality. *The Futurist, Volume 30, Issue 5*, 13-18.

Browning, L. D., Saetre, A. S., Stephens, K. K., & Sornes, J.-O. (2008). *Information and communication technologies in action: Linking Theory and Narratives of Practice*. New York, NY: Routledge.

Burden, D. (2009, May 13). *Toward Semantic Virtual Worlds - A Thinkpiece*. Retrieved October 18, 2009, from Converj.com: http://www.converj.com/sites/converjed/2009/05/toward_semantic_virtual_worlds.html

Burke, T. (2005, May). *Matchmaker, Matchmaker, Make Me a Match: Artificial Societies vs. Virtual Worlds*. Retrieved March 12, 2010, from weblogs.swarthmore.edu: http://weblogs.swarthmore.edu/burke/scholarly-articles/artificial-societies-and-virtual-worlds-digra-2005/html-version-of-my-digra-paper/

Cascio, W. F. (August 2000). Managing a virtual workspace. *Academy of Management Executive*, 81-90.

Caudell, T., & Mizell, D. (1992). Augmented Reality: An Application of Heads-Up Display Technology to Manual Manufacturing Processes. *Proc. Hawaii International Conf. on Systems Science, Vol. 2*, 659-669.

Cherbakov, L., Brunner, R., Lu, C., & Smart, R. (2009, May 29). *Enable far-reaching enterprise collaboration with virtual spaces, Part 1: Introduction to the opportunities and technologies*. Retrieved March 12, 2010, from boulder.ibm.com: http://download.boulder.ibm.com/ibmdl/pub/software/dw/webservices/ws-virtualspaces/ws-virtualspaces-pdf.pdf

Crossman, A., & Lee-Kelley, L. (2004). Trust, commitment and team working: the paradox of virtual organizations. *Global Networks: A Journal of Transnational Affairs*, 375-390.

Daden Limited. (2009). *Cross Sector: Visualisation*. Retrieved October 20, 2009, from daden.co.uk: http://www.daden.co.uk/pages/cross_sector_visualisation.html

Davis, A., Murphy, J., Owens, D., Khazanchi, D., & Zigurs, I. (2009). Avatars, People, and Virtual Worlds: Foundations for Research in Metaverses. *Journal of the Association for Information Systems, Volume 10, Issue 2*, Article 1.

Demster, M. (2005, July). Team-building key for virtual workplace. *Business Edge, Vol. 5, No. 27*.

Ding, L., Finin, T., Joshi, A., Pan, R., Cost, R. S., Peng, Y., et al. (2004, November 9). *Swoogle: A Search and Metadata Engine for the Semantic Web*. Retrieved August 31, 2009, from Proceedings of the Thirteenth ACM Conference on Information and Knowledge Management : http://ebiquity.umbc.edu/_file_directory_/papers/116.pdf

Djorgovski, S. G., Hut, P., McMillan, S., Vesperini, E., Knop, R., Farr, W., et al. (2009). Exploring the Use of Virtual Worlds as a Scientific Research Platform: The Meta-Institute for Computational Astrophysics (MICA). In J. Lehmann-Grube, J. Sablating, & a. et, *Facets of Virtual Environments*. Berlin: Springer Verlag .

Driver, E., & Jackson, P. (2008, February 7). *Getting Real Work Done In Virtual Worlds.* Retrieved October 13, 2009, from Forrester.com: http://www.forrester.com/Research/Document/Excerpt/0,7211,43450,00.html

Duncan, R. B. (1972). *Administrative Science Quarterly, Volume 17, No. 3,* 313-327.

Fain, N., Kline, M., Vukasinovic, N., & Duhovnik, J. (2010). The impact of management on creativity and knowledge transfer in an academic virtual enterprise. *Technical Gazette, Volume 17, Issue 3,* 347-351.

Fetscherin, M., & Lattemann, C. (2008). User Acceptance of Virtual Worlds. *Journal of Electronic Commerce Research, Vol 9, No 3,* 231-242.

Gerben, C. (2009). Putting 2.0 and Two Together:What Web 2.0 Can Teach Composition About Collaborative Learning. *Computers & Composition Online,* pp. 8-9.

Geumacs. (2009). *VirtualLife D2.1 EndUserDefinitionAndNeeds.* Rome, Italy: VirtualLife.

Ghaoui, C. (2003). *Usability evaluation of online learning programs.* Hershey, PA: Information Science Publishing.

Gintautas, V., & Hübler, A. W. (2007). Experimental evidence for mixed reality states in an interreality system. *Physics Review E, Volume 75, 057201* , 1-4.

Goel, L., & Prokopec, S. (March 2009). If you build it wil they come? - An empirical investigation of consumer perceptions and strategy in virtual worlds. *Electronic Commerce Research,* 115-134.

Goldberg, L. B. (2003, May 1). *Circular Organization Focuses on Cash, Not Personalities .* Retrieved October 12, 2010, from Turnaround.org: http://www.turnaround.org/Publications/Articles.aspx?objectID=1988

Greenlee, D. (2003). Building a Community in the Virtual Workplace. *Home Business Journal,* http://www.homebusinessjournal.net/a/virtual-workplace.asp.

Gruber, T. (February 2008). Collective knowledge systems: Where the Social Web meets the Semantic Web . *Web Semantics: Science, Services and Agents on the World Wide Web,* 4-13.

Haller, M., Billinghurst, M., & Thomas, B. (2007). *Emerging technologies of augmented reality: interfaces and design.* Hershey, PA: Idea Group Publishing.

Hampshire, A., Seichter, H., Grasset, R., & Billinghurst, M. (2006). Augmented reality authoring: generic context from programmer to designer. *OZCHI '06 Proceedings of the 18th Australia conference on Computer-Human Interaction: Design: Activities, Artefacts and Environments,* 409-412.

Harasim, L. (2000). Shift happens: online education as a new paradigm in learning. *The Internet and Higher Educaiton,* 41-61.

Hertel, G., Geister, S., & Konradt, U. (2005). Managing virtual teams: A review of current empirical research. *Human Resource Management Review, Vol. 15, Issue 1,* 69-95.

Howells, J. (1999). Research and Technology Outsourcing . *Technology Analysis & Strategic Management, Volume 11, Issue 1,* 17-29.

Huifang, L., Deng, S., Guo, C., & Chen, G. (2009). Tactical Communication Equipment Simulation Training Platform Based on VR. In *WRI World Congress on Computer Science and Information Engineering 2009* (pp. 19-23). Los Angeles, CA: CSIE.

iReport. (2009, July 20). *White House Speaks in SL on High Technology in Government.* Retrieved November 3, 2009, from ireport.com: http://www.ireport.com/docs/DOC-301274

K Zero. (2009, February 09). *K Zero: 260M Registered Accounts for the 10-15-Year-Old Virtual World Demo.* Retrieved September 16, 2009, from VirtualWorldNews.com:

http://www.virtualworldsnews.com/2009/02/k-zero-260m-registered-accounts-for-the-1015yearold-virtual-world-demo.html

Koehne, B., Redmiles, D., & Fischer, G. (2011). Extending the Meta-design Theory: Engaging Participants as Active Contributors in Virtual Worlds. In M. F. Costabile, Y. Dittrich, G. Fischer, & A. Piccinno, *End-user Development: Third International Symposium, IS-EUD 2011* (pp. 264-269). Berlin-Heidelberg, Germany: Springer-Verlag.

Krause, A. (2007, November 14). *Paraverse Meanderings.* Retrieved March 10, 2010, from worldofusablity.blogspot.com: http://worldofusability.blogspot.com/2007/11/paraverse-meanderings.html

Kroeker, K. L. (2010). Mainstream Augmented Reality. *Communications of the ACM, Vol: 53 Issue: 7,* 19-21.

KZero.co.uk. (2008, September 4). *Connecting Virtual Worlds With Myrl: KZero.* Retrieved October 30, 2009, from kzero.co.uk: http://www.kzero.co.uk/blog/?p=2449

Lesko, C. J., & Pickard, J. L. (2011). Data in Depth: Web 3-D Technologies Provide New Approaches to the Presntation of Course Content. *Journal of Online Engineering Education, Volume 1, Issue 2,* 1-6.

Lesko, C., & Hollingsworth, Y. (2010). Compounding the Results: The Integration of Virtual Worlds With the Semantic Web. *Journal of Virtual Worlds research, VOl. 2, Issue 5,* 3-20.

Liefman, G., Meir, R., & Tal, A. (September 2005). Semantic-oriented 3d shape retrieval using relevance feedback. *The Visual Computer,* 865-875.

Lim, T., & Khalid, H. (2003). A framework on virtual collaborative customization in home modification. *Proceedings of 7th SEAES and 4th Malaysian Ergonomics Conference* (pp. 354-361). Kuching: Unimas: Malaysian Ergonomics Conference.

Madhaven, R., & Grover, R. (1998). From embbedded knowledge to embodied knowledge: New product development as knowledge management. *Journal of Marketing, Vol. 62,* 1-12.

Marica Rhodes. (2009, February 17). *Telework Revs Up as More Employers Offer Work Flexibility.* Retrieved October 12, 2009, from WorkingFromAnywhere.org: http://www.workingfromanywhere.org/news/pr021609.html

Martinez-Moyano, I. J. (2006). Exploring the Dynamics of Collaboration in Interorganizational Settings. In S. Schuman, *Creating a Culture of Collaboration* (pp. 69-84). San Francisco, CA: Jossey-Bass.

Masinsin, R. Q. (May 2008). *Secretary of Defense Corporate Fellows Program: Final Report.* New York, NY: Time Warner/CNNMoney.

Merrill, D. (2009, July 24). *Mashups: The new breed of Web app.* Retrieved October 26, 2009, from www.ibm.com: http://www.ibm.com/developerworks/xml/library/x-mashups.html

Mescon, M. H., Albert, M., & Khedouri, F. (1988). *Management, 3rd Edition.* New York, NY: Harper & Row Publishers.

Mikroyannidis, A. (2007). Toward a Social Semantic Web. *Computer Institute of Electrical and Electronics (IEEE),* 113-115.

Milgram, P., & Kishino, F. (1994). Taxonomy of Mixed Reality Visual Displays. *IEICE Transactions on Information and Systems, E77-D(12),* 1321-1329.

Miller, C., & Ahmad, Y. (1981). Collaboration and partnership: an effective response to complexity and fragmentation or solution built on sand? *International Journal of Sociology and Social Policy, Vol. 20, Issue 5/6*, 1-38.

Miller, P. (2009, September 22). *September 2009: The Semantic Web Gang discuss Government data and data.gov*. Retrieved November 6, 2009, from The Semantic Web Gang: http://semanticgang.talis.com/category/uncategorized/

Mitham, N. (2009, September 12). *Growth forecasts for the Virtual Worlds sector*. Retrieved September 16, 2009, from www.kzero.co.uk: http://www.kzero.co.uk/blog/?m=200909

Montoya, M. M., Massey, A. P., & Lockwood, N. S. (2011). 3D Collaborative Virtual Environments: Exploring the Link between Collaborative Behaviors and Team Performance. *Decision Sciences, Volume 42, Issue 2*, 451-476.

Murphy, D. M. (2008). Strategic Communication: Wielding the Information Element of Power. In B. B. J., *U.S. Army War College Guide to National Security Issues* (pp. 175-187). Carlisle Barracks, PA: Army War College.

Murray, H. (1938). *Explorations in Personality*. New York, NY: Oxford University Press.

Murugesan, S. (July-August 2007). Understanding Web 2.0. *IT Professional*, 34-41.

Myrl.com. (2009). *Myrl - Immersive Entertainment Platform*. Retrieved November 2, 2009, from myrl.com: http://www.myrl.com/

O'Looney, J. (2005). Social Work and the New Semantic Information Revolution. *Administration in Social Work, Vol. 29, Issue 4*, 5-34.

O'Reilly, T. (2005, Sept 30). *What Is Web 2.0: Design Patterns and Business Models for the Next Generation of Software*. Retrieved Sept 7, 2009, from O'Reilly: http://oreilly.com/web2/archive/what-is-web-20.html

Parsons, D., Stockdale, R., Bowles, J., & Kamble, V. (2008). If We Build It Will They Come? Creating a Virtual Classroom in Second Life. *19th Australasian Conference on Information Systems* (pp. 720-729). Christchurch, Australia: 19th Australasian Conference on Information Systems.

Peters, L. (2007). Identifying antecedents of virtual team collaboration. *Team Performance Management, Volume 13, Issue 3/4*, 117-129.

Powell, A., Piccoli, G., & Ives, B. (2004). Virtual teams: a review of current literature and directions for future research. *ACM SIGMIS Database, Vol 35, Issue 1*, 6-36.

Regan, K. (2005, April 4). *Vertical Search Market Quickly Becoming Crowded*. Retrieved October 21, 2009, from ecommercetimes.com: http://www.ecommercetimes.com/story/41982.html

Richards, J. (2007, October 24). *Government to police virtual worlds*. Retrieved November 2, 2009, from Times Online: http://technology.timesonline.co.uk/tol/news/tech_and_web/gadgets_and_gaming/virtual_worlds/article2731497.ece

Ritsos, P. D., Ritsos, D. P., & Gougoulis, A. S. (2011). Standards for Augmented Reality: a User Experience perspective. *International AR Standards Meeting-February 17-19*, 1-9.

Ritzema, T., & Harris, B. (2008). The use of Second Life for distance education. *Journal of Computing Sciences in Colleges*, 110-116.

Robidoux, C., & Andersen, R. (2011). Cultivating a Culture of Collaboration. *Society for Technical Communication Summit: 58th Annual Conference* (pp. 90-98). Sacramento, CA: Society for Technical Communications.

Rosenthal, L. (2001). *Graphical User Interfaces: 2D, 3D, and Web3D*. Retrieved Sept 6, 2009, from 3DeZine: http://www.3dezine.com/3DeZine_01/index.html

Rowley, C., & Jackson, K. (2009). *Human Resource Management: The Key Concepts*. New York, NY: Routledge.

Ruohomaki, V. (2010). Knowledge work in distributed, mobile teams. *Proceedings of the International Conference* (pp. 110-117). Helsinki, Finland: FInnish Institute of Occupational Health.

Schmeil, A., & Eppler, M. J. (2010). malizing and Promoting Collaboration in 3D Virtual Environments - A Blueprint for the Creation of Group Interaction Patterns. In F. Lehmann-Gruge, & J. Sablatnig, *Facets of Virtual Environments: Lecture Notes of the Institute for Computer Sciences, Social Informatics and Telecommunications Engineering, Vol. 33, Part 4* (pp. 121-134). Berlin, Germany: First International Coference, FaVE 2009.

Scott, T. (2009, Spring). *Traversing the giant global graph*. Retrieved October 12, 2009, from www.pwc.com: http://www.pwc.com/us/en/technology-forecast/spring2009/interoperable-data.jhtml

Shafia, M. A., Ebrahim, N. A., Ahmed, S., & Taha, Z. (2009). Innivation process is facilitated in virtual environment of R&D teams. *Proceedings of EDULEARN09 Conference* (pp. 2157-2166). Barcelona, Spain: EDULEARN09.

Shih, J.-L., Nuutinen, J., Hwang, G.-J., & Chen, N.-S. (2010). Building Virtual Collaborative Research Community Using Knowledge Management Approach. *2*(3).

Shillabeer, A., Buss, T. F., & Rousseau, D. M. (2011). *Evidence-Based Public Management: Practices, Issues, and Prospects*. Armonk, NY: M. E. Sharpe, Inc.

Simeon, S. (2003). Discovering Business networks in Virtual Marketplaces. *Proceedings of the 14th Australasian Conference on Information Systems* (pp. 1-8). Perth, Australia: 14th Australasian Conference on Information Systems.

Smart, J., Cascio, J., & Paffendorf, J. (2007). *Metaverse Roadmap: Pathways to the 3D Web, A Cross-Industry Public Foresight Project*. Retrieved March 11, 2010, from Metaverseroadmap.org: http://www.metaverseroadmap.org/MetaverseRoadmapOverview.pdf

Smith, M. K., Welty, C., & McGuinness, D. L. (2004, February 10). *OWL Web Ontology Language Guide*. Retrieved August 31, 2009, from World Wide Web Consortium: http://www.w3.org/TR/owl-guide/

Sole, D., & Edmunson, A. (2002). Situated Knowledge and Learning in Dispersed Teams. *British Journal of Management, Volume 13, Issue S2*, S17-S34.

Staikos, K. S. (2009). *History of the Private, Royal, Imperial, Monastic and Public Libraries*. Retrieved October 13, 2009, from www. libraries.gr: http://www.libraries.gr/nonmembers/en/main.htm

Steuer, J. (1992). Defining Virtual Reality: Dimensions Determining Telepresence. *Journal of Communication, 42(4)*, 73-93.

Strickland, J. (2009). *Is there a Web 1.0?* Retrieved Sept 6, 2009, from computer.howstuffworks.com: http://computer.howstuffworks.com/web-10.htm

Sullivan, D. (2007, May 16). *Google 2.0: Google Universal Search*. Retrieved October 22, 2009, from searchengineland.com: http://searchengineland.com/google-20-google-universal-search-11232#what

Sweeny, P. (2009, May 18). *Web 3.0: The Web Goes Industrial.* Retrieved September 3, 2009, from SocialComputingJournal.com: http://socialcomputingjournal.com/viewcolumn.cfm?colid=837

Tech-Faq. (2011). *Augmented Reality.* Retrieved September 19, 2011, from Tech-faq.com: http://www.tech-faq.com/augmented-reality.html

Terry, J. B. (October 2002). *Use of Intranet Technology has had an Increasingly Positive Effect on Corporate Communications.* Largo, MD: University of Maryland University College.

Thomas, J. C., & Streib, G. (2005). E-Democracy, E-Commerce, and E-Research: Examining the Electronic Ties Between Citizens and Governments. *Administration & Society, Vol. 37, No. 3,* 259-280.

Thompson, D. (2009, March 08). *Coming of Age in Second Life: An Anthropologist Explores the Virtually Human.* Retrieved October 20, 2009, from blogoehlert.typepad.com: http://blogoehlert.typepad.com/eclippings/2009/03/coming-of-age-in-second-life-an-anthropologist-explores-the-virtually-human-dusan-writers.html

Toolbox for IT. (2007, June 19). *Virtual Workspace.* Retrieved October 15, 2010, from It.toolbox.com: http://it.toolbox.com/wiki/index.php/Virtual_Workspace

Twine.com. (2009). *The Technology: Twine.* Retrieved November 2, 2009, from www.twine.com: http://www.twine.com/technology

van Krevelen, D., & Poelman, R. (2010). A Survey of Augmented Reality Technologies, Applications and Limitations. *The International Journal of Virtual Reality, 9(2),* 1-20.

VanLeuven, L. J. (March 2009). *Optimizing Citizen Engagement during Emergencies Through Use of Web 2.0 Technologies.* Monterey, CA: Naval Postgraduate School.

Vartiainen , M., & Hyrkkänen, U. (2010). Changing Requirements and Mental Workload Factors in Mobile Multi-Locational Work. *New Technology, Work and Employment, Vol. 25, Issue 2,* 117-135.

Vashistha, A., & Vashistha, A. (2006). *The offshore nation: strategies for success in global outsourcing and offshoring.* New York, NY: McGraw-Hill Professional.

W3C. (2008, January 15). *W3C Opens Data on the Web with SPARQL.* Retrieved July 10, 2009, from www.w3.org: http://www.w3.org/2007/12/sparql-pressrelease

W3C. (2009). *Semantic Web Activity Statement.* (W3C) Retrieved July 9, 2009, from www.w3.org: http://www.w3.org/2001/sw/Activity

Wagner, C. S. (2005). *International Collaboration in Science and the Formation of a Core Group.* Amsterdam, Netherlands: Amsterdam School of Communications Research (ASCoR).

Wang, X. (2009). An Experimental Study on Collaborative Effectiveness of Augmented Reality Potentials in Urban Design. *CoDesign, Volume 5, Issue 4,* 229-244.

Watkins, K. (1995). Workplace Learning: Changing Times, Changing Practices. *New Directions for Adult and Continuing Education, n68,* 3-16.

Watts, S. A. (2007). Evaluative Feedback: Perspectives on Media Effects. *Journal of Computer-Mediated Communication, Volume 12, Issue 2,* 384-411.

White, J. (2010, September 22). *The ripple effect of workplace empowerment.* Retrieved October 11, 2010, from Hrmreport.com: http://www.hrmreport.com/editors-blog/The-ripple-effect-of-workplace-empowerment/

Wickens, C. D., Lee, J. D., Liu, Y., & Gordon-Becker, S. E. (2004). *An Introduction to Human Factors Engineering (2nd Edition).* Upper Saddle River, NJ: Pearson Prentice Hall.

6

Optical Touch Screen and Its Application as a Next Generation Classroom Response System

Hong Zhang
Rowan University
USA

1. Introduction

The way we interact with computers strongly influences how we use the technology. The traditional input methods such as using a keyboard or a computer mouse (Forlines et al, 2007) are still in dominance. Meanwhile, new methods have been explored and developed to provide more diversified or more intuitive user experiences. These include touch screen (Albinsson & Zhai, 2003), voice recognition (Krishnaraj et al, 2010) and brain wave detection (Li et al, 2010; Kaul, 2008). Inspired by the market success of Palm Pilot, and more recently Apple iPhone and iPad, touch screen based devices are becoming increasingly popular (Ostashewski & Reid, 2010) and are expanding their applications to many traditionally non-computing intensive fields, such as health care (Astell et al, 2010; Clark et al, 2009), driving (Lenné et al, 2011) and education (Willis & Miertschin, 2004; Zurn & Frolik, 2004).

A traditional touch screen covers the entire displaying surface with a matrix of resistors or capacitors (Ritchie & Turner, 1975; IEEE Software, 1991). Special circuits are used to capture the changes of the resistances or capacities of the matrix due to the user's touch. The changes are then converted to cursor positions accordingly. The resistive or capacitive technology requires the use of special materials such as indium tin oxide to be both transparent and conductive. However, the supplies of such materials are dwindling fast and the costs are increasing dramatically. Meanwhile, the amount of materials used on such touch screens is almost proportional to their sizes. In compact equipment such as PDAs and cell phones, or in special applications such as public information kiosks, costs of such touch screens can be justified. In regular office or household use, price is often a hurdle that prevents them from being widely adopted.

Different approaches of touch screen technology are developed to overcome the difficulties associated with the resistive or capacitive technologies. For example, an ultrasonic method was proposed to take advantage of surface acoustic waves (Katsuki et al, 2003). Meanwhile, optical based touch screen technology gained renewed interest. It was introduced early but did not gain momentum due to the cost of the digital cameras decades ago. More recently, the prices of single chip digital cameras have dropped significantly. At the level around $1 a piece, it becomes feasible to take cameras as the building blocks of today's input technology.

Several algorithms have been introduced within the optical input technology. Some examples include using frustrated total internal reflection (Han, 2005) or using two cameras to transform an acrylic plastic to a touch screen (Wilson, 2004). However, these two methods require the cameras to be placed on the opposite side of the screen from the user. They inevitably increased the thickness of the display and are not suitable for household, office, or classroom use.

Another popular approach is to put the camera at the user's side and use it to track a laser pointer or a fingertip (Cheng & Takatsuka, 2006). Meanwhile, a popular do-it-yourself project hacking the infrared camera of a WII remote to track the motion of an infrared pointer (Lee, 2007) have won applauses in the Internet. Nevertheless, the view of the user side cameras can be easily blocked by the body of the users and needs calibrations whenever the display is moved. Except for the fixed large projector screens, these methods are difficult to be adopted on regular desktops or laptops.

Meanwhile, stereovision has long been used in robot navigation to control manipulation or maneuver (Hager, 1995). A virtual touch screen using stereovision and see-through head mounted display was also proposed (Koh et al, 2008). However, the set up of the approaches is not suitable for daily application and the image processing is complicate due to the unstructured and noisy background.

In this article, we will describe the concept of using stereo- or mono-vision from the corners of the displays and track the motions of the pointer from sides. As we will explain later, this approach is simple to implement, inexpensive to equip, and not sensitive to the wear and tear of the screen. Comparing to existing touch screen technologies, it is also easy to scale up or down for different sizes or height/width ratios. Further, we can even generate virtual forces in the active input space and provide more vivid and intuitive user experiences. What's more, one of the most outstanding capabilities of the optical method is that it will superimpose but not obstruct the existing surface. This makes it ideal to be used on non-traditional displaying applications, such as a whiteboard, desktop, or even a regular writing pad, which is a staple stationary in a student's backpack.

Further, we will briefly introduce our application of touch screen in the next generation Classroom Response System (CRS) (Langman & Fies, 2010; Suchman et al, 2006). It takes advantage of the superimposing capability of the optical touch screen on a regular writing surface and can obtain instantaneous feedback from the students beyond multi-choice questions provided by traditional Clickers (Nicol et al, 2003; Siau et al, 2006). That is, the students can write or sketch their answers using touch screen devices or touch screen modified writing pads employing the technology described in this chapter.

The structure of this article is as follows. After this introduction, we will provide two approaches of optical touch screens, one based on stereovision and the other one on pseudo-stereovision. Then we will introduce the idea of virtual force to be used in touch screen input and further the superimposed optical touch screen as a next generation CRS. After that, a quick conclusion and discussion will be followed in the final section.

2. Pointer Locator Using Stereovision (PLUS)

The first metheod is to use two digital cameras simultaneously. It is called Pointer Locator Using Sterovision (PLUS) system.

2.1 System set up

In a PLUS system, each of the two cameras comes with a viewing angle that is equal to or greater than 90 degrees. As shown in Figure 1, a supporting structure encloses the flat screen display. At two adjacent corners, two cameras are mounted just above the surface of the display. They are positioned toward the center of the display such that the overlapped viewing field covers the entire screen surface. For convenience of illustration, we assume the cameras are located at the lower left and lower right corners as depicted in Figure 2. In the real-life applications as we will show later in this artical, the cameras are generally put on the top two corners to prevent occlusions by hand and to keep the camera lenses from collecting dust.

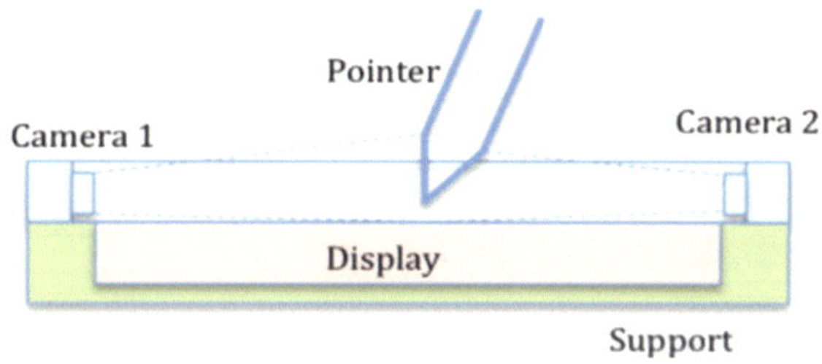

Fig. 1. Set up of the pointer locator using stereovision.

For convenience of analysis we first build a coordinate system. As seen in Figure 2, the origin of the system is at the focal point of the lower left camera. Its X and Y axes are parallel to the horizontal and vertical edges of the screen respectively. At this section, we only analyze the pointer positions. That is, we will only study the planar (X-Y) movement of the pointer projected at the surface of the display. Therefore, we assume a linear camera method

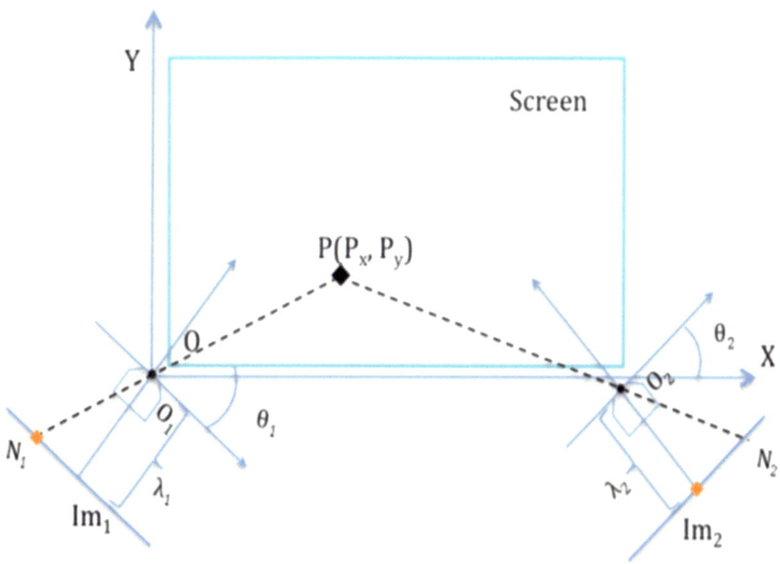

Fig. 2. Coordinate System for Pointer Locater Using Stereovision.

at this point and ignore the Z-coordinate. The focal point of the camera is offset by $-s_{1x}$ and $-s_{1y}$ at horizontal and vertical directions respectively from the lower left corner of the screen. Then the position of the corner is $\mathbf{s}_1=[s_{1x}, s_{1y}]^T$. The lower right corner is $\mathbf{s}_2=[s_{2x}, s_{2y}]^T=[L_H+s_{1x}, s_{1y}]^T$ where L_H is the width of the screen. Likewise, the upper right corner is $\mathbf{s}_3=[s_{3x}, s_{3y}]^T=[L_H+s_{1x}, L_V+s_{1y}]^T$ where L_V is the height of the screen.

2.2 Pointer location using stereovision

Assuming the optical axis of the left camera is rotated from X-axis by angle θ_1, we can obtain the rotation matrix of the camera from screen-based coordinate system to camera-based coordinate system as

$$A_1 = \begin{bmatrix} \cos\theta_1 & -\sin\theta_1 \\ \sin\theta_1 & \cos\theta_1 \end{bmatrix}. \tag{1}$$

Likewise, assuming the focal point of the right camera is located at $\mathbf{d}_2=[d_{2x}, d_{2y}]^T$ with angle θ_2, the transformation (rotation and translation) matrix is

$$A_2 = \begin{bmatrix} \cos\theta_2 & -\sin\theta_2 & d_{2x} \\ \sin\theta_2 & \cos\theta_2 & d_{2x} \\ 0 & 0 & 1 \end{bmatrix}. \tag{2}$$

Please note that we implied the use of homogeneous coordinates in Eq. 2. We will change back and forth between $[x, y]^T$ and $[x, y, 1]^T$ in calculations and in expressions whenever necessary. Therefore any point $P=[P_x, P_y]^T$ in the screen can be transformed to

$$P_1 = \begin{bmatrix} P_{1x} \\ P_{1y} \end{bmatrix} = A_1 P = \begin{bmatrix} P_x\cos\theta_1 - P_y\sin\theta_1 \\ P_x\sin\theta_1 + P_y\cos\theta_1 \end{bmatrix} \tag{3}$$

at camera 1 and

$$P_1 = \begin{bmatrix} P_{2x} \\ P_{2y} \end{bmatrix} = A_2 P = \begin{bmatrix} P_x\cos\theta_2 - P_y\sin\theta_2 \\ P_x\sin\theta_2 + P_y\cos\theta_2 \end{bmatrix} \tag{4}$$

at camera 2. We assume a pinpoint camera model with the focal length as λ_1.

For camera 1, the projection of the point P on the image plane can be easily measured from the image as $N_1=n_1*c_{px1}$ where n_1 is the pixel position at the image plane and c_{px1} is the size of each pixel for camera 1. Hence, we can easily obtain the following relationship using similar triangles:

$$\frac{P_x\sin\theta_1 + P_y\cos\theta_1}{P_x\cos\theta_1 - P_y\sin\theta_1} = \frac{-\lambda_1}{N_1} \tag{5}$$

Likewise, we can find similar result for camera 2 as:

$$\frac{P_x \sin\theta_2 + P_y \cos\theta_2 + d_{2y}}{P_x \cos\theta_2 - P_y \sin\theta_2 + d_{2x}} = \frac{-\lambda_2}{N_2} \quad . \tag{6}$$

By solving Equations 1 and 2 we can get the original position of $[P_x, P_y]^T$ as

$$\begin{cases} P_x = \dfrac{C_1B_2 - C_2B_1}{A_1B_2 - A_2B_1} \\ P_y = \dfrac{A_1C_2 - A_2C_1}{A_1B_2 - A_2B_1} \end{cases} \tag{7}$$

where

$$A_1 = N_1 \sin\theta_1 + \lambda_1 \cos\theta_1, \quad A_2 = N_2 \sin\theta_2 + \lambda_2 \cos\theta_2,$$
$$B_1 = N_1 \cos\theta_1 - \lambda_1 \sin\theta_1, \quad B_2 = N_2 \cos\theta_2 - \lambda_2 \sin\theta_2,$$
$$C_1 = 0, \quad C_2 = -\lambda_2 d_{2x} - N_2 d_{2y}.$$

The corresponding cursor position of the pointer is obtained as $P_s=[P_{sx}, P_{sy}]^T=[(P_x-s_{1x})/s_{px}, (P_y-s_{1y})/s_{py}]^T$ where s_{px} and s_{py} are pixel sizes of the display unit at both X and Y directions. Please note that the values of s_{1x}, s_{1y}, d_{2x}, d_{2y} can be obtained from initial calibration. However, they will not change even if the display is moved since the cameras and the screen are both fixed to the same supporting structure.

3. Pointer Locator Using Monovision (PLUM)

3.1 Pseudo-stereovision

In normal stereovision, the surroundings of the interested features is often full of image noises. However, the scenes observed by the point-detecting cameras are simple and constructed. Therefore, we can use one camera instead of two to achieve the same result.

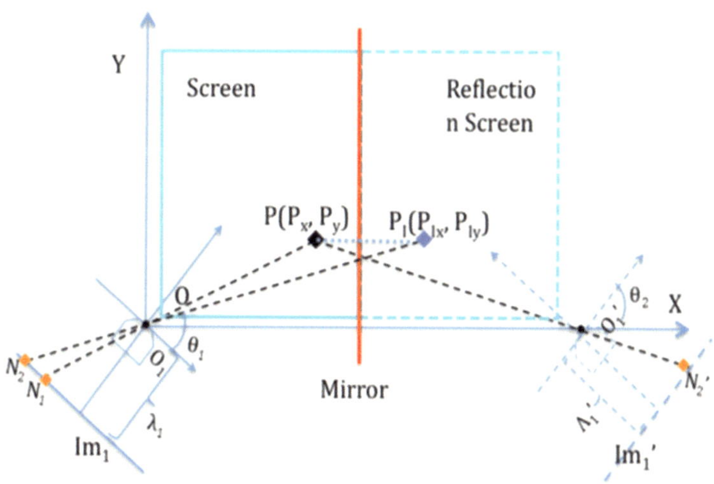

Fig. 3. One configuration of Pointer Locator Using Pseudo-Stereovision.

As seen in Figure 3, the camera on the right is removed. Instead, a mirror is put on the edge of the screen. For the convenience of illustration, we cut the width of the screen to half of that is shown in Figure 2. The mirror is configured to be parallel to the left edge of the screen, or the Y-axis of the screen-based coordinate system. Therefore we can have a mirror image of the camera (virtual camera) with the exact same physical characters as the real one. By combining the physical camera and its reflection (the virtual camera) together, we can obtain a pseudo-stereovision.

From the set up shown in Figure 3, it is obvious that

$$\begin{cases} \theta_2 = -\theta_1 \\ \lambda_2 = \lambda_1 \end{cases} \tag{8}$$

The focal point or origin of the virtual camera frame is at $[d_{2x}, d_{2y}]^T=[2L_H+2s_{1x}, 0]^T$. Meanwhile, as seen from Figure 3, the mirror image of the pointer $P=[P_x, P_y]^T$ is $P_1=[P_{1x}, P_{1y}]^T$. Its projection to the image plane of the physical camera is N_2. As depicted from Figure 3, the mirror image of the projection of P_1 on the physical camera is the projection of the point P on the virtual camera. It is clear that $N'_2=-N_2$.

If we substitute the above values to Equation 5, we can easily find the position of pointer $P=[P_x, P_y]^T$ and its corresponding cursor position $P_s=[P_{sx}, P_{sy}]^T$.

3.2 Monovision with mirror image

Alternatively, we can use a different approach. That is, instead of using the virtual camera and convert back to the case of stereovision, we can process the mirror image of the pointer at the physical camera directly.

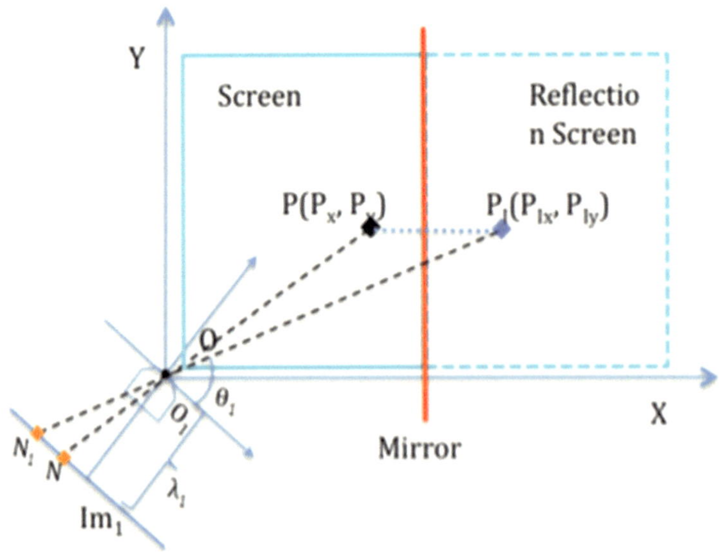

Fig. 4. An alternative configuration of Pointer Localization Using Monovision with mirror image.

First, using the same set up of the coordinate system, the position of $P_1=[P_{1x}, P_{1y}]^T$ can be found as $[2L-P_x, P_y]^T$ where L is the horizontal distance from the origin O to the mirror. Then we can obtain the equations similar to Equations 3 and 4:

$$\frac{P_x \sin\theta + P_y \cos\theta}{P_x \cos\theta - P_y \sin\theta} = \frac{-\lambda}{N_1} \tag{9}$$

$$\frac{(2L - P_x)\sin\theta + P_y \cos\theta}{(2L - P_x)\cos\theta - P_y \sin\theta} = \frac{-\lambda}{N_2} \tag{10}$$

where λ is the focal length of the physical camera, θ is the angle of the camera, and N_1 and N_2 are the projected positions of P and P_1 on the image plane.

Solve for P_x and P_y, we have

$$\begin{cases} P_x = \dfrac{(\lambda^2 - N_1 N_2)\sin 2\theta + 2N_2\lambda \sin^2\theta - 2N_1\lambda\cos^2\theta}{(\lambda^2 - N_1 N_2)\sin 2\theta - (N_1 + N_2)\lambda\cos 2\theta} L \\ P_y = \dfrac{N_1 \sin\theta + \lambda\cos\theta}{\lambda\sin\theta - N_1\cos\theta} P_x \end{cases} . \tag{11}$$

Note that the result is simpler compare to the true stereovision method due to the equality of focal length λ and rotation angle θ between the physical and virtual cameras. Meanwhile, we need to cover the combined surface of both the physical screen and the reflected one, so we can calibrate the angle θ to be $\pi/4$. In this case, the result can be further simplified as

$$\begin{cases} P_x = \dfrac{(\lambda - N_1)(\lambda + N_2)}{\lambda^2 - N_1 N_2} L \\ P_y = \dfrac{\lambda + N_1}{\lambda - N_1} P_x \end{cases} \tag{12}$$

4. Application considerations

4.1 Virtual boundary

Sometime, the pointer is away from the vicinity of the screen but is still close enough to be picked up by the cameras. This can easily happen when a user is pondering for the next action or is talking in front of the screen. As shown in Figure 5A, in true stereovision, a virtual boundary can be set up in the algorithm to filter out the unwanted movements. Any point P within the virtual boundary is considered legitimate and is processed accordingly. Its motion will be reflected as the movement of the cursor on the screen. If the pointer is outside the virtual boundary, like the position P' in Figure 5A, it can be considered idle and an update is not necessary. However, in the background, the video stream is constantly processed to extract the positions of P at both cameras. The distance of the pointer from the screen surface needed to be constantly calculated and compared with the virtual boundary.

On the other hand, with the method of monovision using mirror, we can set up a virtual boundary by combining the height of the mirror and the viewing angle of the camera. As shown in Figure 5B, when the pointer is above the virtual boundary, the image of the pointer P'_1 will not be picked up by the camera even the pointer P' itself is within the range. That is, only one image feature will be obtained instead of two. A quick on-off logic can be easily used to dismiss this single point without calculating the position and distance first. Since the duration of the pointer in use is often far less than when it is not, demand on computing power will be greatly reduced.

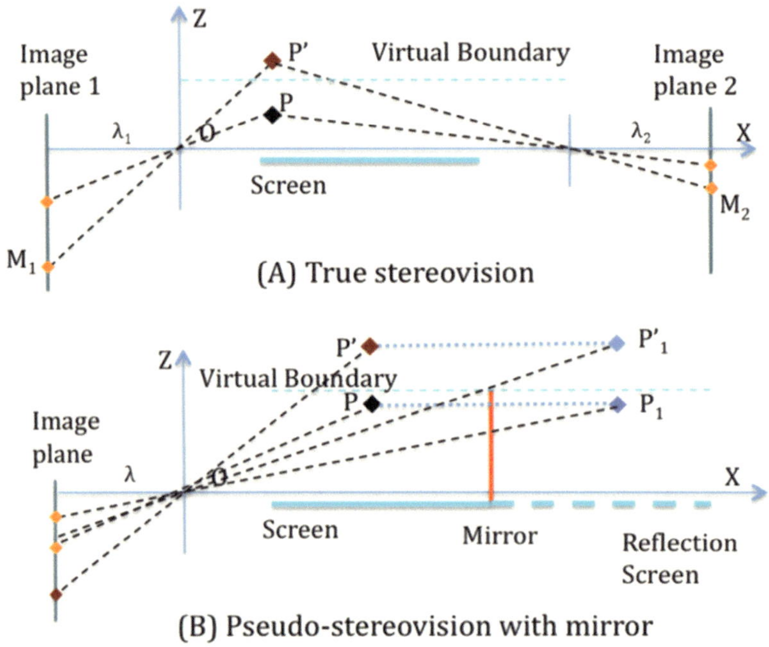

Fig. 5. Virtual boundary with pseudo-stereovision.

4.2 Action space and virtual force

In previous methods, only the X-direction projection (parallel to the screen) on the camera image plane is used. It only provides information on the position of the pointer. Move one step forward, we can take advantage of the Z-direction projection (perpendicular to the screen) of the image and the time derivatives of the projections for more advanced features. One such application is to set up an action space immediately outside the touch screen. In the action space, we can construct virtual forces and use them to achieve the results such as push, pull, stroke, or other similar motions.

First, let us expand the aforementioned model to a 3-dimensional space with the Z-axis perpendicular to the display screen and pointing away from it. This 3D action space is enclosed by the display screen on bottom and the virtual boundary on top. As seen in Figure 6, the pointer can freely move in this space. The projection of the pointer gives a planar trajectory on the camera image plane.

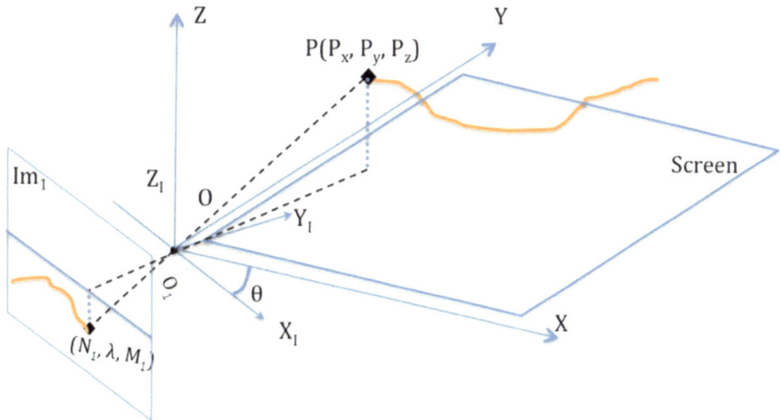

Fig. 6. 3D trajectory in the action space.

Then the z position P_z can be easily obtained as

$$P_z = \frac{M}{\lambda} P_x \tag{13}$$

where M is the vertical position of the pointer projected on the image plane.

With the 3D image features obtained, we can easily construct a virtual force function at both directions. A virtual stroke force can be obtained as

$$F_s = K_s \sqrt{a_x^2 + a_y^2} \tag{14}$$

and a virtual push or pull can be considered as

$$F_p = K_p a_z \tag{15}$$

where K_s and K_p are to be obtained from experiment and to be further adapted using self learning algorithms, a_x and a_y are accelerations of pointer at x and y directions, while a_z is its acceleration at the z direction. The variables a_x, a_y and a_z can all be calculated through second order finite differentiation from P_x, P_y, and P_z.

We should point out that a virtual force can be considered as a function of any subset of the position variables and their derivatives. For example, a simple position based force feedback can be obtained as

$$F = K_p P_z^{-1} \tag{16}$$

while a more sophiscated one may look like

$$F = \sum_{i=1}^{3} K_{pi} P_i^{-ai} + K_{vi} V_i^{-bi} \tag{17}$$

where K_{pi}, P_i, a_i, K_{vi}, V_i, and b_i should be determined by the specific program needs.

Comparing with the force sensing of traditional touch screens, the virtual force can give a much greater force range. The depth of the action space can be easily adjusted by the virtual boundary. By using cameras with wide viewing angles, the action space can be large enough to yield many interesting 3D motions, which can be important for active computer games or on screen calligraphy or painting. Currently, the pull, push, or similar motions are absent in many applications. If used, they can greatly improve the user experiences.

Further, the users do not even need to physically touch the screen. As long as the pointer or finger is in the action space, its movement will be monitored and reflected on the movement of the corresponding cursor or object in the program.

5. Touch screen in the next generation Classroom Response System (CRS)

As we explained earlier, optical touch screen described in this article is simple to implement, inexpensive to equip, and not sensitive to the wear and tear due to the pointers scratching on the touch screen. A commercial version of this device can be used to superimpose but not obstruct the existing writing surface. This makes it ideal to be used on non-traditional displaying applications, such as a whiteboard, desktop, or even a regular writing pad. Here we will briefly introduce our application of touch screen in the next generation Classroom Response System (CRS).

5.1 Need of the next generation CRS

Actively engaging students in classrooms is always a challenge to the teachers (Smith, 1996; Zhang, 1993). People have tried various ways to improve the interactions even from the early days of chalk and board (Bransford et al, 2000). Choosing a volunteer from raised hands and picking a name from the roll book of the class are two most common traditional methods. However, these methods only give teachers feedback from a small fraction of the class. The sample is often not typical or representative. Many students will not volunteer for fear of public mistake and embarassment. As the result, a small vocal minority will skew the view of the teacher of how the entire class understand the topic (Caldwell, 2007). To increase the sample size, people also tried methods such as shouting the answers, applause, or response cards (Karen et al, 2001), all with their pros and cons. More recently, computer based technologies are introduced to classrooms. They enabled teachers to explore more options (Patten, 2006; Richard et al, 2007; Roschelle, 2003).

The first technology used is computer-based visuals such as Powerpoint (Anderson, 2004; Bannan-Ritland, 2002; Liang et al, 2005). It has become ubiquitous today, but with mixed results. The slide shows help to provide strong graphical impact as "one picture worth a thousand words". However, the interactions and feedbacks from the students are still greatly limited. Sometime, the situation is even worse when the light is dimmed to improve the visual contrast.

Recently, a small gadget called Clicker, or the first generation CRS, is gaining momentum among teachers throughout the K-12 and higher education, and to anywhere with a group of audience (Nicol et al, 2003; Siau et al, 2006). A clicker is a remote-like device that comes with a number of buttons and a wireless transmitter. After the instructor giving out a multi-choice or true/false question, the students punch the buttons on their Clickers to select their answers. The answers then are instantly transmitted to the host computer operated by the teacher. A program will collect and summarize the answers and present the aggregated result to the teacher using a chart or graphic.

Both teachers and students welcomed the use of CRS. The engagement is bi-directional. The teacher can continuously assess the level of student understanding or mis-understanding. They can then give targeted clarifications or adjust the course material or pace to address the problems arisen. At the same time, the students can quickly apply the knowledge they just learned and answer the questions without raising hands, which can be intimidating to many. Since the answers are transmitted anonymously, the students will be free from the fear of peer pressure and public embarrassment.

However, still more features are desired for the Clickers. One major drawback of the current Clickers is its dependence on multi-choice or true/false questions (Siau et al, 2006). The teachers make up generally three or four possible wrong answers and mix them with the right one. As a legacy from the early computer-based standardized test, it is easy to grade. However, multi-choice or true/false questions are not the best or the only assessing tools. The number of choices is limited; the result can be skewed by test-taking techniques; and the teachers cannot directly know what the mistakes the students make from the answers.

Meanwhile, since the students can only choose from a limited list of options, their creativities are often ignored or discouraged. In any subject, there are always multiple solutions to a question, especially an open-ended question. In Science, Technology, Engineering, Art & Mathematics (STEAM) and many other fields, we often encourage students to focus on problem-solving progress instead of the final answer. Unfortunately, the multi-choice questions provide no room for the students to derive their own answers. It would be great if we can have a better tool that will encourage open-ended questions and promote problem-solving skills.

One attempt of improvement over clicker is to use touch sensitive tablets (Berque et al, 2004) or touch screen tablets. A touch sensitive tablet digitizes the strokes of the stylus on its surface and send the data stream to the host computer. However, due to the seperation of writing and displaying, the use of this kind device is unnatural and did not gain wide acceptance in the classrooms.

The touch screen pads include Tablet PCs (Koile & Singer, 2006; Willis & Miertschin, 2004; Zurn & Frolik, 2004) or iPad and its competitors (we denote them as xPads). A user can write on the touch screen of the tablet with a stylus or a finger. Then the hardware and software will convert the writing to either the text or graphics, and then display them back on the screen. Once networked together, tablets can be a great tool for a teacher to get instant feedback from the students. The feedback will not be limited to multiple choices, but on every part of the knowledge assessment that can be conducted with a regular paper test.

However, there are still several major drawbacks of these touch screen tablets. First is its cost. For example, the price of a tablet PC starts from $1k and costs much more with rugged design. xPads are generally more affordable, but still costs hundred dollars each. The prices can easily rule out most classroom use, especially when they are under the stress of young students at their active years. Second is the different platforms of the tablet devices in the market. It is able to recommend but difficult to require all the students using the same operating system in one classroom unless they are provided for free. Third is the distraction of the other software, especially the communication and entertainment software installed in the tablets. When a student is having an electronic device in hand, it is not easy to resist the temptation of returning a quick text message or playing a small game while the teacher is not around.

5.2 Set up of a CRS using optical touch screen devices

With the above needs in mind, we applied the optical touch screen to the development of the next generation CRS, or Z-Writers. The major part of the Z-Writer is a clipboard style writing surface. Students can put a regular notepad or a stack of test paper on it. They can write on the paper just like what they are doing in the regular test. The difference of the Z-Writer from the regular clipboard is that a sensor bar is installed at the top of the pad. The sensor bar can take either the PLUS or PLUM configuration as shwon in Figure 7A or Figure 7B.

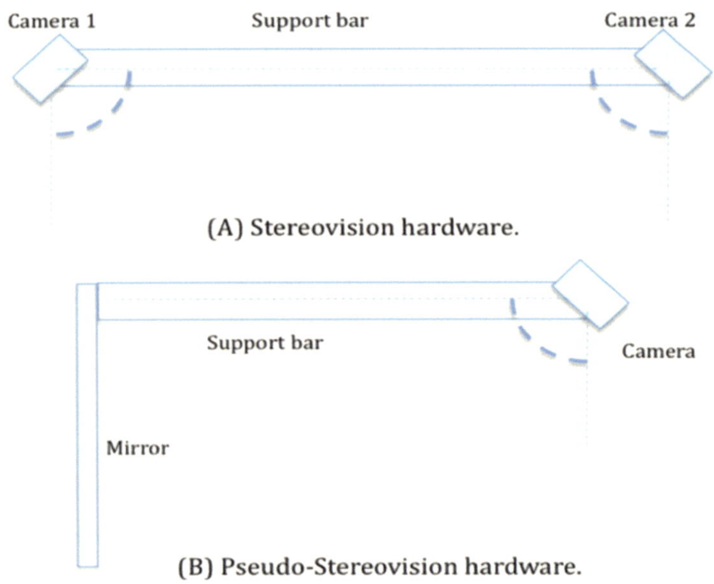

Fig. 7. Hardware setup.

Like tablet PCs or xPads, the Z-Writer can be used by individual users. That is, each Z-Writer is associated with a computer via Bluetooth wireless connection. Since only the movement of the pen tips will be recorded and transmitted, no high capacity data transmission is required. Off-the-shelf mainstream Bluetooth 2.1 transmitters are capable of sending and receiving data without delay.

We can also network Z-Writers in a CRS setting. Each Bluetooth master can only handle up to 7 devices with today's technology. In Linux set up, we can simply add extra Bluetooth dongles to increase the number of devices the computer can handle. For Windows or Mac OS, the operating systems can not handle more than one Bluetooth master. Therefore, we developed a special Scatternet (Mockel et al, 2007) to expand the capacity of the Z-Writers.

As seen in Figure 8, we divide all the Z-Writers in a classroom to groups of 6. One of them equips a sub-server with an enhanced antenna. It acts as both a receiver and a relay. It collects the data from the group and relay them to the Bluetooth master in the host computer. In this network, each computer can handle up to 7 groups or 42 Z-Writers. That is enough for most classes and more than the maximum capacity that a teacher can handle at the individual level without a teaching assistant. For the larger classes with the help of teaching assistants, a local network of multiple computers or an outright change to using 802.11 can be employed. However, these are beyond the topic of this discussion.

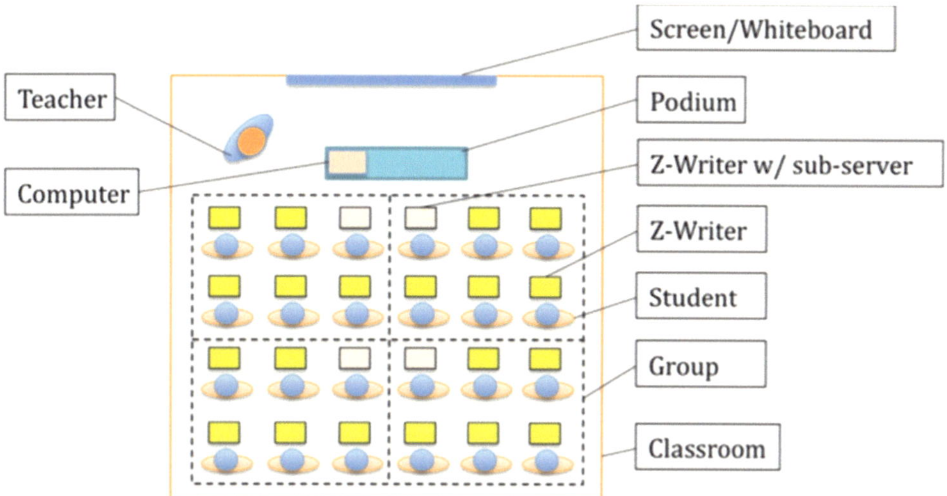

Fig. 8. Set up of a Classroom Response System.

The host computer on the teacher's side collects all the data from the sub-servers and save them into a database. A preview program converts the data into pixel points and display them in a preview window like the left part of Figure 9. With a quick glance, the teachers can have an instant view of how the students are performing. When the teachers need to annotate an individual student's work, they can select and magnify the one of interest and display it as seen in the right half of Figure 9 for in-class review and analysis.

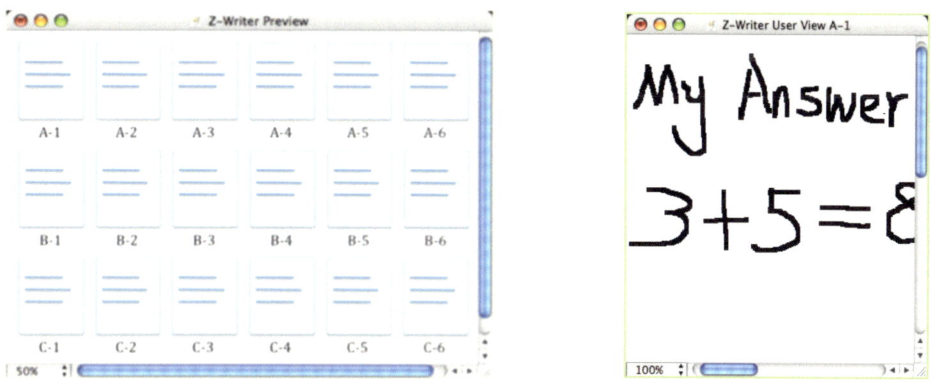

Fig. 9. Display in teacher's computer screen. Left: Real-time preview with all inputs. Right: Magnified view of individual answers.

Figure 10 is a sample course material common to Physics or Engineering majors. One main topic of such majors is load analysis with Free Body Diagrams (FBD). Figure 10 gives a typical example of the force analysis. On left is a block resting on a slanted surface. As shown on right, students need to set up a proper coordinate system, draw the forces, and then write down the governing equations on each direction to find out the magnitudes of the forces.

Before the class, the teacher prepares questions like the one shown in the left part of Figure 10 and makes copies on regular paper. In the class time, the teacher first explains the concepts of FBD and provides examples. Then the handouts with the questions will distributed to the class. The students put the handouts on the writing surfaces of the Z-Writers and then write their answers on the paper just like any other classes. The Z-Writers transfer the results to the host computer for the teacher to review in real time. The teacher is then able to adjust the next step accordingly, such as revisiting the subject, moving on to the next topic, or giving annotations to selected answers. At the end of the class, the students will carry their own paper home while the teacher keeps a soft copy of all answers for future reference.

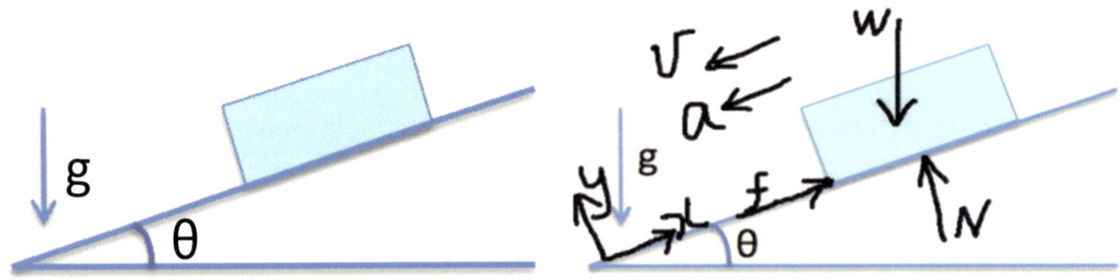

Fig. 10. A typical example of load and motion analysis. Left: Given by teacher. Right: Student answer.

6. Conclusion

In this article, we introduced a novel method of using stereovision (PLUS) and monovision (PLUM) to locate the position of a pointer on a display unit.

6.1 Benefits of the optical touch screen with virtual force

There are many advantages of the algorithms proposed in this article.

1. **Low cost**. It is relatively easy and inexpensive to implement. Thanks to the ubiquitous camera phones and webcams, low-cost high-resolution single-chip digital cameras are widely available today.
2. **Durable**. There is no physical contact between the camera and the pointer. Therefore, the functionality of the screen will not deteriorate due to wear and tear. Even when the screen is scratched or broken, the touch function will still work.
3. **Easy to scale up**. The complexity and cost of existing touch screens increase quickly when the screens become larger. For example, when the size of a screen doubles, its

viewable area quadruples, so is the material used and the computing power needed. In contrast, in the methods introduced in this article, the same two cameras or camera and mirror combination can be easily scaled up or down to screens with different sizes and height-width ratios.

4. **3D input**. As mentioned earlier in this article, the action space and virtual force can be used to achieve the effect of 3D input and to obtain virtual force feedback.
5. **Multi-touch**. Existing computer software can easily detect and follow multiple image features. It will be easy to include multi-touch functions. Combined with virtual force, the multi-touch function can make inputting more versatile and powerful.
6. **Compact and light weight**. Comparing to the existing optical touch screen using behind screen or user side camera, this side camera method is compact and can save precious space. The cameras are generally small and will not increase the weight or size of the computer display like many existing touch screens.

6.2 Benefit of the next generation CRS using touch screen writers

1. **Real-time feedback.** All educators are facing the perpetual challenge of assessing how well the students understand each course, each example, or even each sentence. Homework, quizzes and exams evaluate each individuals but with latency. Group discussion, flash cards, and the original Classroom Response Systems (Clickers) provide instant but collective feedbacks. The Z-Writer Group combines the benefits of the two by providing instant individual feedbacks to the teachers.
2. **Progress monitor.** From one computer display, teachers can monitor not only the answers but how the students proceed from start to finish at both collective and individual levels.
3. **After-class evaluation.** Teachers can replay the writings of every answer after the class. Therefore, they can analyze each student and address their specific needs with higher accuracy.
4. **Open-ended questions.** Many in-class assessment tools rely on multi-choice questions, which are not enough for STEAM subjects. The Z-Writer Group will enable teachers to give open-ended questions in classes and obtain real-time feedbacks. This will greatly encourage creativities from the students.

6.3 Future work

Currently we are working on improving the stability and noise reduction on the optical touch screen algorithm and its use on classroom response system described in this paper. We are also working on expanding the applications of the optical touch screen to art and calligraphy field for paperless painting with realistic strokes. We are also exploring the use of 802.11 for the auditorium size CRS settings.

7. References

Albinsson, P & Zhai, S. (2003). High Precision Touch Screen Interaction, *Proceedings of the SIGCHI conference on Human factors in computing systems*, ISBN:1-58113-630-7, Fort Lauderdale, FL, April 5-10, 2003

Anderson, R. (2004). Beyond PowerPoint: Building a New Classroom Presenter. *Syllabus*, pp. 31-33. June, 2004

Astell, A.; Ellis, M.; Bernardi, L.; Alm, N.; Dye, R.; Gowans, G. & Campbell, J. (2010) Using a touch screen computer to support relationships between people with dementia and caregivers, *Interacting with computers*, Vol. 22, Issue 4, Pages 267-275, July 2010

Bannan-Ritland, B. (2002). Computer-mediated communication, elearning, and interactivity: A review of the research. *Quarterly Review of Distance Education*, Vol. 3. No. 2, pp. 161-179, 2002.

Berque, D.; Bonebright, T. & Whitesell, M. (2004). Using Pen-Based Computers Across the Computer Science Curriculum, *Proceedings of Special Interest Group on Information Technology Education (SIGITE'04)*, Norfolk, VA, USA, March 3-7, 2004

Bransford, J.; Brown, A. & Cocking, R. (2000). *How People Learn: Brain, Mind, Experience, and School*, National Academy Press, Washington, DC, 2000

Caldwell, J. (2007). Clickers in the Large Classroom: Current Research and Best-Practice Tips. *CBE Life Sciences Education*, Vol. 6, No. 1, pp. 9-20. 2007

Cheng, K. & Takatsuka M. (2006). Estimating Virtual Touchscreen for Fingertip Interaction with Large Displays. *Proceedings of 20th conference of the computer-human interaction special interest group (CHISIG) of Australia on Computer-human interaction: design: activities, artefacts and environments (OZCHI'06).* pp. 397-400. Sydney, Australia, November 20-24, 2006

Clark, K.; Bardwell, W.; Arsenault, T.; DeTeresa, R. & Loscalzo, M. (2009), Implementing touch-screen technology to enhance recognition of distress. *Psycho-Oncology*, Vol. 18, No. 8, pp. 822–830, ISSN: 1057-9249, 2009

Forlines, C.; Wigdor, D.; Shen, C. & Balakrishnan, R. (2007). Direct touch vs mouse input for tabletop displays. *Proceedings of the SIGCHI Conference on Human factors in computing systems*, ISBN: 978-1-59593-593-9, San Jose, CA, USA, April 28-May 3, 2007

Hager, G. (1995). Calibration-free visual control using projective invariance. *Proceedings of 5th International Conference of Computer Vision*, pp. 1009-1015, Cambridge, MA, USA, June 20-23, 1995

IEEE Software Staff, Touch Screens Now Offer Compelling Uses, *IEEE Software*, Vol. 8, No. 2, pp. 93-94, March 1991

Han, J. (2005). Low-cost multi-touch sensing through frustrated total internal reflection. *Proceedings of the 18th annual ACM symposium on User interface software and technology*, pp. 115 - 118 , Seattle, WA, USA, October 23-27, 2005

Jaimes A. & Sebe N. (2007). Multimodal human–computer interaction: A survey. *Computer Vision and Image Understanding*, Vol. 108, Issues1-2, pp.116-134, October-November 2007

Karen, K; Carr, J. & Dozier, C. Dozier. (2001). Response-Card Instruction and Student Learning in a College Classroom. *Teaching of Psychology*, Vol. 28, No. 2, pp. 101-104, May 2001

Katsuki, T.; Nakazawa, F.; Sano, S.; Takahashi, Y. & Satoh, Y. (2003). A Compact and High Optical Transmission SAW Touch Screen With ZnO Thin-Film Piezoelectric Transducers. *Proceedings of the 2003 IEEE Symposium on Ultrasonics*, Vol. 1, pp. 821-824, Honolulu, HI, Oct. 5-8, 2003

Kaul, P. (2008). Brain Wave Games and E-Learning. *Innovative Techniques in Instruction Technology, E-Learning, E-Assessment*, ISBN 978-1-4020-8739-4_72, pp410-415, 2008

Koh, E.; Won, J. & Bae C. (2008). Vision-Based Virtual Touch Screen Interface. *Proceedings of International Conference on Consumer Electronics,* pp. 1-2. ISBN: 978-1-4244-1458-1. Las Vegas, NV, USA, Januarary 9-13, 2008

Koile, K. & Singer, D. (2006). Development of a Tablet-PC-Based System to Increase Instructor-Student Classroom Interactions and Student Learning. [book auth.] J. Prey and R. Reed D. Berque. *The Impact of Pen-based Technology on Education: Vignettes, Evaluations and Future Directions,* Purdue University Press, ISBN 9781557534347, June 11, 2006

Krishnaraj, A.; Lee, J.; Laws, S.; & Crawford, T. (2010), Voice Recognition Software: Effect on Radiology Report Turnaround Time at an Academic Medical Center, *American Journal of Roentgenology,* Vol. 195, No. 1, pp. 194-197, July, 2010

Langman, J & Fies, C. (2010). Classroom response system-mediated science learning with English language learners. *Language and Education,* Vol. 24, Issue 2, 2010

Lee, J. (2007). Low-Cost Multi-point Interactive Whiteboards Using the Wiimote. Available from http://johnnylee.net/projects/wii

Lenné, M.; Salmon, P.; Triggs, T.; Cornelissen, M. & Tomasevic, N. (2011). How Does Motion Influence the Use of Touch Screen In-Vehicle Information Systems? *Proceedings of the Human Factors and Ergonomics Society Annual Meeting,* vol. 55 no. 1 1855-1859 September 2011

Li, Y.; Nam, C.; Shadden, B. & Johnson, S. (2010). A P300-Based Brain–Computer Interface: Effects of Interface Type and Screen Size. *International Journal of Human-Computer Interaction,* Vol. 27, Issue 1, pp. 52-68. December 2010

Liang, J.; Liu, T.; Wang, H.; Chang, B.; Deng, Y.; Yang, J.; Chou, C.; KO, H.; Yang, S. & Chan, T. (2005) A Few Design Perspectives on One-On-One Digital Classroom Environment. *Journal of Computer Assisted Learning,* Vol. 21. Issue 1. pp181-189. 2005

Mockel, R.; Sprowitz, A.; Maye, J. & Ijspeert, A. (2007). An easy to use bluetooth scatternet protocol for fast data exchange in wireless sensor networks and autonomous robots. *IEEE/RSJ International Conference on Intelligent Robots and Systems (IROS) 2007,* pp. 2801-2806, October 29-November 2, 2007

Nicol, J.; Boyle, T. & David, J. (2003). Using Classroom Communication Systems to Support Interaction and Discussion in Large Class Settings. *Research in Learning Technology,* ISSN 0968-7769,Vol. 11, pp. 43-57. April, 2003

Ostashewski, N. & Reid, D. (2010). iPod, iPhone, and now iPad: The evolution of multimedia access in a mobile teaching context, *In Proceedings of World Conference on Educational Multimedia, Hypermedia and Telecommunications 2010,* pp. 2862-2864. ISBN 1-880094-81-9, Chesapeake, VA, Toronto, Canada, June 29, 2010

Patten, B. (2006). Designing collaborative, constructionist and contextual applications for handheld devices. *Computers & Education,* Vol. 46. No. 3, pp. 294-308, April 2006

Richard, A.; Ruth, A.; Davis, K; Linnell, N.; Prince, C. & Razmov, V. (2007). Supporting Active Learning and Example Based Instruction with Classroom Technology. *Proceedings of the 38th SIGCSE technical symposium on Computer science education,* ISBN:1-59593-361-1. Covington, Kentucky, 2007

Ritchie, G & Turner, J. (1975). Input devices for interactive graphics. *International Journal of Man-Machine Studies,* Vol. 7, Issue 5, pp. 639-660, September 1975

Roschelle, J. (2003). Unlocking the learning value of wireless mobile devices. *Journal of Computer Assisted Learning,* Vol. 19, No. 3, pp. 260-272. 2003

Smith, D. (1996). Developing a More Interactive Classroom: A Continuing Odyssey. *Teaching Sociology*, Vol. 24. pp. 64-75, 1996

Suchman, E.; Uchiyama, K.; Smith, R. & Bender K. (2006). Evaluating the impact of a classroom response system in a microbiology course. *Journal of Microbiology & Biology Education*, ISSN: 1935-7885, Vol. 7, 2006

Siau, K.; Sheng, H. & Nah, F. (2006). Use of a Classroom Response System to Enhance Classroom Interactivity. *IEEE Transactions on Education*, Vol 49, No.3, pp. 398-403, August 2006

Willis C. & Miertschin, L. (2004). Tablet PCs as Instructional Tools or the Pen is Mightier than the Board! *Proceedings of Special Interest Group on Information Technology Education (SIGITE'04)*, pp.153-159. Salt Lake City, Utah, USA, October 28-30, 2004

Wilson, A. (2004). TouchLight: An Imaging Touch Screen and Display For Gesture-Based Interaction. *Proceedings of 6th International Conference On Multimodal Interfaces*, pp. 69-76. State College, PA, USA, October 13-15, 2004

Zhang, C. & Fulford, S. (1993). Perceptions of interaction: The critical predictor in distance education. *American Journal of Distance Education*, Vol. 7. pp. 8-21, 1993

Zurn, J. & Frolik J. (2004). Evaluation of Tablet PCs for Engineering Content Development and Instruction. *American Society for Engineering Education Annual Conference & Exposition*, Salt Lake City, Utah, June 20-23, 2004

7

Personalization of Virtual Environments Navigation and Tasks for Neurorehabilitation

Dani Tost, Sergi Grau and Sergio Moya
CREB-Polytechnical University of Catalonia
Spain

1. Introduction

The use of "serious" computer games designed for other purposes than purely leisure is becoming a recurrent research topic in diverse areas from professional training and education to psychiatric and neuropsychological rehabilitation. In particular 3D computer games have been introduced in neuropsychological rehabilitation of cognitive functions to train daily activities. In general, these games are based on the first person paradigm. Patients control an avatar who moves around in a 3D virtual scenario. They manipulate virtual objects in order to perform daily activities such as cooking or tidying up a room. The underlying hypothesis of Cognitive Neuropsychological Virtual Rehabilitation (CNVR) systems is that 3D Interactive Virtual Environments (VE) can provide good simulations of the real world yielding to an effective transfer of virtual skills to real capacities (Rose et al., 2005). Other potential advantages of CNVR are that they are highly motivating, safe and controlled, and they can recreate a diversity of scenarios (Guo et al., 2004). Virtual tasks are easy to document automatically. Moreover, they are reproducible, which is useful for accurate analyses of the patients behavior.

Several studies has shown that leaving tasks unfinished can be counterproductive in a rehabilitation process (Prigatano, 1997). Therefore, CNVR systems tend to provide free-of-error rehabilitation tasks. For this, by opposite to traditional leisure games, they integrate different intervention mechanisms to guide patients towards the fulfillment of their goals, from instruction messages to automatic realization of part and even all the task.

The main drawback of CNVR is that the use of technology introduces a complexity factor alien to the rehabilitation process. In particular, it requires patients to acquire spatial abilities (Satalich, 1995) and navigational awareness (Chen & Stanney, 1999) in order to find ways through the VE and perceive relative distances to the patient's avatar. In addition, interacting with virtual objects involves recognizing their shape and semantics (Nesbitt et al., 2009). Moreover, pointing, picking and putting virtual objects is difficult, especially if the environments are complex and the objects size is small (Elmqvist & Fekete, 2008). Finally, steering virtual objects through VEs needs spatio-temporal skills to update the perception of the relative distance between objects through motion (Liu et al., 2011). These skills vary from one individual to another, and they can be strongly affected by patient's neuropsychological impairments. Therefore, it is necessary to design strategies to make technology more usable and minimize its side effects in the rehabilitation process. These strategies, combined with customized intervention strategies, can contribute to the success of CNVR.

In this paper, we propose and discuss several strategies to ease the navigation and interaction in VEs. Our aim is to remove technological barriers as well as to facilitate therapeutic interventions in order to help patients reaching their goals. Specifically, we present mechanisms to help objects picking and placement and to ease navigation. We present the results of these strategies on users without cognitive impairments.

2. Related work

Several studies have shown that virtual objects manipulation improves the performance of visual, attention, memory and executive skills (Boot et al., 2008). This is why typical 3D CNVR systems aimed at training these functions reproduce daily life scenarios. The patients exercises consist mainly in performing virtually domestic tasks. The principal activity of patients in the virtual environments is the manipulation of virtual objects, specifically, picking, dragging and placing objects (Rose et al., 2005). These actions can be performed through a simple user interaction, in general a user click having the cursor put onto the target. More complex actions can be performed, such as breaking, cutting, folding, but in general, all can be implemented as pre-recorded animations that can also be launched with a simple user click (Tost et al., 2009).

The intervention strategies that help patients in realizing these activities by their own consist in reminding the goal through oral and written instructions and attracting the patients attention to the target through some visual mechanisms. Difficulties arisen from the use of the technology are related to the users ability in recognizing target objects, understanding the rules and limitations of virtual manipulation in comparison to real manipulation and managing the scale of the VE. In particular, the selection of small objects in cluttered VE can be difficult. To overcome this problem, a variety of mechanisms has been proposed (Balakrishnan, 2004), mainly based in scaling the target as the cursor passes in front of it. Another interesting question is the convenience of decoupling selection from vision by using the relative position of the hand to make selections, or by applying the hand-eye metaphor and computing the selected objects as those intersected by the viewing ray (Argelaguet & Andújar, 2009).

To be able to reach the objects and manipulate them, patients must navigate in the environment. However, navigation constitutes another type of activity that involves by itself a lot of cognitive skills, some of them different that those needed for objects manipulation. It requires spatial abilities, namely spatial orientation, visualization and relations (Satalich, 1995) and temporal skills to perceive the direction of movement and the relative velocity of moving objects. Moreover, navigation is closely related to way-finding. It requires not only a good navigational awareness, but also logic to perform selective searching of the target in semantically related locations, visual memory to remember the places already explored and strategy to design efficient search. In fact, although some controversy exists on if virtual navigation enhances or not real navigation abilities (Richardson et al., 2011), virtual navigation by itself is being used for the rehabilitation of spatial skills after brain damage (Koenig et al., 2009).

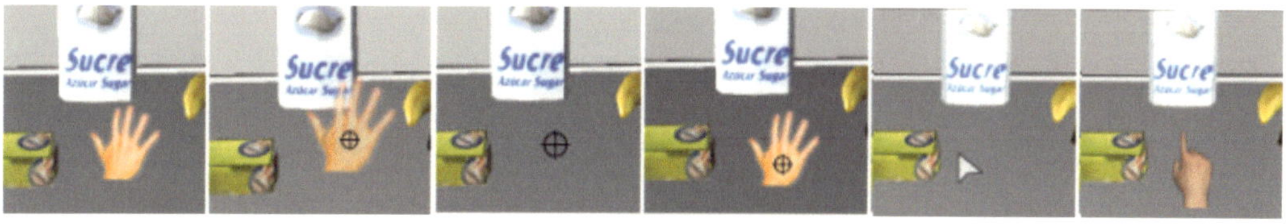

Fig. 1. The six cursors tested. From left to right: opaque hand, transparent hand + spy-hole, spy-hole, opaque hand + spy-hole, arrow, pointing finger

From a technological point of view, navigating interactively is far more complex than clicking. It involves various degrees of freedom and a non-trivial translation of the input device data into 3D motion. Therefore, in objects manipulation tasks, navigation interferes with the foreseen development of the activity. It can hinder it, delay it, and even make it impossible. In order to decouple navigation from object manipulation, automatic camera placement methods must be designed. This topic has been largely addressed by the computer graphics community (Christie & Olivier, 2008) in order to compute automatically the best camera placement for the exploration of virtual environments (Argelaguet & Andújar, 2010) and for the visualization and animation of scientific data (Bordoloi & Shen, 2005). Two main approaches have been proposed: reactive and indirect methods. Reactive methods apply autonomous robotics strategies to drive the camera from one point to the other through the shortest possible path, avoiding obstacles. They apply to the camera the navigation models that are used for the animation of autonomous non-player characters (Reese & Stout, 1999). Indirect approaches translate users needs into constraints on the camera parameters, which they intend to solve (Driel & Bidarra, 2009).

In leisure video games, camera positioning cannot be totally automatic, because camera control is usually an essential part of the game. The camera is placed automatically at the beginning of the game or at the transition between scenarios. In this case, automating positioning must preserve the continuity of the game-play, while providing the best view of the environment. A specially challenging problem is the computation of the camera position in third person games, in which the camera tracks the user's avatar. In this case, it is necessary to avoid collisions of the camera that may produce disturbing occlusions of parts of the environment (Liu et al., 2011).

The aim of our work is to design methods that reduce the technological barriers of VEs for memory, attention and executive skills rehabilitation. We extend existing techniques to ease objects manipulation, and we explore their use as intervention strategies. Moreover, in order to decouple navigation from objects manipulation, we provide automatic and semi-automatic camera placement. We show that automatic camera control provides mechanisms of intervention in the task development that ease a free-of-error training.

3. Objects manipulation

3.1 Technological assistance

We apply the eye-hand metaphor. We propose several strategies to ease pointing, picking and putting: cursor enrichment, objects outlining and free surfaces highlighting.

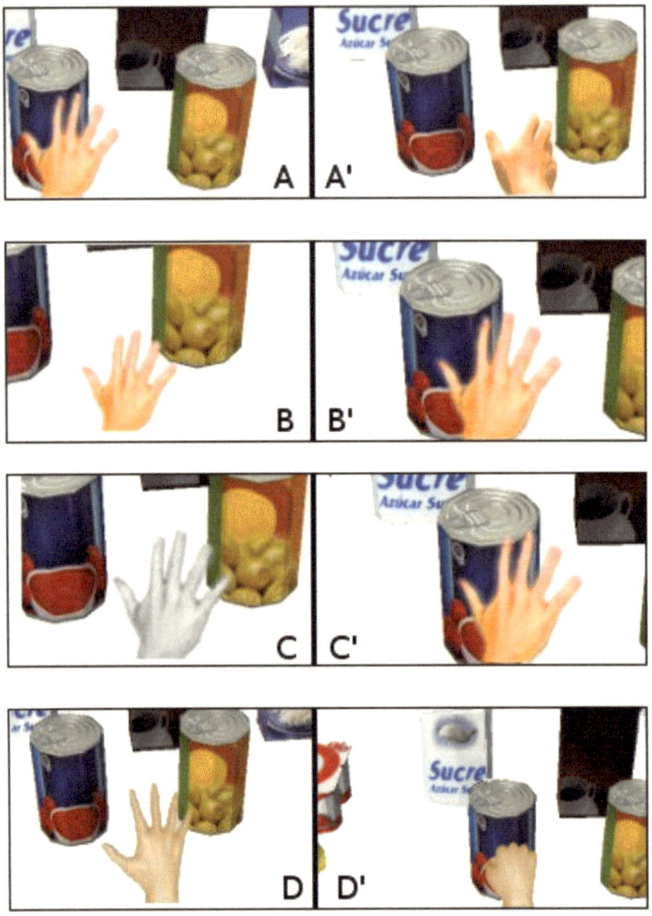

Fig. 2. The four cursor strategies to help pointing; A to A′ changing shape; B to B′ changing size; C to C′ changing color; D to D′ animating.

We have tested six different types of widgets for the cursor (see Figure 1): an opaque hand, a spy-hole, an arrow, an opaque hand with a spy-hole over-impressed, a transparent hand with a spy-hole over-impressed and a pointing finger. The hand and the finger have the advantage of helping users to understand that they are able to interact with the environment. The main drawback of the hand is that it can occlude objects. This can be corrected making it transparent. Another inconvenient is its lack of precision, which can be corrected over-impressing a spy-hole on it. The pointing finger solves this problem. The arrow has the advantage of being small and precise. However, it has a low symbolic value. The spy-hole is precise and little occlusive but it gives a non-desirable aggressive look to the task.

We have proposed two different mechanisms to help pointing: cursor-based mechanisms and object-based mechanisms. The aim of these techniques is to signal in a way or another that the object under the cursor is selectable. For the cursor, we have analyzed four different possibilities (see Figure 2): changing its shape, when it is in front of selectable objects, (ii) enlarging it, (iii) changing its color, and (iv) launching a small animation. For the

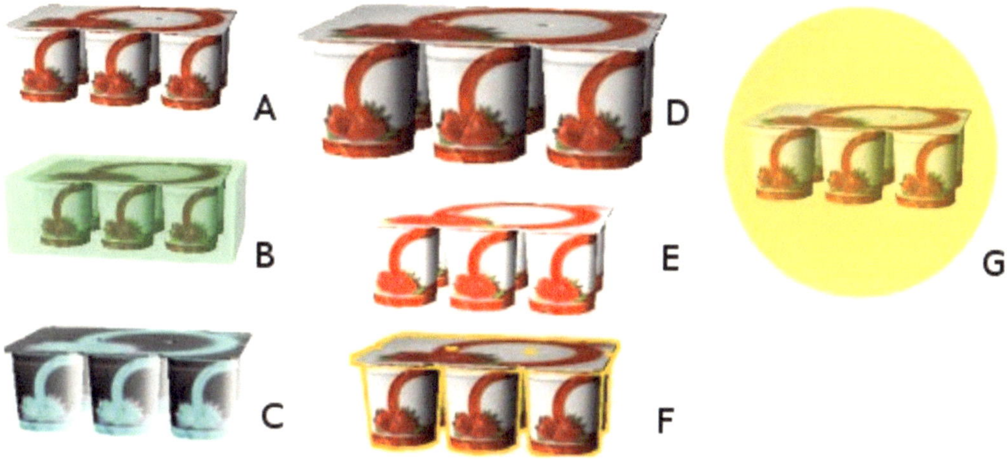

Fig. 3. The six target object strategies to help pointing; A: normal object; B: with rectangular halo; C: with complementary colors; D: enlarged; E: with increased luminance; F: with silhouette edges; G: with spherical halo.

selectable objects, we have tested 6 different ways of highlighting them (see Figure 3): (i) with bounding box halo,(ii) a circular halo, (iii) enlarging size, (iv) changing their color by their complementary color, (v) drawing silhouette edges and (iv) increasing luminance.

In a first person game with the eye-hand metaphor, dragging objects at their real scale in the VE can cause collision problems with the other elements of the scenario and occlusions in the view fustrum. Therefore, instead of moving the geometric model of the object, we actually move a scaled version of the object projected onto the image plane. We have tested three different strategies: (i) to substitute the cursor by the object when it is dragged, to keep the cursor and show the dragged object (ii) centered under the cursor and (iii) separated from the cursor, at right and below it. We have tested two variants of the three strategies with and without transparency. Figure 4 illustrates these modes.

A drawback of not moving the actual object is that when users must put it down on a surface, they don't have a good spatial perception of the free space left. Therefore, we highlight the free space able to lodge the held object as users move the cursor. We have tested different ways of highlighting the surface applying different colors and drawing the 3D bounding box that the object would occupy in the surface or only its projected area (see Figure 5).

3.2 Cognitive assistance

Technological aids can also be used to assist patients at the cognitive level. In particular, to assist patients in picking a specific object, instead of outlining all the pickable objects, we can outline only those related to the task goal. In this case, outlining fulfills two different functions: technological aid and cognitive assistance. The number of visual stimuli is reduced to only those that are related to the task. As a consequence, the range of strategies to outline objects is larger: in addition of appearance changes, we can apply sounds and animations that are not suitable when there is a large number of objects to be outlined.

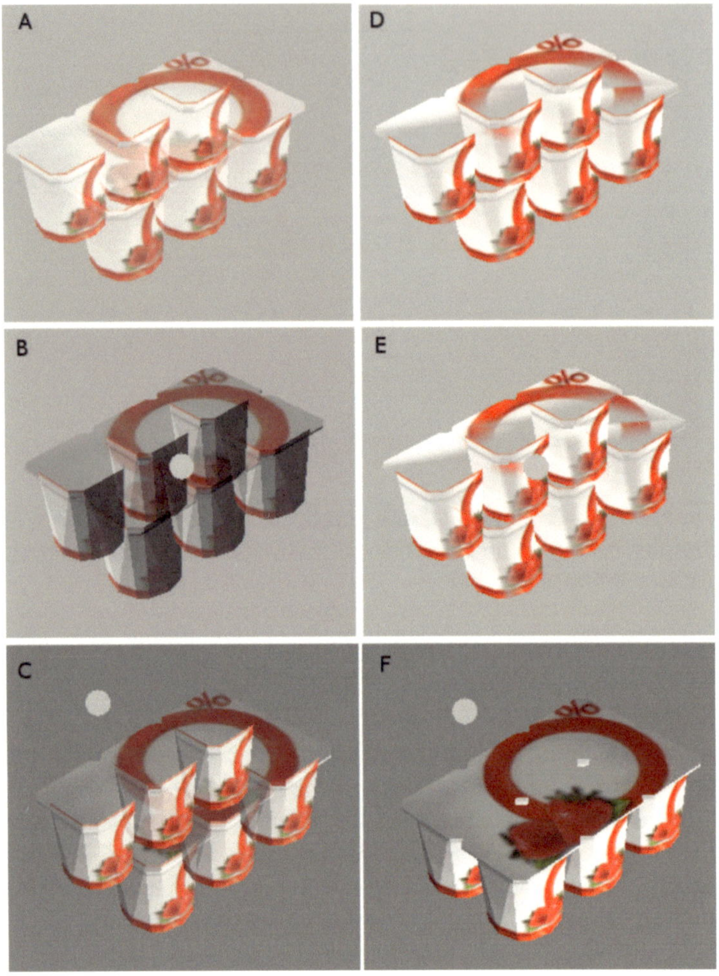

Fig. 4. Different strategies fo give feedback of the dragged object: left column transparent feedback, right column opaque feedback; first row the cursor is substituted by the object; seond row, the cursor is centered on the object ; third row, the object is at bottom right of the cursor.

Cognitive assistance can also be provided through game-master actions. The game-master is a component of the game logics that simulates the intervention of an external observer. It helps the patient by emitting instructions and feedback messages, removing objects of the scenario to simplify it, demonstrating the required action or doing it automatically partially or totally. This way, if focus of the task is put on picking objects and not placing them anywhere else, the picking action can be implemented as a pick-and-place: users pick and the game-master places them.

4. Navigation methods

We propose four different modes of navigation: free navigation, two user-assisted navigation modes and a fully automatic navigation.

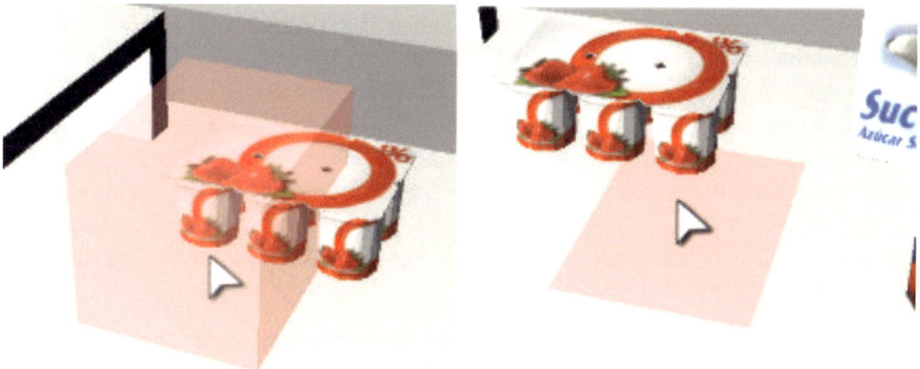

Fig. 5. Two different strategies of highlighting the space that a dragged object would occupy on a surface: at right the 3D bounding box, at left the projected area.

4.1 Free navigation

The free navigation is the classical first person four degrees of freedom model. Users control the viewing vector orientation through the yaw and pitch angle. As usual in computer games, rolling is not allowed. The pitch angle is restricted within a parameterized range between -50 to 50 degrees to allow looking at the floor and ceiling but forbidding complete turns. In addition, users control the camera position by allowing its movement in a plane parallel to the floor at a fixed height. Jumping and crouching down are not allowed. The movement follows the direction of the projection of the viewing vector in that plane, therefore it is not possible to go back. Users can also stop and restart the camera movement. The movement has constant speed except for a short acceleration at its beginning and deceleration at its end. The camera control is done using the mouse to specify the viewing vector and camera path orientation and the bar-space key to start and stop the motion. This system has the advantage that it requires to control only two types of input (mouse movement and space bar key), which is suitable for patients with neuropsychological impairments.

4.2 Assisted navigation

The aim of the assisted navigation mode is to provide means for users to indicate where they want to go, and then automatically drive them to this location. This way, the focus is put on the destination and not on the path towards it. Therefore, navigation is decoupled from interaction.

This assistance can be implemented in two ways: by computing only the final camera position, or by calculating all the camera path towards this position. In the first case, the transition from one view to the next is very abrupt. Therefore, we reserve it for the transition between one scenario to the other. In this work, we focus on the second mode. We compute all the camera path and orientation.

To indicate the target location, users click onto it. If the target location is reachable from the avatar's position, i.e. if it is at a smaller distance than the avatar's arm estimated length, the system interprets the user click as a petition of interaction (to open, pick, put or transform), and it realizes it according to the task logics. However, if the object is not reachable, the system interprets that the user wants to go towards it, it computes the corresponding path and follows it automatically. To provide more user control on the navigation, the system allows users to stop and restart the navigation at any time. Observe that the target location may not be directly the object that the user needs to manipulate, but a container in which the object is hidden. For instance, if the goal of the task is to take out a chicken from the oven, the target direction is the oven's door in order to open it. Depending on the current level of difficulty of the task user will have more or less precise instructions on their goal. This is precisely one of the objectives of the rehabilitation.

The main difficulty with this strategy is that clicking onto the target requires to have it in the view fustrum and to put the cursor onto it. However, both things require a previous navigation or camera orientation process. We distinguish two cases: (i) when the target can be seen without need of modifying the camera position, but only its orientation, and (ii) when the camera position must be modified. In the former case, we propose two strategies: *free camera orientation* and *restricted camera orientation*. The *free camera orientation mode* has two degrees of freedom: yaw and pitch. The camera position is fixed, and users move the viewing direction until the target is in the center of the view fustrum. The *restricted camera orientation mode* has one degree of freedom. The system performs an automatic rotation of the yaw angle. Users only modify the pitch angle. To select the desired orientation, users stop the rotation with a mouse click.

When the target location is invisible from the current camera position, users indicate movement by steps, giving a first path direction, stopping the movement to reorient the camera and clicking again to specify a new direction. In this case, although navigation is removed, way-finding cannot be eliminated. Therapists must be aware of that in the design of their tasks. To overcome this problem, inside rooms, we design the scenarios avoiding the presence of occluders. When the scenario is composed of various rooms, we avoid corridors, we design doors from one room to the other and put the name of the room on the doors. This way, to indicate the direction to another room, users click onto the corresponding door.

4.3 Automatic navigation

The automatic navigation method removes the camera control from users. The system computes the target destination according to the task logics. It puts the camera in front on the next object with which users must interact. For instance, if users are asked to pick a tomato, the application places the camera in front of one.

With this mode, the system intervenes in the task development: it takes decisions on the places to go, and therefore eases the task. It is part of the possible intervention strategies that therapists can design to help their patients.

4.4 Implementation

In order to manage the described alternatives, the system needs to know the position of all interactive objects. The position of static objects is part of the scene model. Objects that can be moved can be on top of or inside other objects. We use a system of grids that allows us to control the exact position of all the objects at any time of the play. Then, when an object is the

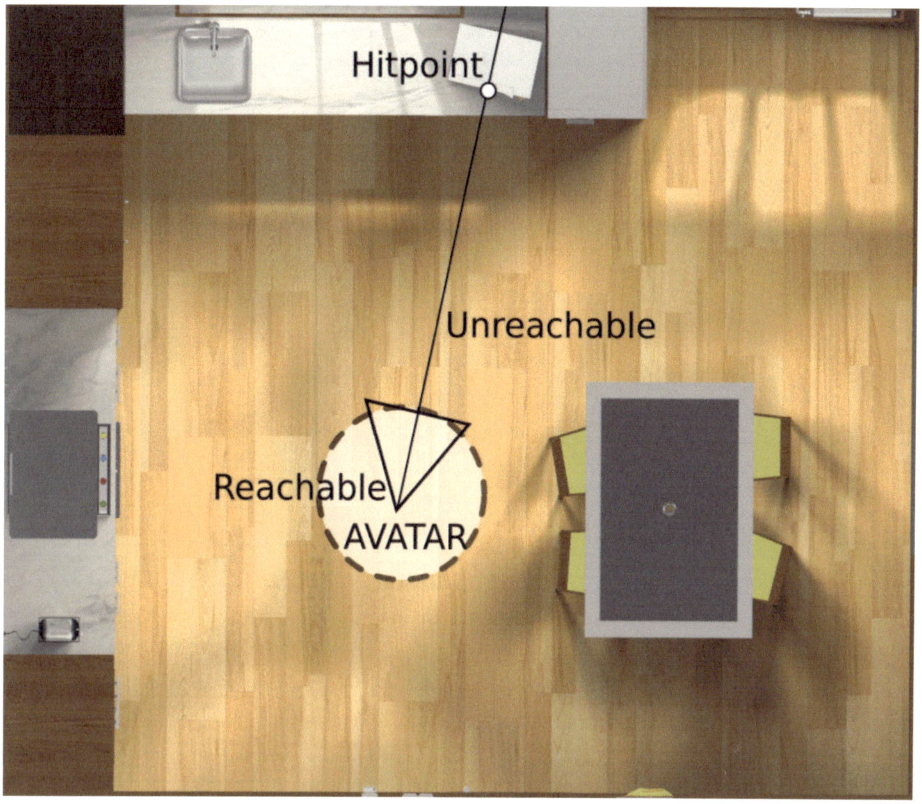

Fig. 6. VE example that shows the avatar's position and the first intersection of the view-vector with the scene. In this case the hit-point is the microwave, and it is not reachable for interaction at the current position.

user's target, the system has the ability to compute the best position to reach it, computing the best path to arrive there and the best camera's orientation.

When the user does a mouse click, the system detects the first object that intersects the view vector (hit-point). Figure 6 shows an example where the hit-point is a microwave. The object is reachable if the distance between its position and the avatar is smaller than a fixed value. In this case, the interaction with the object is performed. When the distance is greater, the system interprets that the user wants to perform the interaction, and it moves the avatar to a position that allows the interaction with the object.

The system uses the object's position to determine the best avatar's location to reach it. This location lays on the grid of the VE's floor. Figure 7 shows a grid example of a kitchen. The cells of the floor can be classified as occupied (red), unreachable (orange) or reachable (green). The unreachable cells are free cells where the avatar cannot go, because it would collide with other elements of the VE. Thus, the avatar is only allowed to be in a position inside reachable cells. The system uses the grid to determine which of the reachable cells is the best to interact with the target object. The naive strategy consists of finding the closest cell to the target. However, it does not take into account the possible occlusions. Therefore, we choose the closest cell

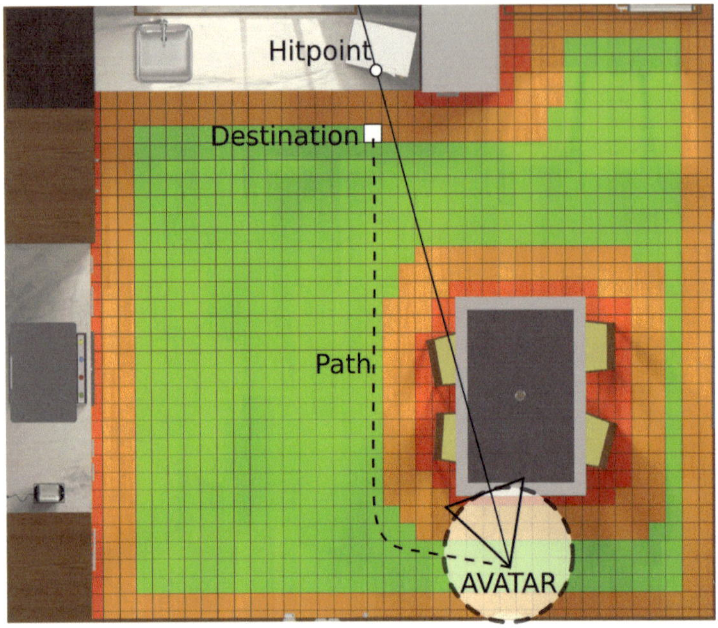

Fig. 7. Example of the navigation strategy. The system use the floor's grid to determine the best path to reach the hit-point. The destination cell is draw in white, and the cells are classified as occupied (red), unreachable (orange) and reachable (green).

from which the target is visible. We compute these cells in a pre-process, casting rays from the surfaces cells to virtual camera positions centered at the grid floor cells. Our scenario model stores the cells associated to each surface cell. Then, when the system wants to determine the best destination for a target, it selects the closest cell that belongs to the set of the target's surface cell. Taking into account that the objects during the task can change their positions, it is possible that all the cells are occupied, and then the avatar cannot reach the target. In those cases, the system's logic is the responsible of asking the user to move some objects to be able to reach the target.

Once the system has the current position of the avatar and the destination position, it computes the path that allows the avatar to move inside the VE without colliding with any object. The method used is an implementation of the A* path-finding method that minimizes the Euclidean distance, and uses the floor's grid to compute a discrete path. After this process, the system computes a Bezier path that follows the discrete path computed before. This new path allows the system to perform softer movements and keep a constant speed.

5. Results and discussion

In order to test the suitability of the proposed technological assistance strategies, we have created a set of specific tasks in a virtual scenario representing a kitchen. We have asked 30 volunteers without cognitive impairments to realize these tasks. We have recorded their results and asked them to fill a questionnaire about different aspects of these assistance strategies. The profile of the users can be categorized according to three different criteria:

Fig. 8. A task example to test the suitability of the different types of cursors.

gender, age (below and over 30) and 3D-game players or not. The groups were approximately of the same size except for women over 30 and game-player and men below 30 non 3D game-players that were smaller (only 1 and 2 users, respectively).

5.1 Object manipulation tests

To test the strategies to help picking, we put the camera in front of an open virtual fridge full of objects. The camera movement was inhibited. User could only rotate the camera but not change its position. All the objects were accessible from the camera position. The task consisted of clicking onto objects to remove them. Figure 8 shows an example of this task. We measured the number of objects that users could remove during a fixed time interval. Users answered questions about their preferred mechanism according to three different criteria: visibility, precision and visual appearance. We tested the different cursors as well as the objects highlighting mechanisms. The results showed that the cursor that allowed a larger number of selections was the spy-hole. However, users preferred the pointing finger because they found it more meaningful. Their second preference was the arrow. In addition, users preferred the animation of the cursor to indicate the nature of the interaction that objects support, for instance, a rotation of the hand on doors, and opening and closing the hand for grasping objects.

To test objects grabbing, we set a task in which users had to move objects from the fridge to the kitchen marble at a side. The marble was also reachable, so it was not necessary to move the camera but only to rotate it. We measured the number of objects that users were able to move

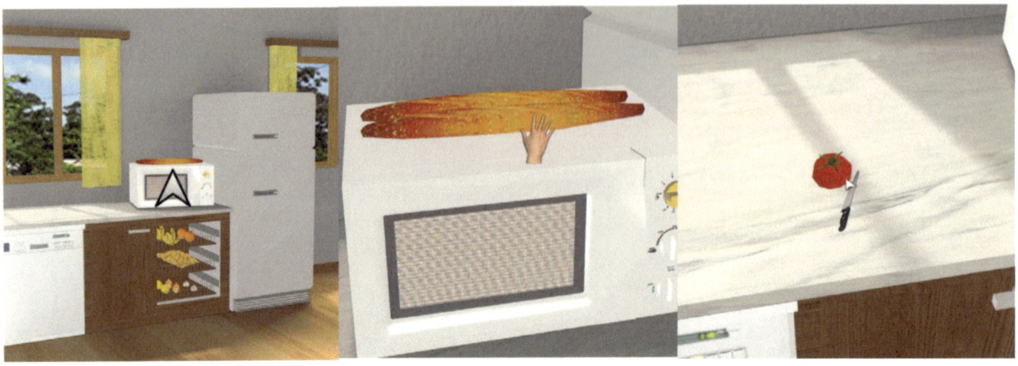

Fig. 9. The three cursor modes: at left an arrow on unreachable objects, in the middle an animation of the hand on reachable objects and, for dragging, the arrow and the held object conveniently scaled, here, the knife.

during a fixed time interval. Users answered questions about visibility, precision and visual appearance. The results showed the more effective mechanism was to show the grasped object at a side of the cursor. Surprisingly, the opaque mode was preferred to the semi transparent one, because it was found more natural.

Taking into account these results, we finally chose to have three cursor modes (see Figure 9): when the object under the cursor is not reachable or an object is being held, we use an arrow and when the object is reachable the animated hand.

Finally, to test the feedback mechanisms to help putting objects, we used a task consisting in placing objects on the kitchen marble. Users did not need to pick them. As soon as they put one, another was automatically grasped. We measured the number of objects that users were able to leave on the marble, and users answered a questionnaire about precision and comfort. The preferred mechanism was to color the 2D free space nearer the cursor.

5.2 Navigation methods test

To test the navigation methods we proposed a task consisting in touching two objects strategically placed in the scenario (see Figure 10): an orange (dashed in blue) and a dish (dashed in pink). The task is segmented in three stages. The first stage is to reach the orange. In this stage, it is necessary to avoid the table, which is an obstacle that does not prevent from seeing the target object. The next stage is to go to the cabinet's door, which consists of walking in a straight line near the marble without obstacles. The last stage is to open the cabinet door and walk around to reach the dish, which is an object placed into a container. Thus, the cabinet door is an obstacle that prevents from seeing the target object. Figure 11 represents the paths performed by the users in free navigation mode using a temperature range color encoding. Temperatures are represented with a blue-to-red color scale. The most transited is the place that represents the higher temperature. In other words, places where users stay during a long time are colored in red.

Clearly, it can be seen that areas containing obstacles (near the table in the first stage and near the door in the third stage) are critical for users. The area corresponding to the second stage is also colored in red because when there are no obstacles, they all choose the same

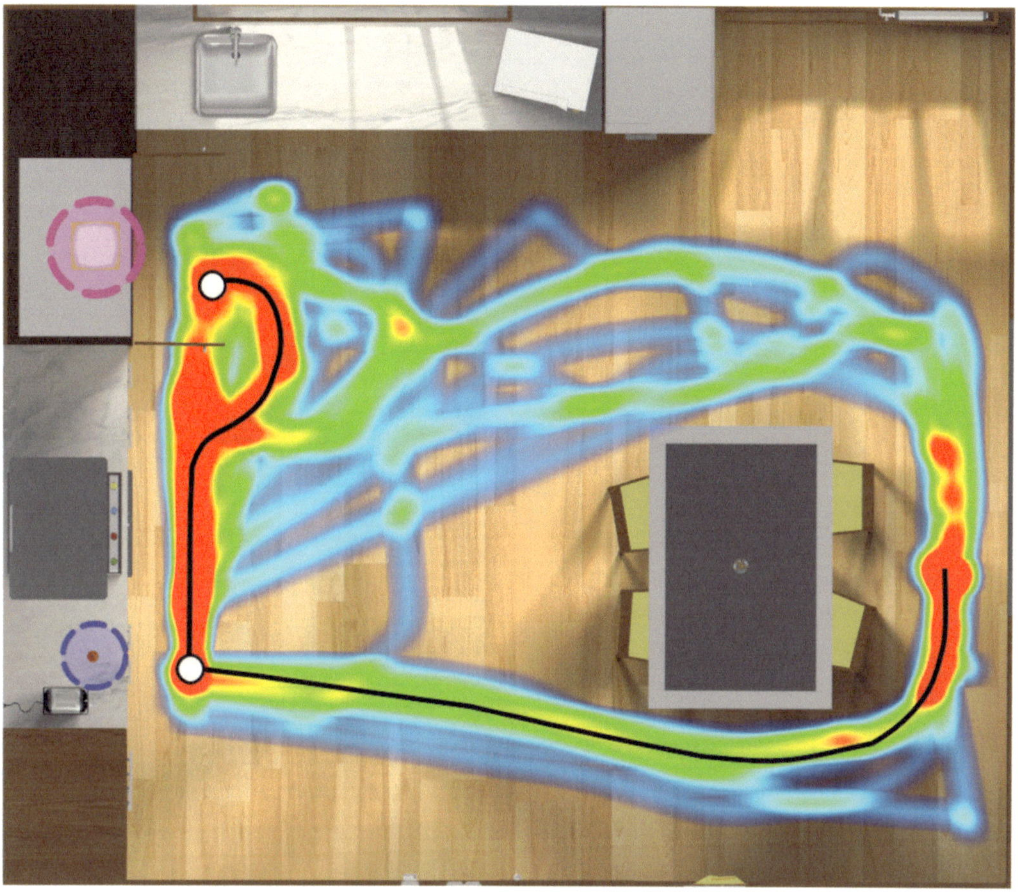

Fig. 10. Results of the paths used by the users to perform the task.

option: to walk in a straight line near the marble. The black line represents the automatic path computed by the system. Our method keeps constant speed along the path and avoids the obstacles automatically without errors. Note that some of users chose the other side of the table which is the longest way. These users had, in general, more difficulties in navigating, as it can be seen from their paths sparser and more erratic.

The temperature diagram in Figure 11 represents the head deviation in the pitch angle in free navigation mode. The figure shows that users tend to look down to see where they are going.

Users ranked the navigation method easiness in the following order: automatic, assisted, assisted rotation and free. As expected, they found the automatic method very easy or easy (100% of users). The assisted mode was also considered as easy and very easy by 95% of users. However, the assisted rotation was less valued (only 80% scored it as easy or very easy). Users reported that not being able to rotate the camera was disturbing. The sensation was the same in all groups. The free navigation mode was found easy and very easy by 67% of users in general, but only by 20% of non 3D-gamers, who were, however, 2D-gamers. We conclude, as expected, that free navigation is difficult for non-gamers. Concerning the preferred navigation mode, all groups of users chose the assisted mode, even the 60% of game players.

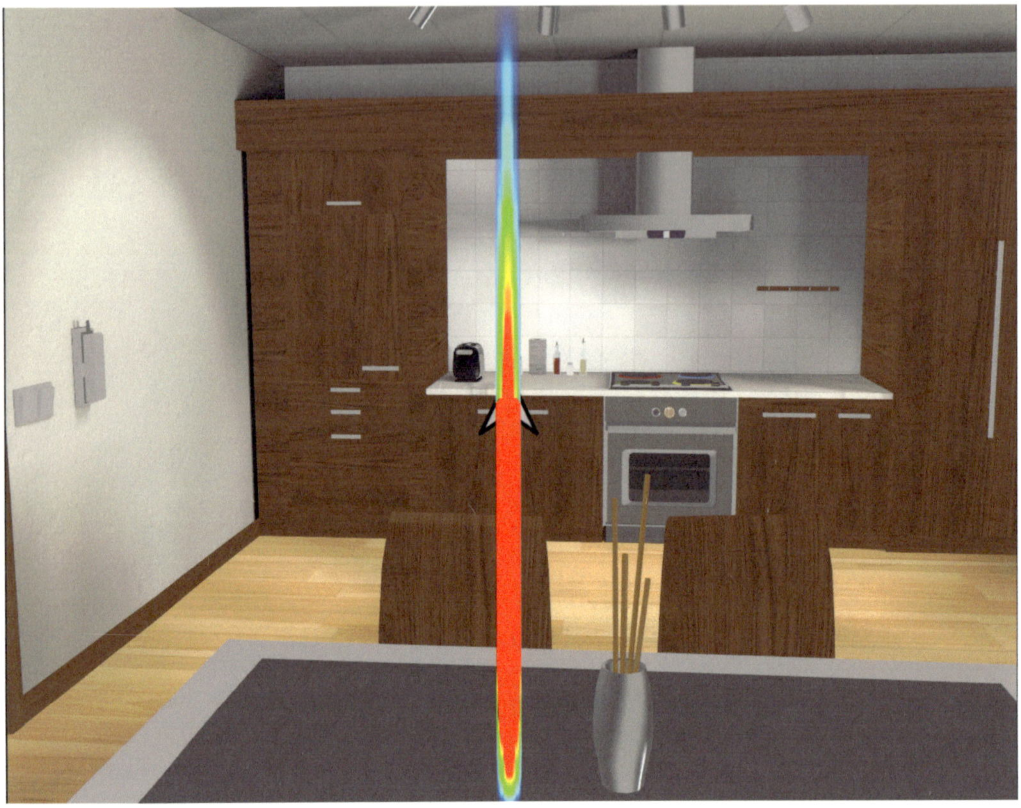

Fig. 11. Results of the camera movements performed by the users to encountering the task.

In relation to the quality of the paths, 90% of users valued them as good and very good. About 75% of users described the camera orientation during movement as good and very good whereas 25% found it regular or bad. The bad scores came from users that reported being disturbed by the fact that the camera didn't look at the target when it was avoiding an obstacle. They affirmed that the target object should always be in the view. For this reason, we modified the system to allow users to control the camera rotation if they wish during the automatic camera movement. In this way, the system is more flexible and satisfies the desires of passive users as well as more active ones.

6. Conclusions

Serious games in 3D virtual environments can greatly contribute to rehabilitation. However, to be usable by patients with cognitive impairments, many technological barriers must be broken that are disturbing for all kind of users as well. In particular, it is important to separate objects manipulation from navigation. In this paper, we have proposed and analyzed several strategies to ease manipulation in 3D. We have designed visual mechanisms to enhance the perception of objects. Our aim is to help users in picking, dragging and putting objects. In addition, we have proposed a mechanism for the semi-automatic navigation inside VEs. Our goal is to allow users to move in the VE without having the technological difficulties of controlling a virtual camera. We have tested these strategies with volunteer users and seen that they were effective and well accepted. Our next step is to use them on patients.

7. References

Argelaguet F. & Andújar C. (2009). Efficient 3D pointing selection in cluttered virtual environments, *IEEE Computer Graphics and Applications* 29(6): 34–43.

Argelaguet F. & Andújar C. (2010). Automatic speed graph generation for predefined camera paths, *Smart graphics*, pp. 115–126.

Balakrishnan R. (2004). "Beating" Fitts' law: virtual enhancements for pointing facilitation, *International Journal on Human-Computer Studies* 61: 857–874.

Boot W., Kramer A., Dimons D., Fabiani M. & Gratton G. (2008). The effects of video game playing on attention, memory, and executive control, *Acta Psychologica* 129(3): 387–398.

Bordoloi U. & Shen H.-W. (2005). View selection for volume rendering, *IEEE Visualization'05*, pp. 487–494.

Chen J. L. & Stanney K. M. (1999). A theoretical model of wayfinding in virtual environments: Proposed strategies for navigational aiding, *Presence* 8: 671–685.

Christie M. & Olivier P. (2008). Camera control in computer graphics, *Computer Graphics Forum* 27(8): 1–197.

Driel L. & Bidarra R. (2009). A semantic navigation model for video games, *Proceedings of the 2nd International Workshop on Motion in Games*, MIG'09, Springer-Verlag, pp. 146–157.

Elmqvist N. & Fekete J. (2008). Semantic pointing for object picking in complex 3D environments, *Proceedings of Graphics Interface 2008*, GI '08, pp. 243–250.

Guo W. Lim S. Fok G. & Chan, G. (2004). Virtual reality for memory rehabilitation, *International Journal of Computer Applications in Technology* 21(1–2): 32–37.

Koenig S., Crucian G., Dalrymple-Alford J. & Dunser A. (2009). Virtual reality rehabilitation of spatial abilities after brain damage, *Studies for Health Technological Information* 144: 105–107.

Liu L., Jean-Bernard J. & Van Liere R. (2011). Revisiting path steering for 3D manipulation tasks, *International Journal on Human-Computer Studies* 69: 170–181.

Nesbitt K., Sutton K., Wilson J. & Hookham G. (2009). Improving player spatial abilities for 3D challenges, *Proceedings of the 6th Australasian Conference on Interactive Entertainment*, pp. 1–6.

Prigatano G. (1997). Learning from our successes and failures: Reflections and comments, *International Neuropsychological Society* 3: 497–499.

Reese B. & Stout B. (1999). Finding a pathfinder, *Symposium on arificial intelligence and computer games*, pp. 69–72.

Richardson A., Powers M. & Bousquet L. (2011). Video game experience predicts virtual, but not real navigation performance, *Comput. Hum. Behav.* 27: 552–560.

Rose F., Brooks B. & Rizzo A. (2005). Virtual reality in brain damage rehabilitation: Review, *CyberPsychology & Behavior* 8(3): 241–271.

Satalich G. (1995). Navigation and wayfinding in virtual reality: Finding the proper tools and cues to enhance navigation awareness, Http://www.hitl,washington, edu/publications/satalich/.

Tost D., Ferré M., Garcia P., Tormos J., Garcia A., Roig T. & Grau, S. (2009). Previrnec: a cognitive telerehabilitation system based on virtual environments, *Virtual Rehabilitation*, pp. 1–8.

8

Vision for Motor Performance in Virtual Environments Across the Lifespan

Patrick Grabowski and Andrea Mason
University of Wisconsin, Madison
USA

1. Introduction

Current trends in neuroscience research are heavily focused on new technologies to study and interact with the human brain. Specifically, three-dimensional (3D) virtual environment (VE) systems have been identified as technology with good potential to serve in both research and applied settings. For the purpose of this chapter, a virtual environment is defined as a computer with displays and controls configured to immerse the operator in a predominantly graphical environment containing 3D objects in 3D space. The operator can manipulate virtually displayed objects in real time using a variety of motor output channels or input devices. The use of VEs has almost exclusively been limited to experimental processes, utilizing cumbersome equipment well suited for the laboratory, but unrealistic for use in everyday applications. As the evolution of computer technology continues, the possibility of creating an affordable system capable of producing a high-quality 3D virtual experience for home or office applications comes nearer to fruition. However, in order to improve the success and the cost-to-benefit ratio of such a system, more precise information regarding the use of VEs by a broad population of users is needed. The goal of this chapter is to review knowledge relating to the use of visual feedback for human performance in virtual environments, and how this changes across the lifespan. Further, we will discuss future experiments we believe will contribute to this area of research by examining the role of luminance contrast for upper extremity performance in a virtual environment.

2. Background

The following sections identify the well-known physiologic changes that occur in the sensorimotor system as part of the natural human aging process. Further, we discuss some of the limited work that has been done to understand the implications of these changes for the design of VEs.

2.1 Changes to the human sensorimotor system across the lifespan

The human body is a constantly changing entity throughout the lifespan. Most physiologic processes begin to decline at a rate of 1% per year beginning around age 30, and the sensorimotor system is no exception (Schut, 1998). There is a general indication from the research that both the processing of afferent information and the production of efferent signals steadily change as a function of age. Multiple authors demonstrate physical changes in brain tissues (Andersen, Gundersen, & Pakkenberg, 2003; Kuo & Lipsitz, 2004; Raz & Rodrigue, 2006), changes in excitability of the corticospinal tract and anterior horn cells (Rossini, Desiato, & Caramia, 1992), and changes in neurotransmitter systems. There is a general loss of neural substrate, including grey and white matter. This has been demonstrated in both the cerebral cortex (Raz & Rodrigue, 2006) and the cerebellum (Andersen et al., 2003). These tissue changes then result in a myriad of functional changes within the central nervous system (CNS). There is a general deterioration of motor planning capabilities (Sterr & Dean, 2008;Yan, Thomas, & Stelmach, 1998) and feed-forward anticipatory control (Hwang et al., 2008) with aging. Along with this decrease in planning ability, there also appears to be slowing of central processing (Chaput & Proteau, 1996; Inui, 1997; Light, 1990; Shields et al., 2005). This change in processing is partially due to neurophysiologic changes within the CNS resulting in a decrease in the available resources of the processing pool (Craik & McDowd, 1987; Schut, 1998). Loss of attentional resources also contributes to this slowing of central processing (Goble et al., 2008; Kluger et al., 1997; Sparrow, Begg, & Parker, 2006). This in itself results from a multifactorial process relating to neurophysiologic changes in the CNS and degradation of afferent information arriving from compromised peripheral receptors (Chaput & Proteau, 1996; Goble et al., 2008). The result of these attentional and processing changes is a decline in the ability to integrate multiple sensory modalities causing a relative decrease in the use of proprioceptive feedback and an increased use of vision (Adamo, Martin, & Brown, 2007; Chaput & Proteau, 1996; Goble et al., 2008; Lemay, Bertram, & Stelmach, 2004). This shift to the use of visual resources is due to the tendency of the CNS to re-weight sensory information when one source of feedback is compromised (Horak & Hlavacka, 2001), as well as a general systems neuroplasticity effect (Heuninckx, Wenderoth, & Swinnen, 2008; Romero et al., 2003). These compensatory neuroplastic changes are the end manifestation of the normal aging process within the CNS.

The peripheral nervous system (PNS) undergoes concordant neurophysiologic changes as well (Chaput & Proteau, 1996; Goble et al., 2008; Roos, Rice, & Vandervoort, 1997). These changes occur in both the afferent and efferent pathways. Studies have shown both a decrease in number and density of proprioceptors (Goble et al., 2008), as well as a slowing of sensory receptors in general (Light, 1990). In the efferent systems, research demonstrates a loss of motor units and a decrease in firing rate and increased discharge variability of intact motor units (Roos et al., 1997). The available literature also demonstrates a loss of larger motor neurons resulting in a net decrease of alpha motor neurons, a slowing in the conduction velocity of remaining motor neurons, and changes in the excitability of alpha motor neurons (Leonard et al., 1997; Roos et al., 1997).

The changes in the CNS and PNS with age are accompanied by changes in the muscular system as well. In the aging adult, research shows a loss of muscle fibers and a decrease in size of remaining fibers resulting in a net loss of muscle mass (Roos et al., 1997). Changes in motor units in the PNS result in fiber type changes, causing a loss of fast-twitch fibers and a proportional increase of slow-twitch fibers.

Transformations in the sensorimotor system have a resultant detrimental effect on motor performance in daily life. This decrease has a physiologic basis in aging and is amplified by disuse and dysfunction. In general, aging adults demonstrate decreases in movement speed (Light, 1990; Mankovsky, Mints, & Lisenyuk, 1982; Poston et al., 2008; Yan et al., 1998), accuracy of movement (Chaput & Proteau, 1996), reaction time (Light, 1990; Sparrow et al., 2006; Yan et al., 1998), strength (Roos et al., 1997; Vandervoort, 2002), hand dexterity (Contreras-Vidal, Teulings, & Stelmach, 1998; Seidler, Alberts, & Stelmach, 2002), and postural control (Jonsson, Henriksson, & Hirschfeld, 2007; Koceja, Allway, & Earles, 1999; Mourey et al., 1998; Romero & Stelmach, 2003). En masse, these changes have the potential to contribute to a spiral of disuse and loss of function that often characterizes the process of aging. Due to the tendency for visual dominance in aged humans (Lemay et al., 2004), and the task specificity of human movement (Proteau, 1992), the fact that visual sensory feedback is much less rich in a virtual than natural environment makes it imperative to study human performance in such surroundings. Research is needed to improve our understanding of sensorimotor changes, and their consequences for performance, for an aging population interacting in three-dimensional environments.

2.2 Three-dimensional virtual environments and human computer interaction (HCI) across the lifespan

Today, the users of computers include people from all age groups. Very little information is available on how the performance of individuals in a VE changes throughout the lifespan as a function of the natural aging process. Prior to designing programs for individuals in special subgroups, such as rehabilitation programs designed for patients with neurological lesions, it will be important to understand what age-specific requirements will be beneficial to the user. For instance, because there is a paucity of information on how healthy adults in the older age groups commonly affected by stroke interact in VEs, it is likely that a system designed as an adjunct to standard rehabilitation will struggle to gain success without a foundation of baseline knowledge. This level of information regarding subjects of various age groups will greatly assist in producing successful, cost-effective VEs. Unfortunately, although computers have been commonplace in homes and work-environments for decades, the literature on interface design as it relates to age is only very recent, and is limited in scope. Early computer interface design relied primarily on the intuition of the designer (Hawthorn, 2001; Hawthorn, 2007). There was a distinct disparity between what designers recognized as necessary interface components and what was truly usable by the lay population. As access to computer technology improved and allowed the spread of computers into the hands of consumers, a necessary change to user-centered design followed. Typically, however, in order to be a feasible process, the representative users must have a basic level of proficiency with computer skills and language. This resulted in a general exclusion of both young and old age groups from the design process. In the late 1990's, interest in age-specific design increased, and there is now a reasonable body of knowledge on the design of standard computer interface systems for various age groups.

While the bulk of age-specific computer design information relates to ways to improve cognitive performance through specific training or tutorial methods (Hawthorn, 2007), there is some scientific literature which explores the areas of human motor control (Laursen, Jensen, & Ratkevicius, 2001; Smith, Sharit, & Czaja, 1999). Most of this information centers on the input device, specifically mouse usage in older adults. Smith et al. (1999) reported that there are many age-related changes in performance, and in general, it is quite difficult for older individuals to use a mouse. The act of double-clicking seems to consistently be the most problematic. Difficulty with cursor control is also named as a top complaint among older individuals (Hawthorn, 2001; Hawthorn, 2007). It has also been shown that performance within a standard computer interface is slower and results in a greater number of errors with increased age of the operator. These specific limitations point to the need to develop new interfaces that capitalize on natural manipulation, thereby eliminating difficulties with the functional abstraction of input devices.

Contrary to standard computer interface systems, little is known about the age-related variance of HCI within three-dimensional virtual environments. The literature in this subject area is nearly non-existent. There is some evidence of age-related differences in performance between children and adults, as well as young adults and older participants. This research indicates relevant disparities in reactions to environmental immersion, usage of various input devices, size estimation ability, navigational skills and completion time for gross motor tasks (Allen et al., 2000). According to these authors, "these results highlight the importance of considering age differences when designing for the population at large." Currently, the International Encyclopedia of Ergonomics and Human Factors (Karwowski, 2006) leaves the explanation of age-related differences in virtual environments to a short, two sentence description recommending that equipment be tailored to physically fit the smaller frames of children, and for designers to take into consideration the changes in sensory and motor functions of the elderly. Other than these works, very little specific knowledge regarding age and motor control in virtual environments has been elicited through research, especially as it relates to precision movements with the upper extremities. This fact has led us to begin a series of experiments investigating the use of vision for precise sensorimotor control of the upper extremity in virtual environments, and how that usage changes as a function of age.

3. Research methods, design, and results

In the next sections, we describe the specific methodology used in our lab, followed by a brief review of the most recent findings.

3.1 Physical apparatus

For our research, we utilize a tabletop virtual environment located in the Human Motor Behavior laboratory at the University of Wisconsin-Madison (Figure 1). This system has been used in a number of studies investigating the role of visual feedback for upper extremity movement in young adults, as well as the first phase of data collection on subjects across the lifespan. This single-user VE is specifically designed to permit detailed and highly accurate kinematic measurements of human performance. Paradigms from the Human Motor Control and Biomechanics disciplines are used to provide detailed descriptions of human movement and to make inferences about the cognitive processes controlling those movements. More recently, our research has focused on how these processes change throughout the lifespan. Our virtual environment has been designed to focus on natural manipulation, allowing users to employ their hands to manipulate and explore augmented objects located within the desktop environment (i.e. Tangible user interface or TUI) (MacLean, 1996; Mason & MacKenzie, 2002; Mason et al., 2001; Sturman & Zeltzer, 1993; Y. Wang & MacKenzie, 2000).

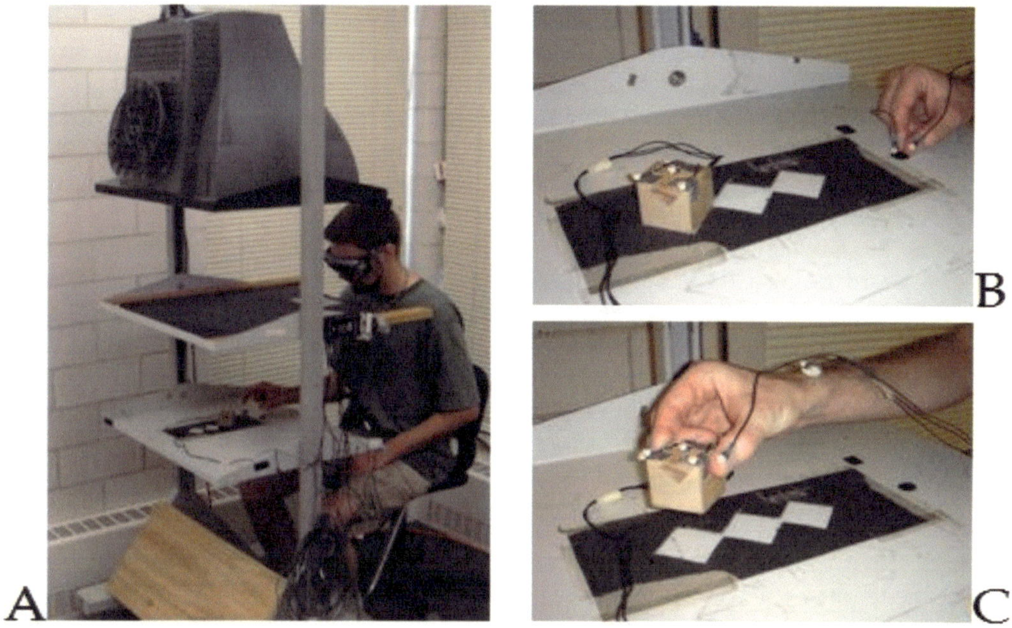

Fig. 1. Wisconsin virtual environment (WiscVE). Panel A shows the apparatus with downward facing monitor projecting to the mirror. Images are then reflected up to the user wearing stereoscopic LCD shutter goggles, and thus the images appear at the level of the actual work surface below. Panels B and C demonstrate a reach to grasp task commonly utilized in this environment. The hand and physical cube are instrumented with light emitting diodes (LEDs) that are tracked by the VisualEyez (PTI Phoenix, Inc) system, not shown.

This type of interface gives investigators complete control over the three-dimensional visual scene (important in generalizeability to natural environments), and makes for maximal use of the naturalness, dexterity and adaptability of the human hand for the control of computer mediated tasks (Sturman & Zeltzer, 1993). The use of such a tangible user interface removes many of the implicit difficulties encountered with standard computer input devices due to natural aging processes (Smith et al., 1999). The exploitation of these abilities in computer-generated environments is believed to lead to better overall performance and increased richness of interaction for a variety of applications (Hendrix & Barfield, 1996; Ishii & Ullmer, 1997; Slater, Usoh, & Steed, 1995). Furthermore, this type of direct-manipulation environment capitalizes on the user's pre-existing abilities and expectations, as the human hand provides the most familiar means of interacting with one's environment (Schmidt & Lee, 1999; Schneiderman, 1983). Such an environment is suitable for applications in simulation, gaming/entertainment, training, visualization of complex data structures, rehabilitation and learning (measurement and presentation of data regarding movement disorders). This allows for ease of translation of our data to marketable applications.

The VE provides a head-coupled, stereoscopic experience to a single user, allowing the user to grasp and manipulate augmented objects. The system is configured as follows (Figure 1):

- 3-D motion information (e.g. movement of the subject's hand, head and physical objects within the environment) is monitored by a VisualEyez (PTI Phoenix, Inc.) motion analysis system connected to a Windows PC workstation. The VisualEyez system monitors the 3-D positions of small infrared light emitting diodes (LEDs) located on landmarks of interest. We typically utilize the tips of the thumb and index finger along with the radial styloid at the wrist to demarcate the hand. Objects in the environment are also equipped with three LEDs for motion tracking.

- Once the motion information is obtained by the VisualEyez system, it is broadcast on a subnetwork to a scene rendering Linux-based PC.
- Using the motion capture information the scene is calculated and then rendered on a downward facing CRT monitor, placed parallel to a work surface. A half-silvered mirror is placed parallel to the computer monitor, midway between the screen and the workspace. The image on the computer monitor is reflected in the mirror and is perceived by subjects, wearing stereoscopic goggles, as if it were a three-dimensional object located in the workspace below the mirror.

3.2 Human performance measurement

Human motor control, biomechanics and neuroscience research has provided a comprehensive description of how humans reach to grasp and manipulate objects in natural environments under a variety of sensory and environmental conditions (MacKenzie & Iberall, 1994). By using the same measurement techniques as those employed to monitor human performance in natural environments we can compare movement in virtual environments to decades of existing human performance literature. The comparisons allow the development of comprehensive cognitive models of human performance under various sensory feedback conditions. Simple timing measures such as reaction time and movement time provide a general description of upper limb movements. However, in motor control studies, more complex three-dimensional kinematic measures such as displacement profiles, movement velocity, deceleration time, and the formation of the grasp aperture (distance between the index finger and thumb for a precision pinch grip) have also been used to characterize object acquisition movements (MacKenzie & Iberall, 1994). By observing regularities in the 3D kinematic information, inferences can be made regarding how movements are planned and performed by the neuromotor control system. This detailed movement information essentially provides a window into the motor control system and allows the determination of what sensory feedback characteristics are important for movement planning and production.

3.3 Preliminary experiments: Understanding vision for motor performance in virtual environments across the lifespan

In a study investigating the role of visual feedback about the hand for the control of reach to grasp movements, Mason and Bernardin (2009) demonstrated that young healthy adults could utilize very simple visual feedback of their fingertips to improve motor performance when compared to a condition in which no visual feedback of self was present. The crude visual representation consisted of two 10 mm yellow spheres representing the thumb and index finger tips (see Figure 2B for example). The visual representation of the hand was always provided with moderate contrast. Mason and Bernardin (2009) also noted that vision of the hand was not necessary throughout the movement, but only up to movement onset. If vision of the hand was completely removed, performance deteriorated. The results of this work shed light on ways to minimize the amount of visual feedback necessary for successful control of precision upper extremity movements in virtual environments. While the rendering of complex images capable of simulating the full human hand is now possible in VEs, it remains problematic in two ways. First, the motion capture and computing technology can result in significant increases in equipment costs to render a realistic hand. More importantly, the complexity of the rendering process generally results in significant latency problems, with time lags on the scale of 150+ ms from the movement of the real hand to its represented movement within the virtual environment (Wang & Popović, 2009). Latencies of this magnitude can have a significant negative impact on human performance (Ellis et al., 1997). Further, time delays in the range of 16-33 ms become noticeable to subjects when performing simple visual tasks in virtual reality (Mania et al., 2004). As a result of these problems, a key area of research in the development of successful, cost-effective VEs must relate to simulator validity. That is, the degree of realism the environment provides in approximating a real situation. Simulator validity has been identified as a key parameter for the effectiveness of learning in training simulations (Issenberg et al., 2005). This is extremely important in applications such as neurologic rehabilitation, where the ultimate goal is to ensure that practice in the virtual environment will carry over to function in activities of daily living. We must identify the minimal features of sensory feedback required for valid simulations so that humans can interact in ways sufficiently similar to movements in natural environments. In their initial study, Mason and Bernardin (2009) identified some sufficient visual feedback parameters for young adults. We conducted a follow up study using a similar paradigm to see if these results generalize to older and younger user groups.[1]

In our follow-up study, participants were asked to reach from a designated start position to grasp and lift a target cube. We manipulated three variables. The first was age group membership: children (7-12 years), young adults (18-30 years), middle age adults (40-50 years) and senior adults (60+ years). Each of these groups included 12 participants. Second, we manipulated target distance by placing the target object at either 7.5cm or 15cm from the start mark. Finally we varied visual feedback of the hand by providing the subject with one of five visual feedback conditions (Figure 2). In the no vision (NV) condition, the subject was not given any graphical feedback about the position of the hand. In the full vision crude (FVC) condition, graphical feedback about hand position (10mm spheres at the fingertips) was provided throughout the entire reach-to-grasp movement. For the vision up to peak velocity (VPV) condition, graphical feedback about hand position was extinguished once peak velocity of the wrist was reached. In the vision until movement onset (VMO) condition, graphical feedback of the hand was extinguished at the start of movement. For these conditions, subjects were prevented from seeing the real workspace below the mirror so that vision of the actual limb and surrounding environment was absent. For the final condition (full vision or FV), subjects were given full vision of the real hand as in a natural environment. Computer rendered graphical information about the target size and location was always available. All visual feedback was presented with visual stimuli of moderate contrast in relation to the background.

[1] A preliminary version of these results were published elsewhere (Grabowski & Mason, 2011).

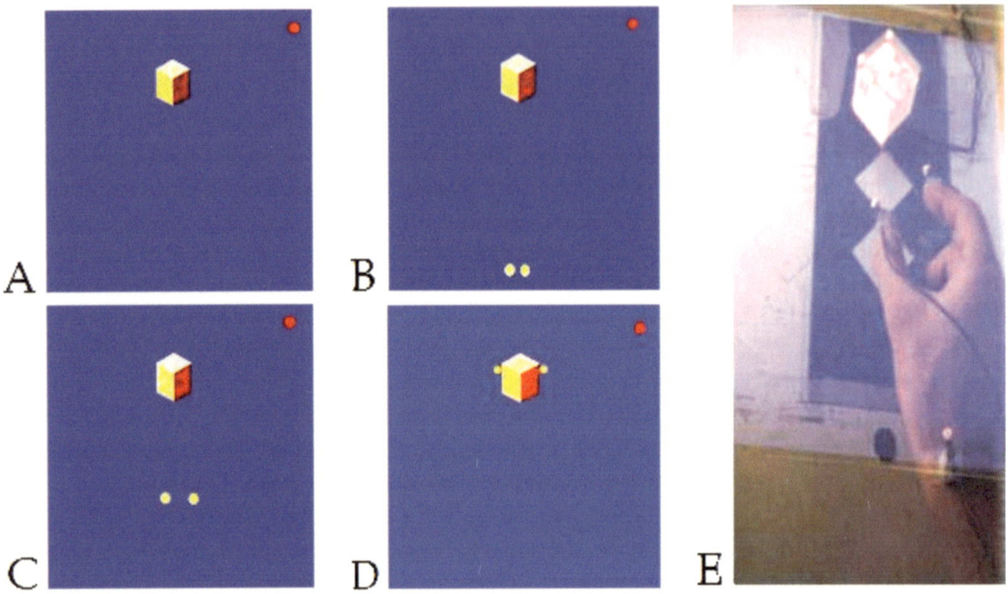

Fig. 2. Visual conditions. A) No vision-NV B) Vision to movement onset-VMO C) Vision to peak velocity - VPV D) Full vision crude-FVC E) Full vision-FV.

Results - Transport Component: Movement time results for young adults showed that crude feedback of the hand (both FVC and VPV) resulted in performance that was not different from performance under natural viewing conditions (FV) (Figure 3B). Conditions where this feedback was provided only to movement onset or not at all (VMO and NV) showed distinct performance deterioration. This pattern of results has been replicated several times in our lab (Mason, 2007; Mason & Bernardin, 2008; Mason & Bernardin, 2009). Older adults did not show any differences between visual conditions, indicating that they used a transport strategy that was independent of visual feedback of self (Figure 3D). While this strategy was effective for performance of the current experimental task, it could result in significant limitations with more complex and continuous tasks. For middle age adults and children (Figure 3C and 3A respectively), results indicated that they make use of full visual feedback of their moving limb to improve performance, but use of any crude feedback failed to provide significant performance enhancements.

The peak velocity of the transport varied with visual condition for all age groups, but children showed the most distinct effect (Figure 4). All conditions with altered feedback (FVC, VPV, VMO, and NV) had significantly lower peak velocities when compared to the natural viewing conditions (FV). Peak-velocity is determined by feed-forward motor planning mechanisms. Therefore, since slower movements are more accurate, it appears that children used a pre-planned strategy of slowing their reach to enhance the accuracy of their transport when they were only provided with crude visual feedback or no visual feedback.

Finally the results from the limb deceleration data, which give an indication of the portion of movement allotted for closed-loop sensory feedback processing, shed light on the same phenomenon mentioned previously in older adults: this age group did not alter their movement patterns based on the visual feedback conditions provided. This finding is

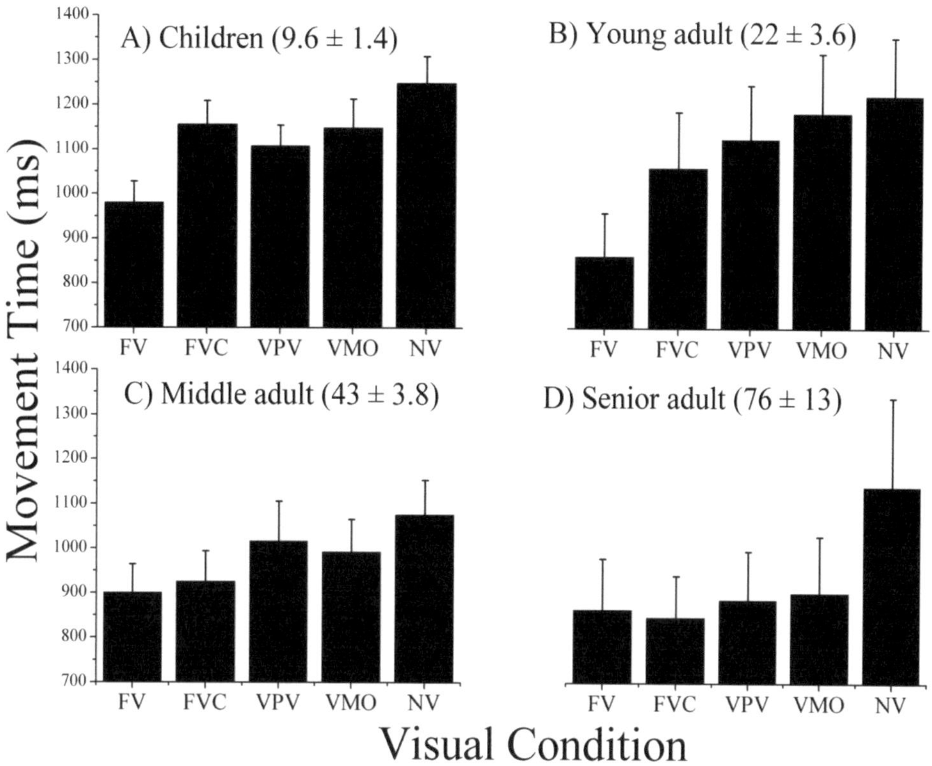

Fig. 3. Effect of visual condition manipulations on average movement times (error bars show ±SE) and mean age ±SE is shown in parentheses: A) Children $F_{4,44}$=10.09, $p<0.01$ B) Young adult $F_{4,44}$=7.24, $p<0.01$ C) Middle age adults $F_{4,44}$= 4.23, $p<0.01$ D) Senior adult $F_{4,44}$= 1.86, $p=0.19$. In young adults, FV was significantly faster than VMO and NV, but not different from the other simple feedback conditions (FVC and VPV). Also of note is the lack of any discernable condition effect in the group of older adults. Adapted from (Grabowski & Mason, 2011).

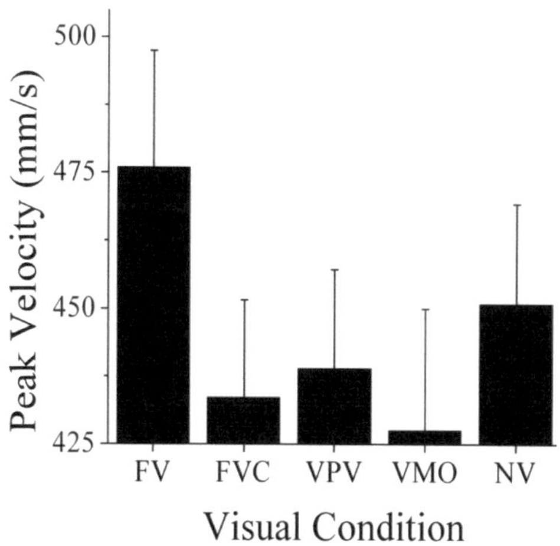

Fig. 4. Peak velocity results for children, $F_{4,44}$=5.32, $p<0.01$. All conditions show a slowing compared to the natural viewing in the FV condition.

consistent with previous work on age and motor control showing that for faster movements, older adults rely on modes of control that are minimally dependent on sensory feedback (Chaput & Proteau, 1996). These results can be interpreted as a manifestation of slowed central processing of sensory information.

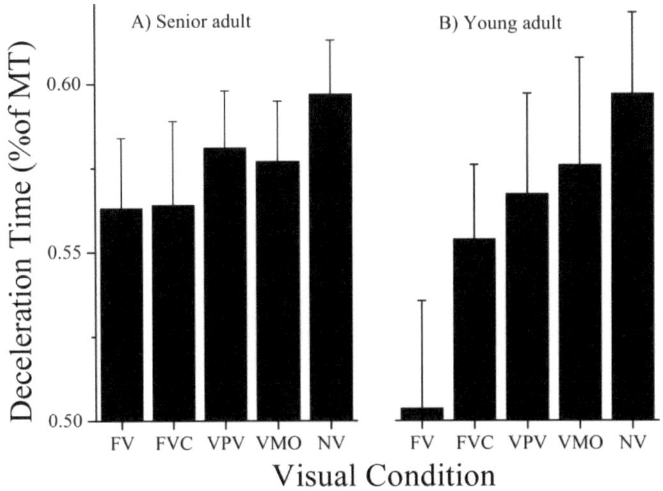

Fig. 5. Time spent in deceleration as a percentage of total movement time. A) Senior adult, $F_{4,44}$=1.84, p=0.15 and B) Young adult , $F_{4,44}$=13.70, p<0.01.

Results – Grasp component: To quantify formation of the grasp component we analyzed peak grasp apertures. Grasp aperture gives an indication of the precision requirements of a task, with larger apertures considered a compensatory strategy present in more demanding tasks with higher levels of uncertainty. In young adults apertures were significantly smaller in the FV, FVC, and VPV when compared to the condition where no visual feedback of the hand was provided (NV). This replicates the results found for movement time and indicates that young adults were able to use some limited visual feedback to reduce uncertainty in planning their grasp. In contrast, older adults used a markedly larger grasp aperture than the rest of the cohorts, and showed a minimal condition effect. Middle age adults did show an effect on grasp measures when provided with crude visual feedback of the hand throughout the movement (FVC). This condition resulted in apertures that were significantly smaller than in the no feedback condition (NV). No other condition resulted in smaller apertures than NV (Figure 5). Therefore, it appears that for middle age adults, the condition with crude feedback available throughout the movement simplified the sensorimotor requirements even more than when participants were provided with natural viewing conditions (FV).

Further inspection of the grasp aperture results shows that, although not statistically significant, the FVC condition resulted in the smallest average grasp apertures for all four age groups. These results provide preliminary evidence that luminance contrast may be an important variable for reducing movement complexity when grasping objects in a virtual environment. In our experiment, due to room lighting, the luminance contrast between the real limb and the background was low in the FV condition. Therefore, aperture planning in this condition may have been more difficult than in the FVC condition where the graphical representation of the fingertips provided greater luminance contrast. All other conditions either had a low contrast representation (FV) or no representation at all (VPV, VMO, NV). Therefore, the quality of the visual representation, specifically the luminance contrast, may serve as a means to further reduce task demands and uncertainty.

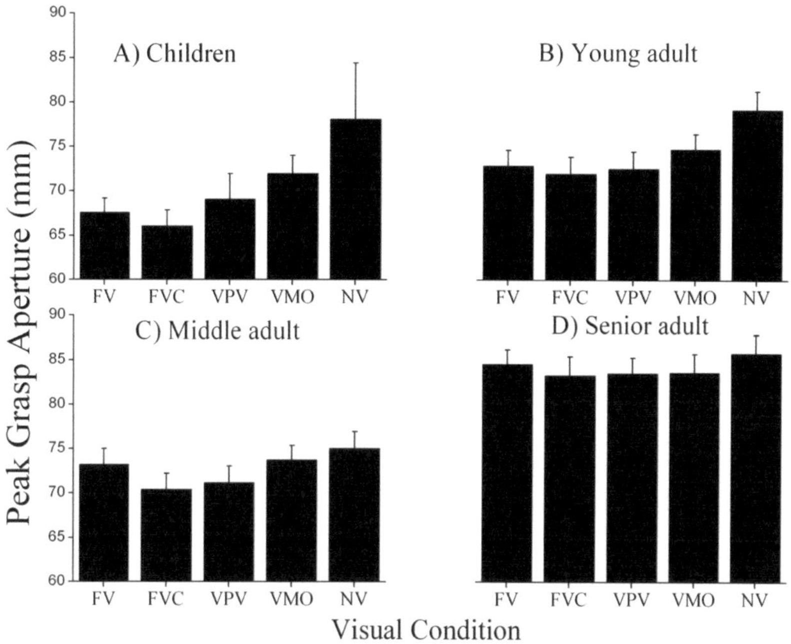

Fig. 6. Effect of visual condition on average peak grasp apertures (error bars show ±SE): A) Children $F_{4,44}=3.061, p=0.102$ B) Young adults $F_{4,44}=10.011, p<0.001$ C) Middle age adults $F_{4,44}=4.144$ $p=0.022$ D) Senior adults $F_{4,44}=1.207, p= 0.320$. For young and middle age adults, aperture in FVC was significantly smaller than in NV. For children and seniors FVC also had the smallest mean aperture, although this did not reach significance at the $p<0.05$ level. Also of note is that in young adults, FV and VPV also had significantly smaller apertures than NV. Note the general lack of visual condition effect among seniors. Adapted from (Grabowski & Mason, 2011).

To summarize, there are a few key findings from these two studies. First, young adults were quite adept at utilizing limited visual feedback for the control of precision grasp tasks in virtual environments. In contrast, senior adults could not make use of limited visual feedback and tended to rely on a feed-forward strategy. While this strategy allowed the older adults to be successful with the experimental task, it may limit the nature of their interactions in such environments when tasks become more complex. Children and senior adults both appeared to make compensatory adjustments in their motor planning for the demands of the experimental task, however they involved different components of the movement. Children altered the transport of their hand in space by using lower peak velocities. Senior adults used a very large grasp configuration to compensate for task uncertainty. Finally, aperture results indicated that there could potentially be some enhancement in performance when augmented feedback about the hand (i.e. the crude finger representation) contrasts at least moderately with the background environment. This was most pronounced in middle age adults, but weakly present in all age groups. While there are many directions to head with future research, the finding regarding the possibility of performance enhancement through the manipulation of luminance contrast is one particular area of interest.

4. Future directions

In the final sections, we will develop a theoretical basis for the importance of understanding the role of luminance contrast for precise, visually guided movements of the upper extremities. Following this, we briefly describe our next set of experiments aimed at a deeper understanding of the role of vision for motor performance in virtual environments across the lifespan.

4.1 Contrast sensitivity and tuning of neuronal populations

The neural processing of sensory information is described by the tuning of neuronal populations to specific stimuli (Desimone & Duncan, 1995). Within areas of the visual cortex, groups of neurons fire in response to the presence of afferent information. This firing rate is tuned to specific aspects of the stimulus, thereby increasing the precision by which the system can differentiate visual information. Within neuronal populations, firing rates differ among neurons. Some neurons will fire constantly with the presence of a stimulus, known as tonic firing. Other neurons fire rapidly at the onset of the stimulus, and rapidly decrease activity thereafter; this is known as phasic activity. This phasic activity makes the general sensorimotor system particularly sensitive to changes in stimulation. The visual cortex is no exception. Phasic neurons located within the visual cortex are sensitive to areas within the visual scene that are actively changing. It is simple to understand this in the case of a moving object, however the border of a stationary object also has this effect. Specifically, when the eye is moving and a stationary image passes over the moving retina, the border of the stationary object causes the visual scene to abruptly change, and phasic neurons react accordingly.

Sensitivity to object borders is dependent on the visual contrast between the object and its background. Contrast is described by two characteristics, luminance (brightness) and chromaticity (color), which are processed differently in the dorsal and ventral visual streams. The two visual stream hypothesis put forth by Goodale and Milner has a wide breadth of experimental support in explaining multiple functions for visual processing (Goodale and Milner 1992 as cited in Milner & Goodale, 2008). Briefly, the ventral stream includes structures along the pathway from the visual cortex in the occipital lobe to the inferotemporal lobe. This circuit has been implicated in the use of vision for perception of the surrounding environment, allowing the conscious experience of seeing the world around us. The dorsal stream includes the pathway from the visual cortex to the posterior parietal lobe. This pathway is responsible for the visuomanual transformations that allow visual information to guide our motor system in interacting with the surrounding environment. The neuronal structure of the ventral stream allows for high spatial resolution and sensitivity to chromaticity (Wade et al., 2002). Processing of color information in the ventral stream plays a role in the perception of objects (Kleinholdermann et al., 2009; Morrone, Denti, & Spinelli, 2002). The role of color contrast in visual processing for motor output has not been clearly elucidated, but it appears the strict dichotomous notion of the two visual stream hypothesis may be overly rigid. Recent investigation has shown that for simple eye movements and pointing tasks, color information can be used to guide movement (White, Kerzel, & Gegenfurtner, 2006). Pisella, Arzi, and Rossetti (1998) studied the ability of humans to utilize color information to quickly update their movements in a perturbation paradigm. While movement reorganization was possible utilizing only color information, the results showed a distinct slowing of movement reorganization. Brenner and Smeets (2004) also studied a similar paradigm, finding that color could in fact be utilized rather quickly for task reorganization; however, they still showed a minor slowing compared with movement reorganization based on luminance information. Luminance contrast, while also important in perception, may have more direct implications for motor output. Motion sensitivity is dependent on contrast sensitivity and motion sensitivity is a hallmark of the neuronal structure of the dorsal stream (Born & Bradley, 2005). Therefore luminance contrast may be an important source of visual sensory feedback for motor output.

Properties of visual feedback are used both in the planning and online control of movement. The specific role of luminance contrast for such processes has not been clearly identified, and previous study of this topic is sparse. Recently Braun et al. (2008) investigated whether initiation of eye movements differed when tracking two types of targets, one with luminance contrast compared to the background and one isoluminant with the background (i.e. defined by color only). They showed a strong and significant effect of target contrast on speed of eye movement initiation, with tracking of isoluminant targets delayed by 50 ms. They also showed lower eye accelerations to these no-contrast targets. For upper extremity control, studies have shown mixed results. White, Kerzel, and Gegenfurtner (2006) showed that there was no difference in accuracy or response latency when comparing simple rapid aiming movements to targets of high luminance contrast versus isoluminant targets. In a more complex task, Kleinholdermann et al. (2009) looked at the influence of the target object's luminance contrast as subjects performed reach to grasp movements within a desktop augmented (physical object with graphical overlay) environment. Participants were not provided with a head-coupled stereoscopic view, nor were they provided any visual representation of the hand. They were given a view of the environment that included only a virtual image overlaying the actual target disk. The independent variables controlled by the experimenters were the visual properties of chromatic and luminance contrast between the target object and the environment background. The results of this study showed only a minimal effect of luminance contrast on the formation of grasp aperture. They concluded that isoluminant targets were as suitable for the motor planning of grasp as targets defined by a luminance contrast or a luminance plus chromatic contrast. However, because current theories of motor control rest on the premise that object location can be precisely identified in relation to limb location (Wolpert, Miall, & Kawato, 1998) we contend that the lack of visual feedback about the limb likely resulted in a ceiling effect for a number of performance measures used by Kleinholdermann et al. Given that neuronal tuning properties make the visual system particularly sensitive to change, it is logical that some property involving a change in visual stimulus may be especially useful in this quick, precise identification of object and limb spatial location. Luminance contrast is such a property. Future experiments should expand upon the work of Kleinholdermann et al. by examining the role of luminance contrast of both the target object and the effector limb for upper extremity performance. Further, the Kleinholdermann et al. paper focused predominantly on motor planning. Future studies should examine kinematic findings at a deeper level to understand the use of vision in both open and closed loop functions. Additionally, since the treatment of visual contrast information by the CNS changes with time, as discussed in the next section, new studies must focus on delineating the role of such information for populations differing by age.

4.2 Aging and luminance contrast

While there are changes at the ocular level with age, the predominant cause of functional decline is due to a slowing of central processing in the brain (Chaput & Proteau, 1996; Inui, 1997; Light, 1990; Shields et al., 2005). The slowing of temporal processing has been specifically implicated in the decline of luminance contrast sensitivity in adults over 60. Motion sensitivity, which is dependent on contrast sensitivity, also declines with age (Spering et al., 2005; Trick & Silverman, 1991). Motion sensitivity is also known to be directly linked to function of dopaminergic circuitry, a system known to play a major role in the aging process (Wild-Wall et al., 2008). Despite these declines, older adults become more dependent on vision over time, resulting from the relative sparing of visual resources when compared to other sources of sensory feedback (Adamo et al., 2007; Chaput & Proteau, 1996; Goble et al., 2008; Lemay et al., 2004). The important concept to note is that this sparing of neurons in the visual systems results in a greater amount of substrate available for positive neuroplastic changes relating to motor output. Indeed, such positive changes have been documented in older adults when trained via the visual system to improve speed of processing (Ball, Edwards, & Ross, 2007; Edwards et al., 2005; Long & Rourke, 1989; Zhou et al., 2006). The key question to consider is how might this potential for plastic changes be manipulated and optimized? Given that the processing of luminance contrast information is linked in multiple ways with speed of processing, and speed of processing is a central theme in aging related functional decline, this visual property may be a useful means to answer the plasticity question. We believe a number of attributes of 3D VEs make them an ideal tool to aid in investigating this question, and believe design of VEs will directly benefit from the information gained. Therefore, we intend to investigate changes in sensorimotor processing of luminance contrast in older adults compared to younger adults. The information gained from this study will be directly applicable to development of technologies to rehabilitate and enhance function in aging and neurologically compromised adults.

4.3 Future research aims

Aim 1 is to test the hypothesis that luminance contrasts of target and limb have an effect on upper extremity kinematics in a virtual environment. This will be investigated using the methodology described previously with a reach to grasp paradigm. We will test a population of adults age 18-25 without history of visual or upper extremity sensorimotor dysfunction. We intend to study five contrast levels ranging from very low to very high. Based on previous studies of visual feedback, we believe that low levels of luminance contrast will negatively affect kinematic markers of upper extremity performance, for example slowed movement time, when compared to moderate and high levels. We also believe that high levels of contrast will not have a significant effect on performance measures when compared to the moderate level for this group of participants.

Aim 2 is to test the interaction of age with visual contrast between the limb/target and background environment. We will use the same reach to grasp paradigm, but collect data on a group of healthy adults age 18-25, a middle age group 40-50, and a group of healthy adults age 60+. We believe that older adults will only effectively use visual feedback of self in the highest contrast condition. This will allow inferences about the age-related processing of luminance contrast as a visual feedback parameter for motor performance.

4.3.1 Application of results

We anticipate the results of this line of research will have implications in numerous fields. First, the information gained will have direct bearing on computer science for the user-specific design of next generation 3D virtual environments. As the world population continues to age, understanding of how to enhance performance with computer interfaces must take into account the physiologic changes that occur over time. Luminance contrast appears to be an important factor in upper extremity control, and one that is known to play a role in performance changes with age in natural environments. It stands to reason then that performance in a primarily visual environment, such as a 3D VE, will rely heavily on the neural processing of contrast. Secondly, we believe the field of rehabilitation will benefit indirectly through improvements in user-centered design. Currently, 3D VEs are regularly studied as a means to improve upon current practices in rehabilitation of patients post-stroke. Unfortunately, one barrier to success continues to be usability and provision of cost-effective, age-appropriate sensory feedback. Information on performance changes in older adults related to manipulation of luminance contrast may be of use to both program designers and rehab clinicians. For example, if older adults perform movements in VEs under certain contrast conditions in a manner equivalent to a natural environment, rehab clinicians may want to capitalize on such parameters to improve functional carryover of training to activities of daily living. Lastly, we believe results from our current and future study will contribute to the fields of gerontology and behavioural neuroscience by expanding our knowledge of visual processing and motor behaviour across the lifespan.

5. Conclusion

User-centered design of virtual environments continues to be an under-studied area with regard to both old and young users. Knowledge of human performance, and the nature of the sensory feedback that guides it, will be imperative in the successful, cost-effective design of tangible user interfaces intended for use by these populations. Recent work has shown that young adults can utilize visual information provided in virtual environments differently than both older adults and young children, and therefore more specific age-group studies are needed. Future studies will focus on specific parameters of visual feedback, such as luminance contrast, and how the provision of such properties in virtual environments impacts the performance of the user.

6. Acknowledgements

We would like to thank Drew Rutherford, Alexandra Skogen, Brandon Bernardin, and Stephanie Ehle for their assistance with data collection and analysis. This work was funded by the National Science Foundation grant No. 0916119.

7. References

Adamo, D. E., Martin, B. J., & Brown, S. H. (2007). Age-related differences in upper limb proprioceptive acuity. *Perceptual and Motor Skills, 104*(3 Pt 2), 1297-1309.

Allen R, C., Singer M, J., McDonald D, P., & Cotton J, E. (2000). Age differences in a virtual reality entertainment environment: A field study. *Human Factors and Ergonomics Society Annual Meeting Proceedings, 44*(5), 542-545.

Andersen, B. B., Gundersen, H. J., & Pakkenberg, B. (2003). Aging of the human cerebellum: A stereological study. *The Journal of Comparative Neurology, 466*(3), 356-365.

Ball, K., Edwards, J. D., & Ross, L. A. (2007). The impact of speed of processing training on cognitive and everyday functions. *Journals of Gerontology Series B: Psychological Sciences and Social Sciences, 62*(Special Issue 1), 19.

Born, R. T., & Bradley, D. C. (2005). Structure and function of visual area MT. *Annu.Rev.Neurosci., 28,* 157-189.

Braun, D., Mennie, N., Rasche, C., Schütz, A., Hawken, M., & Gegenfurtner, K. (2008). Smooth pursuit eye movements to isoluminant targets. *Journal of Neurophysiology, 100*(3), 1287.

Brenner, E., & Smeets, J. B. J. (2004). Colour vision can contribute to fast corrections of arm movements. *Experimental Brain Research, 158*(3), 302-307.

Chaput, S., & Proteau, L. (1996). Aging and motor control. *The Journals of Gerontology.Series B, Psychological Sciences and Social Sciences, 51*(6), P346-55.

Contreras-Vidal, J. L., Teulings, H. L., & Stelmach, G. E. (1998). Elderly subjects are impaired in spatial coordination in fine motor control. *Acta Psychologica, 100*(1-2), 25-35.

Craik, F. I. M., & McDowd, J. M. (1987). Age differences in recall and recognition. *Journal of Experimental Psychology: Learning, Memory, and Cognition., 13*(3), 474-479.

Desimone, R., & Duncan, J. (1995). Neural mechanisms of selective visual attention. *Annual Review of Neuroscience, 18*(1), 193-222.

Edwards, J., Wadley, V., Vance, D., Wood, K., Roenker, D., & Ball, K. (2005). The impact of speed of processing training on cognitive and everyday performance. *Aging & Mental Health, 9*(3), 262-271.

Ellis, S. R., Breant, F., Manges, B., Jacoby, R., & Adelstein, B. (1997). Factors influencing operator interaction with virtual objects viewed via head-mounted see-through displays: Viewing conditions and rendering latency. *Vrais,* 138.

Goble, D. J., Coxon, J. P., Wenderoth, N., Van Impe, A., & Swinnen, S. P. (2008). Proprioceptive sensibility in the elderly: Degeneration, functional consequences and plastic-adaptive processes. *Neuroscience and Biobehavioral Reviews,33*(3), 271-278.

Grabowski, P.J., & Mason, A.H. (2011). Sensory feedback for motor performance in virtual environments across the lifespan. *Proceedings of the IADIS International Multiconference on Computer Science and Information Systems,* Rome, Italy, July, 2011.

Hawthorn, D. (2001). Towards interface design for older users. *Proceedings of the NACCQ,* Napier, New Zealand, July, 2001.

Hawthorn, D. (2007). Interface design and engagement with older people. *Behaviour & Information Technology, 26*(4), 333-341.

Hendrix, C., & Barfield, W. (1996). The sense of presence with auditory virtual environments. *Presence: Teleoperators and Virtual Environments, 5*(3), 290-301.

Heuninckx, S., Wenderoth, N., & Swinnen, S. P. (2008). Systems neuroplasticity in the aging brain: Recruiting additional neural resources for successful motor performance in elderly persons. *The Journal of Neuroscience : The Official Journal of the Society for Neuroscience, 28*(1), 91-99.

Horak, F. B., & Hlavacka, F. (2001). Somatosensory loss increases vestibulospinal sensitivity. *Journal of Neurophysiology, 86*(2), 575-585.

Hwang, J. H., Lee, Y. T., Park, D. S., & Kwon, T. K. (2008). Age affects the latency of the erector spinae response to sudden loading. *Clinical Biomechanics (Bristol, Avon), 23*(1), 23-29.

Inui, N. (1997). Simple reaction times and timing of serial reactions of middle-aged and old men. *Perceptual and Motor Skills, 84*(1), 219-225.

Ishii, H. & Ullmer, B.,. (1997). Tangible bits: Towards seamless interfaces between people, bits and atoms. *In Proceedings of the Conference on Human Factors in Computing Systems,* Atlanta, USA, March, 1997.

Issenberg, S. B., Mcgaghie, W. C., Petrusa, E. R., Lee Gordon, D., & Scalese, R. J. (2005). Features and uses of high-fidelity medical simulations that lead to effective learning: A BEME systematic review*. *Medical Teacher, 27*(1), 10-28.

Jonsson, E., Henriksson, M., & Hirschfeld, H. (2007). Age-related differences in postural adjustments in connection with different tasks involving weight transfer while standing. *Gait & Posture, 26*(4), 508-515.

Karwowski, W. (Ed.). (2006). *International encyclopedia of ergonomics and human factors* (2nd ed.). Boca Raton, FL: CRC Press.

Kleinholdermann, U., Franz, V. H., Gegenfurtner, K. R., & Stockmeier, K. (2009). Grasping isoluminant stimuli. *Experimental Brain Research, 197*(1), 15-22.

Kluger, A., Gianutsos, J. G., Golomb, J., Ferris, S. H., George, A. E., Franssen, E., et al. (1997). Patterns of motor impairement in normal aging, mild cognitive decline, and early alzheimer's disease. *The Journals of Gerontology.Series B, Psychological Sciences and Social Sciences, 52*(1), P28-39.

Koceja, D. M., Allway, D., & Earles, D. R. (1999). Age differences in postural sway during volitional head movement. *Archives of Physical Medicine and Rehabilitation, 80*(12), 1537-1541.

Kuo, H. K., & Lipsitz, L. A. (2004). Cerebral white matter changes and geriatric syndromes: Is there a link? *The Journals of Gerontology.Series A, Biological Sciences and Medical Sciences, 59*(8), 818-826.

Laursen, B., Jensen, B. R., & Ratkevicius, A. (2001). Performance and muscle activity during computer mouse tasks in young and elderly adults. *European Journal of Applied Physiology, 84*(4), 329-336.

Lemay, M., Bertram, C. P., & Stelmach, G. E. (2004). Pointing to an allocentric and egocentric remembered target in younger and older adults. *Experimental Aging Research, 30*(4), 391-406.

Leonard, C. T., Matsumoto, T., Diedrich, P. M., & McMillan, J. A. (1997). Changes in neural modulation and motor control during voluntary movement of older individuals. *The Journals of Gerontology.Series A, Biological Sciences and Medical Sciences, 52*(5), M320-5.

Light, K. E. (1990). Information processing for motor performance in aging adults. *Physical Therapy, 70*(12), 820-826.

Long, G. M., & Rourke, D. A. (1989). Training effects on the resolution of moving targetsdynamic visual acuity. *Human Factors: The Journal of the Human Factors and Ergonomics Society, 31*(4), 443-451.

MacKenzie, C.L. & Iberall, T. (1994). *The grasping hand.*. Amsterdam: Elsevier Science.

MacLean, K. E. (1996). The haptic camera: A technique for characterizing and playing back haptic properties of real environments. *Proceedings of the 5th Annual Symposium on Haptic Interfaces for Virtual Environments and Teleoperator Systems.*

Mania, K., Adelstein, B. D., Ellis, S. R., & Hill, M. I. (2004). Perceptual sensitivity to head tracking latency in virtual environments with varying degrees of scene complexity. *Proceedings of the 1st Symposium on Applied Perception in Graphics and Visualization,* 39-47.

Mankovsky, N. B., Mints, A. Y., & Lisenyuk, V. P. (1982). Age peculiarities of human motor control in aging. *Gerontology, 28*(5), 314-322.

Mason, A. H. (2007). An experimental study on the role of graphical information about hand movement when interacting with objects in virtual reality environments. *Interacting with Computers, 19*(3), 370-381.

Mason, A.H., & Bernardin, B.J. (2008). The role of visual feedback when grasping and transferring objects in a virtual environment. *Proceedings of the 5th International Conference on Enactive Interfaces,* 111-116.

Mason, A.H., & MacKenzie, C.L. (2002). The effects of visual information about self-movement on grip forces when receiving objects in an augmented environment. *Proceedings of the IEEE Conference on Virtual Reality, Haptics Symposium,* 105-112.

Mason, A.H., Walji, M.A., Lee, E.J., & MacKenzie, C.L. (2001). Reaching movements to augmented and graphic objects in virtual environments. *Proceedings of the SIGCHI Conference on Human Factors in Computing Systems,* 426-433.

Mason, A. H., & Bernardin, B. J. (2009). Vision for performance in virtual environments: The role of feedback timing. *International Journal of Human-Computer Interaction, 25*(8), 785-805.

Milner, A. D., & Goodale, M. A. (2008). Two visual systems re-viewed. *Neuropsychologia, 46*(3), 774-785.

Morrone, M. C., Denti, V., & Spinelli, D. (2002). Color and luminance contrasts attract independent attention. *Current Biology, 12*(13), 1134-1137.

Mourey, F., Pozzo, T., Rouhier-Marcer, I., & Didier, J. P. (1998). A kinematic comparison between elderly and young subjects standing up from and sitting down in a chair. *Age and Ageing, 27*(2), 137-146.

Pisella, L., Arzi, M., & Rossetti, Y. (1998). The timing of color and location processing in the motor context. *Experimental Brain Research, 121*(3), 270-276.

Poston, B., Van Gemmert, A. W., Barduson, B., & Stelmach, G. E. (2009). Movement structure in young and elderly adults during goal-directed movements of the left and right arm. *Brain and Cognition, 69*(1):30-38.

Proteau, L. (1992). On the specificity of learning and the role of visual information for movement control. In Proteau, L. & Elliott, D. (Ed.), *Vision and motor control* (pp. 67-103). Amsterdam: Elsevier.

Raz, N., & Rodrigue, K. M. (2006). Differential aging of the brain: Patterns, cognitive correlates and modifiers. *Neuroscience and Biobehavioral Reviews, 30*(6), 730-748.

Romero, D. H., & Stelmach, G. E. (2003). Changes in postural control with aging and parkinson's disease. *IEEE Engineering in Medicine and Biology Magazine : The Quarterly Magazine of the Engineering in Medicine & Biology Society, 22*(2), 27-31.

Romero, D. H., Van Gemmert, A. W., Adler, C. H., Bekkering, H., & Stelmach, G. E. (2003). Time delays prior to movement alter the drawing kinematics of elderly adults. *Human Movement Science, 22*(2), 207-220.

Roos, M. R., Rice, C. L., & Vandervoort, A. A. (1997). Age-related changes in motor unit function. *Muscle & Nerve, 20*(6), 679-690.

Rossini, P., Desiato, M., & Caramia, M. (1992). Age-related changes of motor evoked potentials in healthy humans: Non-invasive evaluation of central and peripheral motor tracts excitability and conductivity. *Brain Research, 593*(1), 14-19.

Schmidt, R.S. & Lee, T.D. (1999). *Motor control and learning: A behavioral emphasis.* Illinois: Human Kinetics.

Schneiderman, B. (1983). Direct manipulation: A step beyond programming languages. *IEEE Computer, 1983. 16(8): P. 57-69.*

Schut, L. J. (1998). Motor system changes in the aging brain: What is normal and what is not. *Geriatrics, 53 Suppl 1,* S16-9.

Seidler, R. D., Alberts, J. L., & Stelmach, G. E. (2002). Changes in multi-joint performance with age. *Motor Control, 6*(1), 19-31.

Shields, R. K., Madhavan, S., Cole, K. R., Brostad, J. D., Demeulenaere, J. L., Eggers, C. D., et al. (2005). Proprioceptive coordination of movement sequences in humans. *Clinical Neurophysiology : Official Journal of the International Federation of Clinical Neurophysiology, 116*(1), 87-92.

Slater, M., Usoh, M., & Steed, A. (1995). Taking steps: The influence of a walking metaphor on presence in virtual reality. *ACM Transactions on Computer-Human Interaction, 2*(3), 201-219.

Smith, M. W., Sharit, J., & Czaja, S. J. (1999). Aging, motor control, and the performance of computer mouse tasks. *Human Factors, 41*(3), 389-396.

Sparrow, W. A., Begg, R. K., & Parker, S. (2006). Aging effects on visual reaction time in a single task condition and when treadmill walking. *Motor Control, 10*(3), 201-211.

Spering, M., Kerzel, D., Braun, D. I., Hawken, M. J., & Gegenfurtner, K. R. (2005). Effects of contrast on smooth pursuit eye movements. *Journal of Vision, 5*(5), 455-465.

Sterr, A., & Dean, P. (2008). Neural correlates of movement preparation in healthy ageing. *The European Journal of Neuroscience, 27*(1), 254-260.

Sturman, D.J. & Zeltzer, D. (1993). A design method for "whole-hand" human-computer interaction. *ACM Transactions on Information Systems, 11*(3), 219-238.

Trick, G. L., & Silverman, S. E. (1991). Visual sensitivity to motion: Age-related changes and deficits in senile dementia of the alzheimer type. *Neurology, 41*(9), 1437.

Vandervoort, A. A. (2002). Aging of the human neuromuscular system. *Muscle & Nerve, 25*(1), 17-25.

Wade, A. R., Brewer, A. A., Rieger, J. W., & Wandell, B. A. (2002). Functional measurements of human ventral occipital cortex: Retinotopy and colour. *Philosophical Transactions of the Royal Society of London.Series B: Biological Sciences, 357*(1424), 963.

Wang, R. Y., & Popović, J. (2009). Real-time hand-tracking with a color glove. *ACM SIGGRAPH 2009 Papers,* 1-8.

Wang, Y., & MacKenzie, C.L. (2000). The role of contextual haptic and visual constraints on object manipulation in virtual environments. *Proceedings of the Conference on Human Factors in Computing Systems.*, 532-539.

White, B. J., Kerzel, D., & Gegenfurtner, K. R. (2006). Visually guided movements to color targets. *Experimental Brain Research, 175*(1), 110-126.

Wild-Wall, N., Willemssen, R., Falkenstein, M., & Beste, C. (2008). Time estimation in healthy ageing and neurodegenerative basal ganglia disorders. *Neuroscience Letters, 442*(1), 34-38.

Wolpert, D. M., Miall, R. C., & Kawato, M. (1998). Internal models in the cerebellum. *Trends in Cognitive Sciences, 2*(9), 338-347.

Yan, J. H., Thomas, J. R., & Stelmach, G. E. (1998). Aging and rapid aiming arm movement control. *Experimental Aging Research, 24*(2), 155-168.

Zhou, Y., Huang, C., Xu, P., Tao, L., Qiu, Z., Li, X., et al. (2006). Perceptual learning improves contrast sensitivity and visual acuity in adults with anisometropic amblyopia. *Vision Research, 46*(5), 739-750.

9

Ergonomics Design Criteria of a Virtual Environment

Zahari Taha[1], Hartomo Soewardi[2,3], Siti Zawiah[2] and Aznijar Ahmad-Yazid[2]

[1]*Faculty of Mechanical Engineering, University Malaysia Pahang Pekan, Pahang*
[2]*Centre for Product Design and Manufacturing, Department of Engineering Design and Manufacture, Faculty of Engineering, University of Malaya, Kuala Lumpur,*
[3]*Department of Industrial Engineering, Faculty of Industrial Technology, Islamic University of Indonesia, Yogyakarta*
[1,2]*Malaysia*
[3]*Indonesia*

1. Introduction

Virtual environment (VE) can be defined as a computer generated three dimensional model environment; in which a user feels as if he/she is present in it and the user can interact intuitively with objects contained within it (Wilson, 1999). While being advantageous in experiencing new environment without having to build the real thing, the experience comes with some side effect for some. When interacting with VE through output and input devices, it has been reported that some users experienced negative side effects by being immersed into the graphically rendered virtual worlds. One of side effect is known as cyber sickness i.e. especially affecting the vision (Stanney *et all*, 1998; Barret, 2004). Stanney *et all* (1998) further mentioned that for VEs to be effective and well received by their users; while avoiding unwanted side effect, human being's limitation needs to be considered during the VE design stage. It is highly essential to ensure that advances in VE technology will not be at the expense of human well being.

Ergonomics is a branch of science that is concerned with the achievement of optimal relationship between workers and their work environment (Tayyari, F. and Smith, J.L., 1997). Since human being's limitation is crucial in the design process of a virtual environment, implementation of ergonomics will bring about an optimal VE experience for users. Good design incorporating ergonomics consideration will enhance the communication between the user and the virtual world. Since several ergonomic factors contribute to good VE design, there is a need to investigate what are the critical ergonomics design criteria.

Most ergonomics researches are related to the ergonomic design criteria of human computer interaction. They are focused on physical ergonomics such as visual display terminal (VDT). Stewart, T. (1995) exhibited the importance of ergonomics standards for computer equipment (IS0 9241), and the necessity in understanding how to use them when selecting or designing visual display unit (VDU) equipment and systems. When Menozzi, M., *et al* (1999) conducted studies comparing cathode ray tube (CRT) display and liquid crystal display (LCD) for their suitability in visual tasks in VDU, it was found that LCD provided better viewing conditions compared to CRT display. Nichols, S. (1999) investigated the design of VR equipment in respect to the physical ergonomics such as head mounted display (HMD) and hand-held input devices and the problems associated with it. Shieh and Lin (2000) investigated the effect of screen type, ambient lighting and colour combination on VDT to visual performance and found that those factors do affect VDT performance. Lin (2003) studied the effects of contrast ratio and text colour on visual performance using TFT-LCD and found that contrast ratio significantly affects visual performance. In 2007, after being approved by ANSI on 14th November, the Human Factor Engineering Society published the new national standard for human factor engineering of computer workstation (ANSI/HFES100), which eventually becomes the comprehensive ergonomics guideline in the design of a VDT.

Ergonomics research related to virtual environment has been conducted in the past, but the focus of the research is only on the use of VE as a tool in ergonomics analysis (Shaikh,I., *et al*, 2004; Colombo and Cugini, 2005; Pappas, M., *et al*, 2005; Dukic, T., *et al*, 2007; Hu, B, *et al*, 2011). Shaikh,I., *et al*, (2004) studied on participatory ergonomics using VR and found that VR system will help towards designing better workplaces. Colombo and Cugini (2005) researched on virtual humans and prototypes, evaluating ergonomics and safety. While Pappas, M. *et al* (2005) investigated on ergonomic evaluation of virtual assembly tasks. Other researchers such as Dukic, T *et al* (2007) researched on the evaluation of ergonomics in a virtual manufacturing process and Hu, B. *et al* (2011) presented preliminary experimental results on the relationship between ergonomic measurements in VE and RE for some typical "drilling" tasks.

It has been noted that no research on ergonomics design criteria for designing a virtual environment has been reported. Thus, the objective of this study in identifying the ergonomics design criteria for designing a Virtual Environment is imperative.

2. Material and methods

2.1 Subjects

Eight university students participated in the study. None of the participants suffered from any vestibular and visual dysfunction and were not taking any medication during the experiments. The mean age was 21.7 years old (aged 19-23 years). Prior to the experiment, informed consent was obtained about the nature of the experiment and the objectives of the experiment as well as participant rights were fully explained. Participants were tested individually during the entire experiment session and received payment for their participation. Ishihara plates for Pseudo Isochromatic test were used to test normal visual of a subject. The test for colour blindness was adapted from Courtney (1986).

2.2 Apparatus

2.2.1 Virtual stimulus

The virtual stimulus system used is a virtual robot manufacturing system (from here onwards to be referred only as the virtual environment (VE)). This Virtual Environment presents a virtual robot activity for storage loading and unloading (SLU) process (shown in Figure 1). It was developed using direct X and Dark Basic Professional. The Autodesk 3DS Max software was used to build the virtual object. The VE was displayed through a projector on a wide screen. The projector was connected via cable to a laptop controlled by a keyboard and mouse. This wide screen allows the projection of stereoscopic images where each eye will see the slightly shifted images.

Fig. 1. Snap shot of Virtual Robot Manufacturing System

2.2.2 Questionnaires

A qualitative assessment was conducted through the use of questionnaire. The questionnaire was developed to identify the visual symptoms of the virtual environment variables / attributes investigated. The questionnaire consists of two principal parts. The first part contains the question with seven response option. This is aimed to identify the visual problems experienced during or after interacting with the VE. The second part contains questions to identify the level of symptoms experienced based on the answers of the previous part. The answers to the questions in the second part were of the ordinal data type.

2.2.3 Statistical analysis

Statistical analysis was conducted to analyse the effect/relationship between independent variable and dependent variable. Non parametric statistic was implemented involving descriptive statistic and statistical binomial test. The tests were on hypotheses about the effect of each attributes or variables of the virtual environment on the incidence of visual symptoms. The hypotheses developed were:

- H1: Colour of background has effect of visual symptoms among immersive environment users
- H2: Virtual lighting has effect of visual symptoms among immersive environment users
- H3: Field of View (FOV) has effect of visual symptoms among immersive environment users
- H4: Flow rate (FR) has effect of visual symptoms among immersive environment users
- H5: Speed of virtual object motion has effect of visual symptoms among immersive environment users
- H6: Resolution of display has effect of visual symptoms among immersive environment users
- H7: Contrast ratio has effect of visual symptoms among immersive environment users

The level of significance was set at $\alpha = 0.05$ for all analyses.

2.3 Experimental design and procedure

2.3.1 Experimental design

The experiments were conducted at the ergonomic-virtual reality laboratory. A sitting position was adopted with the subject sitting at a distance of 15 - 25 cm from the back edge of the table to complete the task. The activity is to operate a virtual robot in the VE using an infrared mouse (wireless mouse) with the motion observed on the wide screen display.

The digital projector was positioned on a table 75 cm in height with an inclination angle of between 5°-10° with respect to the horizontal axis. The projector was connected to laptop with a display set to 1280 x 800 pixels. The distance from the front edge of the table or the digital projector to the center of the wide screen was 300 cm. The size of wide screen display is 170 cm in length and 155 cm in width. The bottom edge of wide screen display was measured at 94 cm above the floor. Prior to conducting the experiment, the subjects were made to adjust their seating positions to make them as comfortable as possible.

2.3.2 Experimental procedure

The subjects were provided with information describing the aims of the study and how the experiment will be conducted. Their health condition and past experience of sickness were also identified and their anthropometric data measured. The colour blind test was then conducted before proceeding to colour selection and the experiment. If a subject cannot complete the test, it means that the subject has some visual problems and is unable to continue the experiment.

Prior to performing the experiment, subjects were trained on how to use the wireless mouse in order to operate the virtual robot in the VE to complete the virtual task. Heart rate and visual acuity was measured before and after the experiment.

In the experiment, subjects were exposed to the virtual environment to view and operate a virtual robot by using a wireless mouse; to pick up a virtual material in a rack and to put it on a conveyor and subsequently to also pick up a virtual product on the conveyor and store in another rack as shown in Fig. 1. The activity was performed for 10 minutes for each attributes and for every subject of the VE studied. All subjects were required to sit in an upright posture and also in a comfortable posture while completing the virtual task. Participants were also instructed to complete the questionnaire immediately after finishing the virtual task.

3. Results

3.1 Effect of colour of virtual background to visual symptoms

Table 1 shows the results of the experiment describing the effect of colour of the virtual background on visual symptoms of the subjects. There are five types of colour used in this experiment, which are Red, Fuchsia, Dark Sky Blue, Medium Slate Blue and White. The colours were identified on the basis of user's preferences. Statistical binomial test at 5% significant level shows that the overall background colour has an effect on the user i.e. eyestrain and blurred vision syndrome. The eyestrain syndrome was experienced by 75% of users when Red and White background colours were used while 63% was experienced by the users when Fuchsia, Dark Sky Blue and Medium Slate Blue background colours were used. The blurred vision syndrome was only experienced by users when Red background colour was used.

No.	Colour	Observation Proportion (%)	Symptoms	Exact Sig. (1-tailed)	Decision
1.	Red	75 63	Eyestrain Blurred Vision	0.633 0.321	Effect Effect
2.	Fuchsia	63	Eyestrain	0.321	Effect
3.	Dark Sky Blue	63	Eyestrain	0.321	Effect
4.	Medium Slate Blue	63	Eyestrain	0.321	Effect
5.	White	75	Eyestrain	0.633	Effect

$p > 0.05$; N = 8

Table 1. Result of Experiment and Binomial Test of Visual Symptoms of Colour Virtual Background

No.	Level of Brightness	Observation Proportion (%)	Symptoms	Exact Sig. (1-tailed)	Decision
1.	10% level	83 50	Eyestrain Dry and Irritated Eyes	0.534 0.169	Effect Effect
2.	25% level	83	Eyestrain	0.534	Effect
3.	50% level	83	Eyestrain	0.534	Effect
4.	100% level	100 67 50	Eyestrain Dry and Irritated Eyes Light Sensitivity	0.178 0.138 0.169	Effect Effect Effect

$p > 0.05$; N = 8

Table 2. Result of Experiment and Binomial Test of Visual Symptoms of Virtual Lighting

3.2 Effect of virtual lighting to visual symptoms

The results of experiments on the effect of virtual lighting on visual symptoms are presented in Table 2. The experiment was conducted for four level of brightness of virtual light from darkest (10% level) to the brightest (100% level). The result of statistical binomial test at 5% significant level exhibiting the different effects of visual symptoms experienced by users is shown in Table 2. Eyestrain symptom was experienced by 83% of the users for all level of brightness. Whereas 50% the users experienced symptoms of dry and irritated eyes at 10% level of brightness and light sensitivity at 100% level of brightness. At the highest level of brightness, dry and irritated eyes were experienced by 67% of the users.

3.3 Effect of field of view

Table 3 presents the result of experiment on the effect of field of view (FOV). There are two types of FOV namely 120^0 and 85^0 FOV. Statistical binomial test at 5% significant level shows the same result of visual symptoms effect experienced by users but at different proportion especially the eyestrain and dry and irritated eyes symptoms. For 120 degree of FOV, 63% of the users experienced dry and irritated eyes while only 50% of the users experienced it for 85 degree of FOV. 75% of the users experienced eyestrain symptom at 85^0 of FOV and 50% of the users experienced it at 120^0 of FOV.

No.	Degree of FOV	Observation Proportion (%)	Symptoms	Exact Sig. (1-tailed)	Decision
1.	FOV 120^0	50	Eyestrain	0.114	Effect
		50	Blurred Vision	0.114	Effect
		63	Dry and Irritated Eyes	0.321	Effect
2.	FOV 85^0	75	Eyestrain	0.633	Effect
		50	Blurred Vision	0.114	Effect
		50	Dry and Irritated Eyes	0.114	Effect

$p > 0.05$; N = 8

Table 3. Result of Experiment and Binomial Test of Visual Symptoms of Field of View

3.4 Effect of flow rate of virtual object

Table 4 shows the result of experiments on the effect of flow rate (FR) of virtual object on visual symptoms of the subjects. There are two types of flow rate studied, which are five

No.	Flow Rate (FR)	Observation Proportion (%)	Symptoms	Exact Sig. (1-tailed)	Decision
1.	Flow Rate 5 (FR5)	75	Eyestrain	0.633	Effect
		50	Dry and Irritated Eyes	0.114	Effect
2.	Flow Rate10 (FR10)	75	Eyestrain	0.633	Effect
		50	Blurred Vision	0.114	Effect
		50	Dry and Irritated Eyes	0.114	Effect

$p > 0.05$; N = 8

Table 4. Result of Experiment and Binomial Test of Visual Symptoms of Flow Rate (FR) of Virtual Object

second per piece (FR 5) and ten second per piece (FR 10); corresponding to virtual object in sight every five second and ten second respectively. Statistical binomial test at 5% significant level shows that both types of flow rates have an effect on the users, in which 75% of the users experienced symptoms of eyestrain and 50% of the users also experienced blurred vision and dry and irritated eyes symptoms.

3.5 Effect of speed of virtual object motion

Table 5 shows the result of the experiment on the effect of speed of virtual object on the subjects. Two levels of speed were investigated, that is slow motion (0.050) and fast motion (0.100). The result of statistical binomial test at 5% significant level proves that both speeds have an effect to the users where both slow and fast motion caused the same visual symptoms i.e. eyestrain, blurred vision, and dry and irritated symptoms.

No.	Level of Speed	Observation Proportion (%)	Symptoms	Exact Sig. (1-tailed)	Decision
1.	Low Speed	83	Eyestrain	0.534	Effect
		50	Blurred Vision	0.169	Effect
		67	Dry and Irritated Eyes	0.466	Effect
2.	High Speed	75	Eyestrain	0.633	Effect
		50	Blurred Vision	0.114	Effect
		50	Dry and Irritated Eyes	0.114	Effect

$p > 0.05$; N = 8

Table 5. Result of Experiment and Binomial Test of Visual Symptoms of Speed of a Virtual Object

No.	Level of Resolution	Observation Proportion (%)	Symptoms	Exact Sig. (1-tailed)	Decision
			LCD		
1.	High Resolution	56	Eyestrain	0.166	Effect
2.	Medium Resolution	89	Eyestrain	0.300	Effect
3	Low Resolution	56	Eyestrain	0.166	Effect
			CRT		
4.	High Resolution	67	Eyestrain	0.399	Effect
5.	Medium Resolution	67	Eyestrain	0.399	Effect
		56	Dry and Irritated Eyes	0.166	Effect
6.	Low Resolution	67	Eyestrain	0.399	Effect
		56	Dry and Irritated Eyes	0.166	Effect

$p > 0.05$; N = 8

Table 6. Result of Experiment and Binomial Test of Visual Symptoms of Resolution of Display Type

3.6 Effect of resolution of display type to visual symptoms

Table 6 shows the result of experiment on the effect of display resolution on the subjects. Three level of resolution were investigated for both the liquid crystal display (LCD) and cathode ray tube (CRT) displays, which are high resolution, medium resolution and low resolution. The result of statistical binomial test at 5% significant level found that the overall level of resolution using either the LCD or CRT displays causes eyestrain symptoms to the users with more than 56% experiencing eyestrain. Others effect such as dry and irritated eyes symptoms were experienced by 56% of users when interacting with medium and low resolution CRT display.

3.7 Effect of contrast ratio

The result on the effect of contrast ratio to visual symptoms is described in Table 7. There are three kind of contrast ratio investigated. They are -50.83%, +24.58% and 0%. The ratio can vary from 100% (positive) to zero for targets darker than the background, and from zero to minus infinity (-∞) for targets brighter than the background (Grether and Baker, 1972). Statistical binomial test at 5% significant level shows that all contrast ratios causes eyestrain symptoms (75% of users). Blurred vision and dry and irritated eyes symptoms were experienced by 63% and 50% of users at contrast ratios of --50.83% and 0% (or -0.56%) respectively.

No.	Ratio of Contrast	Observation Proportion (%)	Symptoms	Exact Sig. (1-tailed)	Decision
1.	-50.83%	75	Eyestrain	0.633	Effect
		63	Blurred Vision	0.321	Effect
2.	+24.58%	75	Eyestrain	0.633	Effect
3.	0% (-0.56%)	75	Eyestrain	0.633	Effect
		50	Dry and Irritated Eyes	0.114	Effect

$p > 0.05$; N = 8

Table 7. Result of Experiment and Binomial Test of Visual Symptoms of Contrast Ratio

4. Discussion

One of the parameters of cyber sickness is visual symptoms (Barret, 2004). In his handbook, Anshel, J. (2005) mentioned that visual symptoms can vary but these mostly include eyestrain, headache, blurred vision, dry and irritated eyes, double vision, colour distortion and light sensitivity. The symptom most often occurs when the viewing demand of the task exceeds the visual abilities of the user. The viewing task is influenced by the design of the virtual environment viewed or interacted. This research has identified some attributes or variables of the VE that may cause the occurrence of visual symptoms.

4.1 Analysis of the colour types for the virtual background design

Statistical binomial test on five types of colour of virtual background (Table 1) shows that the colour type inflicts the users with eyestrain and blurred vision symptoms. Fig. 2 (a) and

(b) exhibit the levels of eyestrain and blurred vision symptoms experienced by users when interacting with the VE. Only the red colour significantly resulted in blurred vision. This might be caused by the red colour causing discomfort to the eyes when a virtual object is in motion. The colour is also quite glaring in such a way that it would be difficult for the eyes

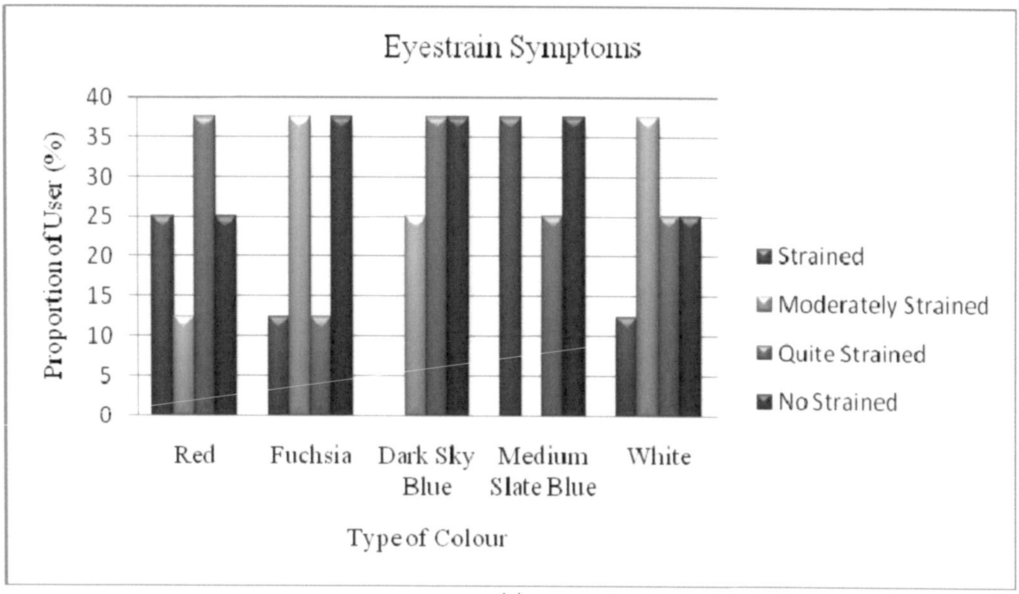

(a)

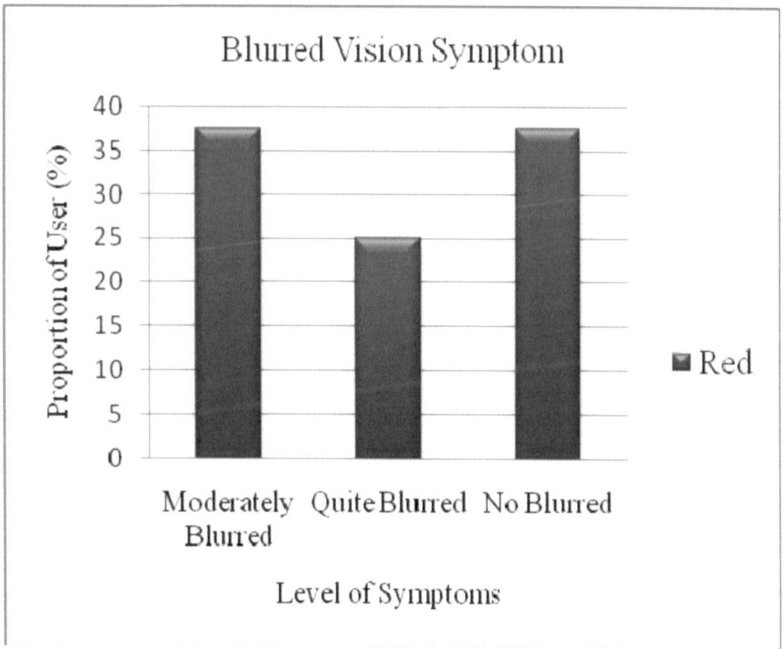

(b)

Fig. 2. (a) Level of eyestrain symptoms (b) Level of blurred vision symptoms to focus on a virtual object. Others types of colours also generally causes eyestrain symptoms. Ergonomics recommendation on background colours stipulates the use of a design that is able to reduce or minimize the incidence of visual symptoms. No strain and no blur level is the target in the design of the background colour. Thus Red, Fuchsia, Dark Sky Blue, Medium Slate Blue and White colours must be changed to a smoother and softer colour type that can alleviate visual symptoms incidence.

4.2 Analysis of the virtual lighting level

Results of statistical binomial test in Table 2 demonstrated the effect of brightness level of the virtual light on the occurrence of visual symptoms incidence. The level of brightness affects the eyes when tracking virtual objects in the VE. A darker light level (10%) or higher bright level (100%) can induce eyestrain and dry and irritated eyes symptoms as well as light sensitivity symptom. This is because the eyes are forced to focus causing strain to the eyes as well as dryness and irritation and decrease the sensitivity to light. Fig.3 (a), (b) and (c) describes the level of symptoms occurring in the human visual system. No effect (no strained, no dry, no glare) is the best condition of virtual lighting to be considered as one of the attributes in designing a VE.

4.3 Analysis of the effect Field of View (FOV)

Table 3 is the result of statistical binomial test of the effect of field of view (FOV) on users. It shows that the degree of visual field can develop incidence of visual disorder especially eyestrain, blurred vision and dry and irritated eyes. Therefore the degree of FOV has to be taken into account when designing a VE. It can be seen that 120^0 of FOV causes 50% of the users to suffer eyestrain symptoms as compared to the 85^0 of FOV. On the other hand, dry

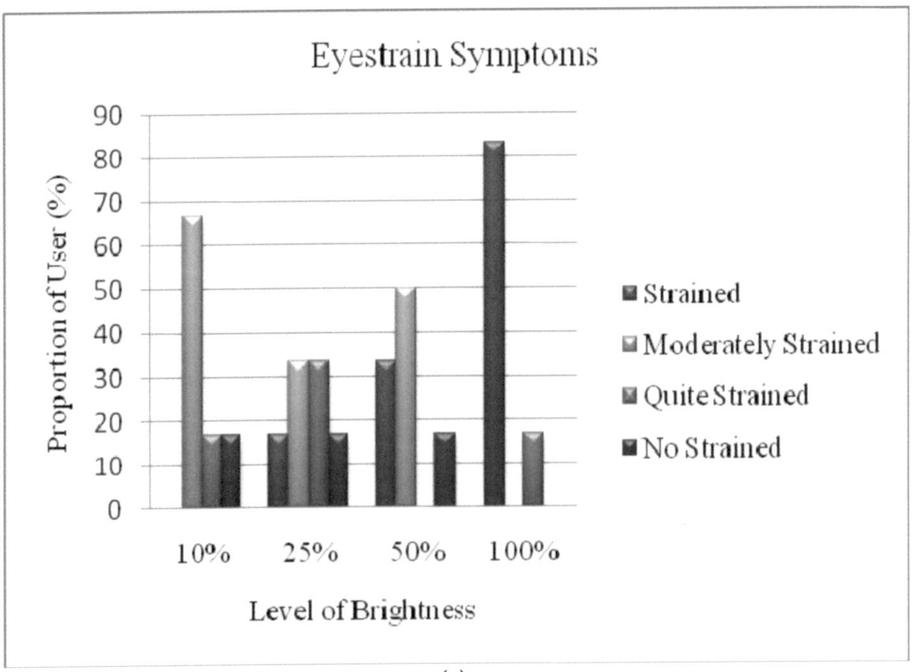

(a)

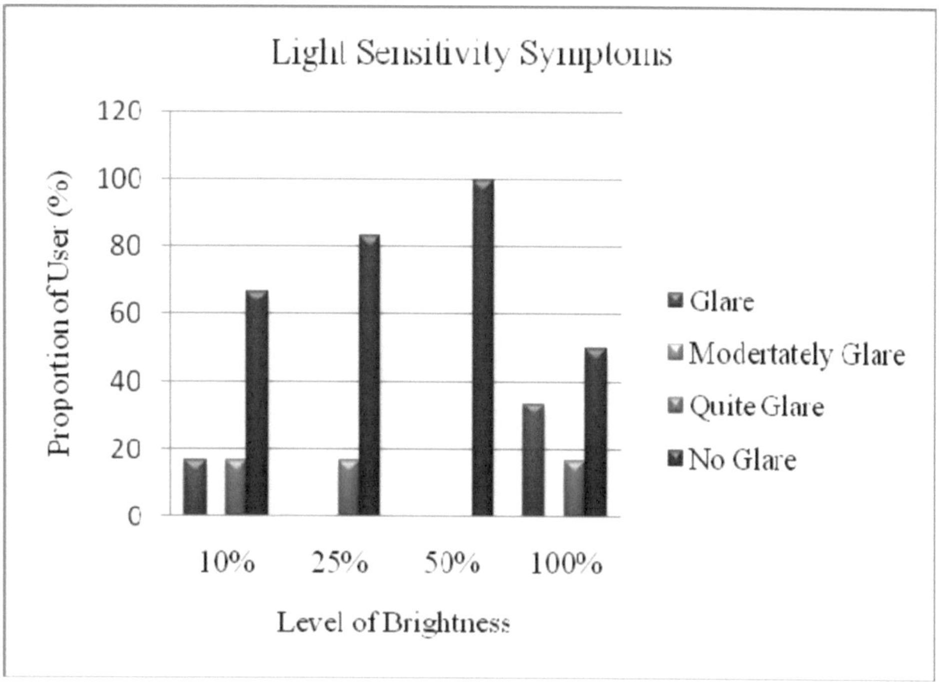

(b)

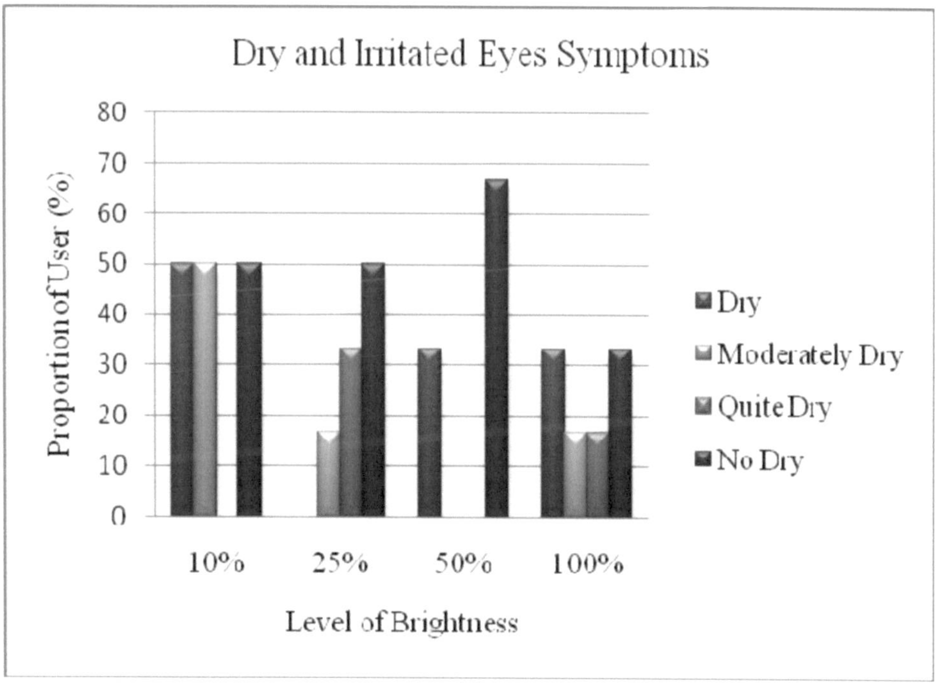

(c)

Fig. 3. (a) Level of eyestrain symptoms (b) Level of Light Sensitivity symptoms (c) Level of dry and irritated eyes symptoms

and irritated eyes symptoms were experienced by 63% of the users when using 120⁰ of FOV higher than they were using 85⁰ of FOV. Thus a wider of FOV or narrower of FOV will cause users to suffer one of the visual symptoms. It is because of both conditions require the eyes to focus. Thus it is essential to determine what FOV is required to reduce these symptoms. Fig.4 (a), (b) and (c) describes the levels of symptoms occurring for eyestrain, blurred vision and dry and irritated eyes symptoms respectively. For the eyestrain symptoms, 120° of FOV is better than 85° because about 50 % users did experience any incidence. On the contrary, 120° of FOV is not acceptable compared to 85° for dry and irritated eyes symptoms. This is because 50% of users did not experience any eye symptoms when using 85° of FOV.

4.4 Analysis of the Flow Rate (FR) of the virtual objects

Flow rate (FR) is the rate at which subsequent flow of the virtual object can be generated per unit time. Result of statistical binomial test in Table 4 have found that the flow rate of virtual object have the effect on the incidence of eyestrain, blurred vision and dry and irritated eyes symptoms. This is because it affects the ability of the eyes to see the virtual objects as it is being generated so that the eyes experienced strain, blur and also dryness or irritation during that period. Fig. 5 (a), (b), and (c) depict the level of the symptoms experienced by users. The effect can be minimized by designing the appropriate flow rate of the virtual object generated. A flow rate at 5 seconds per piece is better than a flow rate of 10 seconds per piece to avoid blurred vision symptoms. This is because more than 69% of users do not suffer this condition at this flow rate.

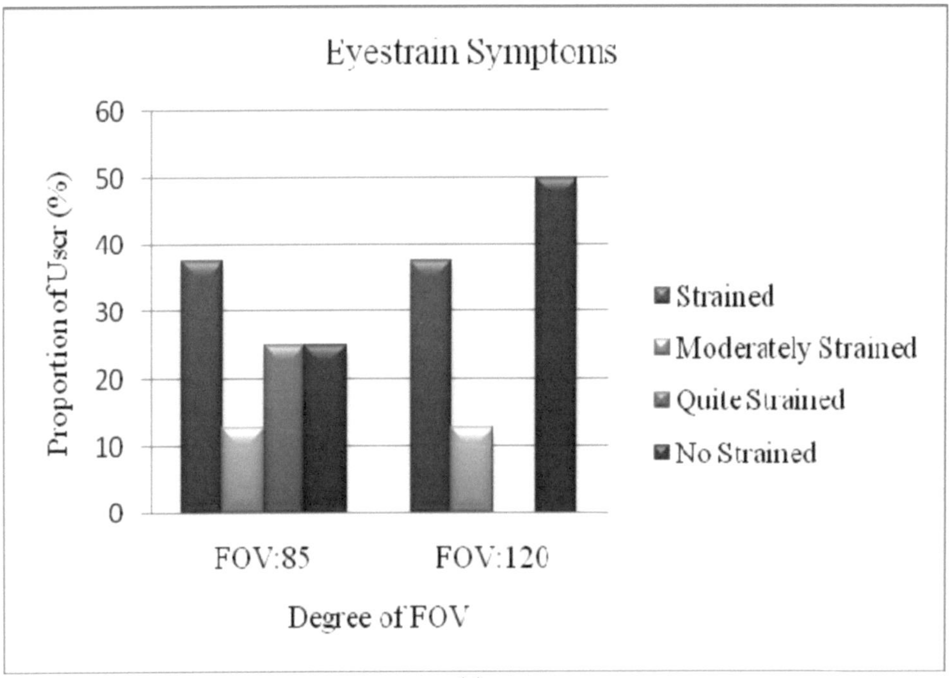

(a)

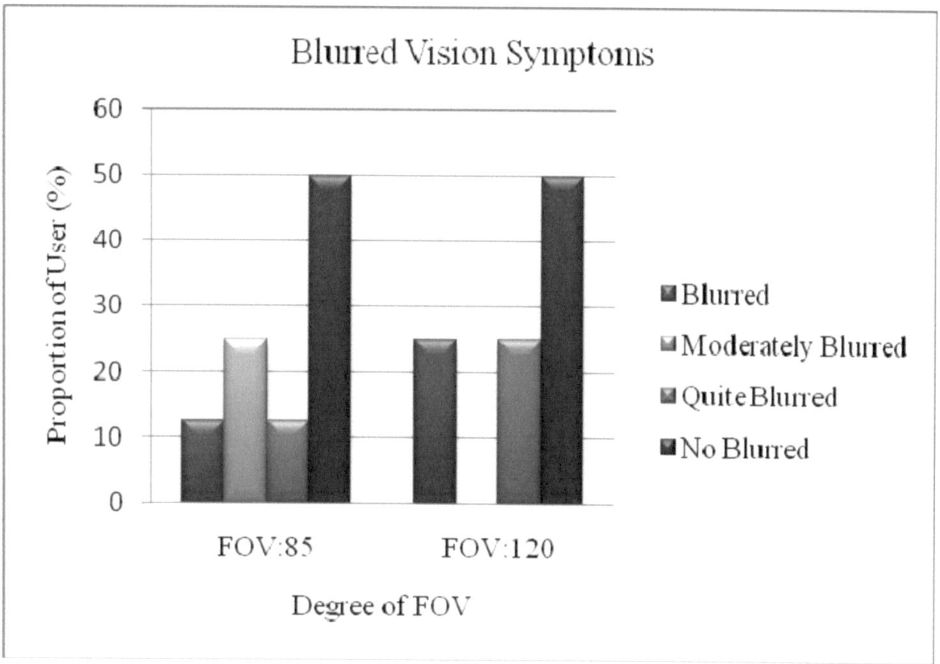

(b)

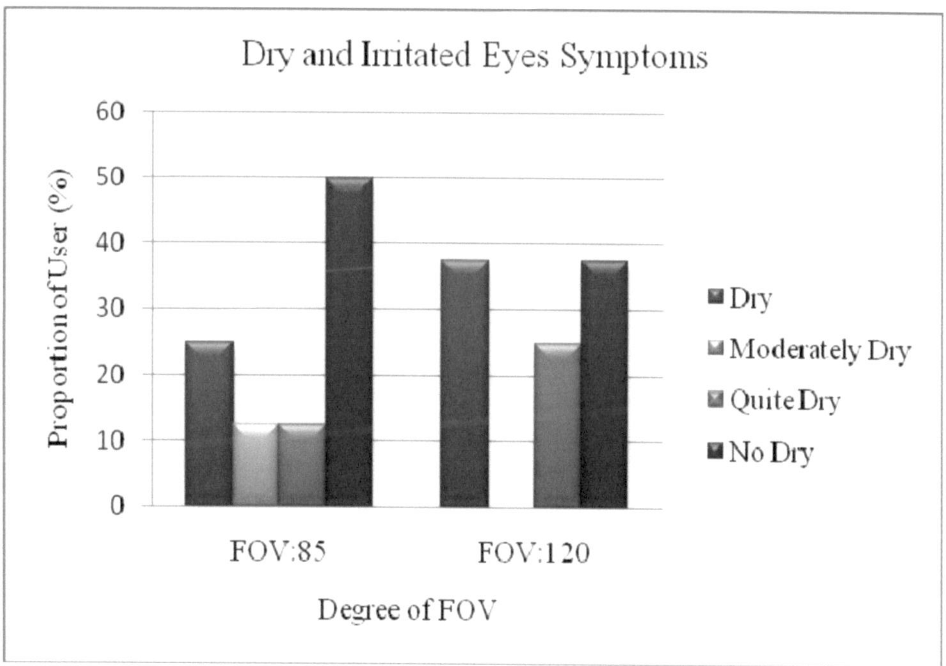

(c)

Fig. 4. (a) Level of eyestrain symptoms (b) Level of blurred vision symptoms (c) Level of dry and irritated eyes symptoms

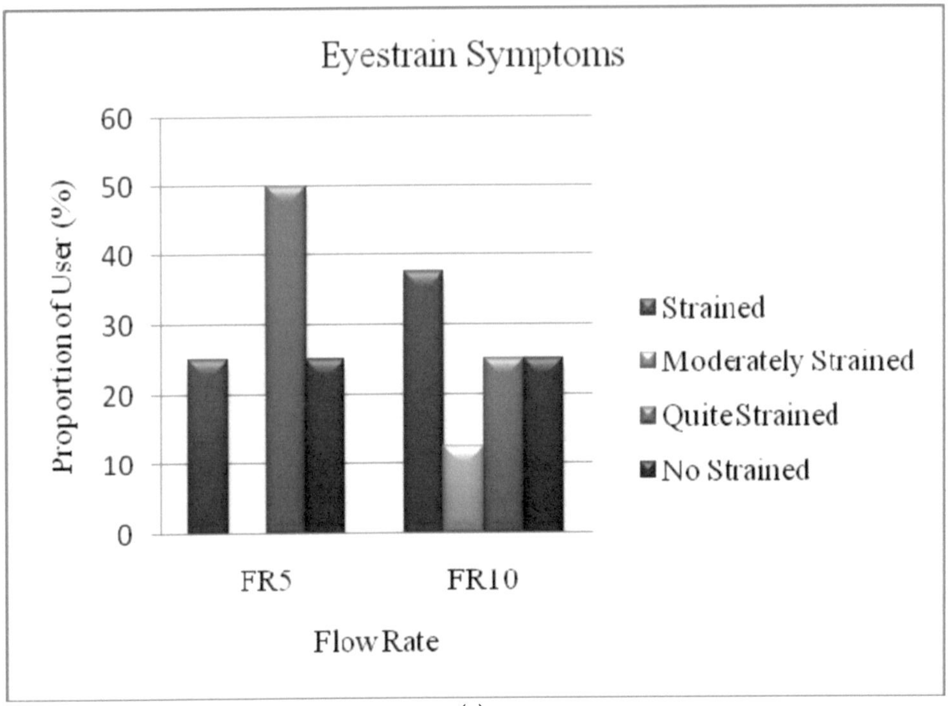
Eyestrain Symptoms
60
50
40
30
20
10
0
Proportion of User (%)
FR5
FR10
Flow Rate
Strained
Moderately Strained
Quite Strained
No Strained

(a)

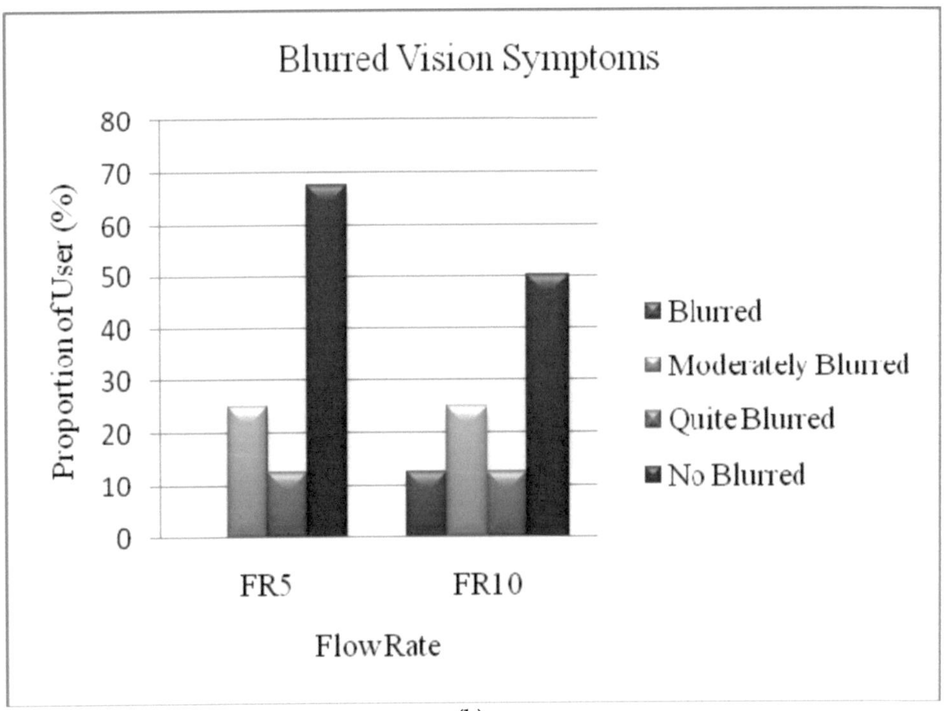
Blurred Vision Symptoms
80
70
60
50
40
30
20
10
0
Proportion of User (%)
FR5
FR10
Flow Rate
Blurred
Moderately Blurred
Quite Blurred
No Blurred

(b)

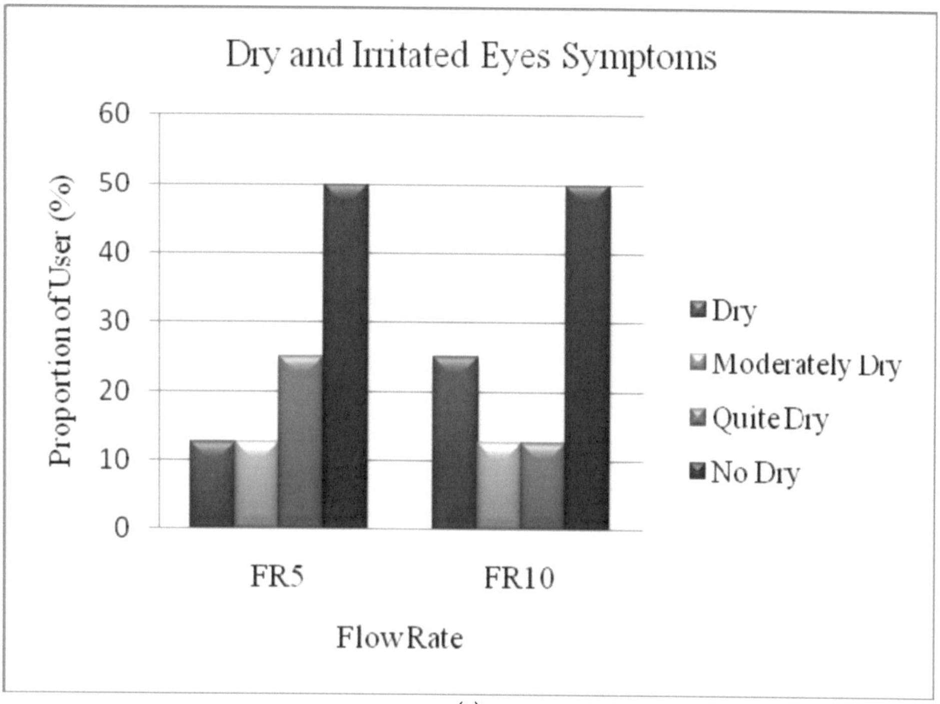

(c)

Fig. 5. (a) Level of eyestrain symptom (b) Level of blurred vision symptoms (c) Level of dry and irritated eyes symptoms

4.5 Analysis of the speed of the virtual objects motion

Different speeds of the virtual object motion in the VE were investigated. Statistical binomial test (Table 5) shows that users suffers from eyestrain, blurred vision and dry and irritated eyes when interacting with virtual objects at low and high speed of motion. This is because the eyes are trying to focus on the virtual object in motion which requires good coordination with the hand when performing task. Figures 6 (a), (b) and (c) shows the level of symptoms experienced by the users. It can be seen that the speed of virtual object motion needs to be considered as an attribute in designing of a VE. A higher speed of the virtual object motion is better than a lower speed. This is because at higher speeds there is no effect on users whether for eyestrain symptoms or dry and irritated eyes symptoms compared with lower speeds.

4.6 Analysis of the resolution of display

Many research have been conducted and have concluded that working with LCD screen is much more comfortable compared to working with CRT screens (Alstrom, et al, 1992; Saito, et al, 1993; Shieh,K.K., and Lin, C.C., 2000). This is contributed to the luminance contrast and limited viewing angle of LCD screens (Snyder, 1988). Additionally, the TFT-LCD screen seems to be the preferred technology by users for identifying letters on VDTs (Shieh, K.K. and Lin, C.C.,2000). In the current research, statistical binomial test (Table 6) have found that eyestrain and dry and irritated symptoms were experienced by users at three different resolution (high, medium and low resolution) whilst dry and irritated eyes incidence were experienced by users with the CRT screens at medium and low level of resolution only. This indicates that the resolution of display needs to be considered as one of the attributes in designing a VE.

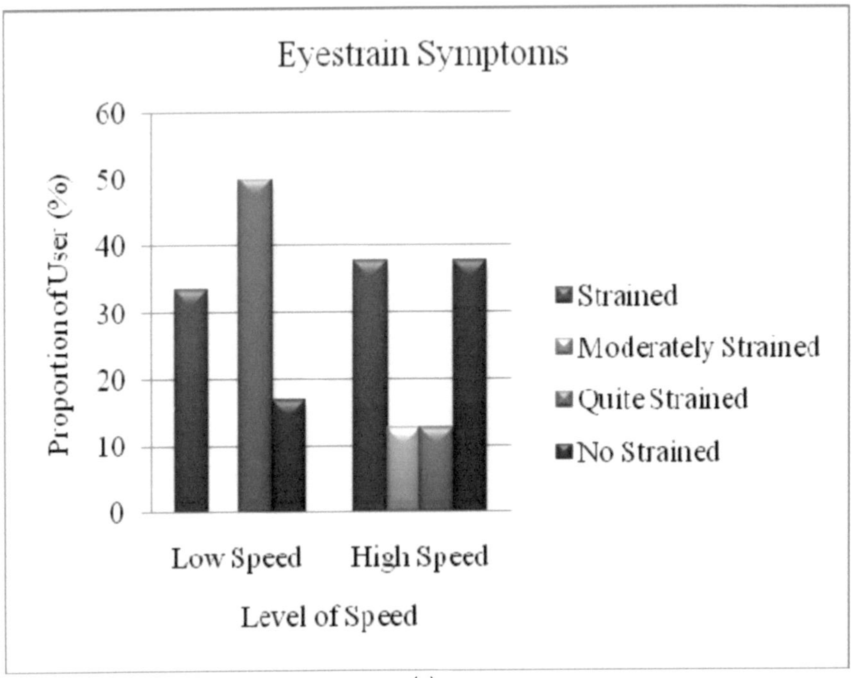

(a)

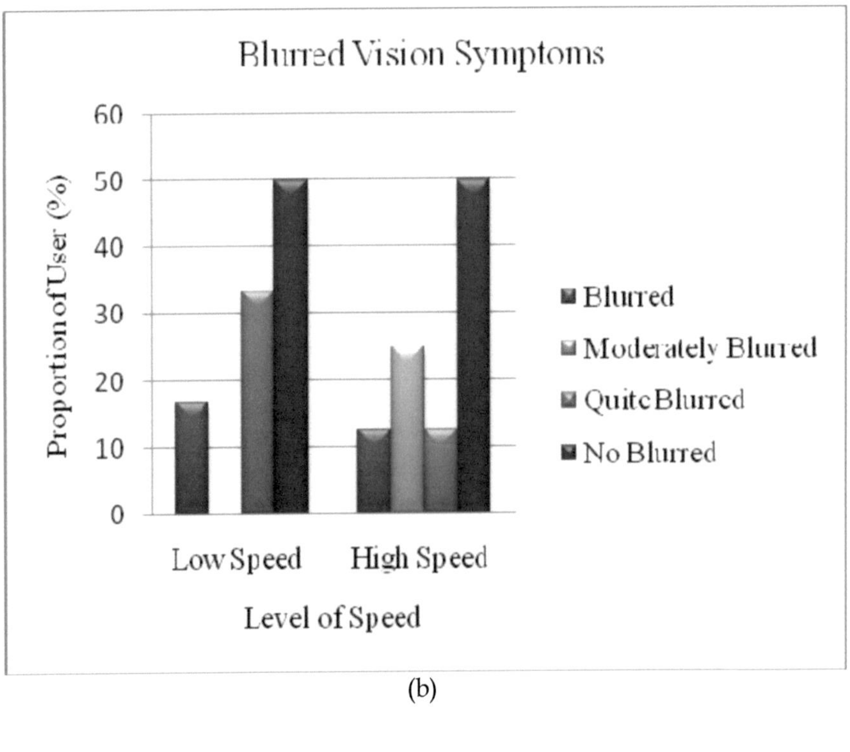

(b)

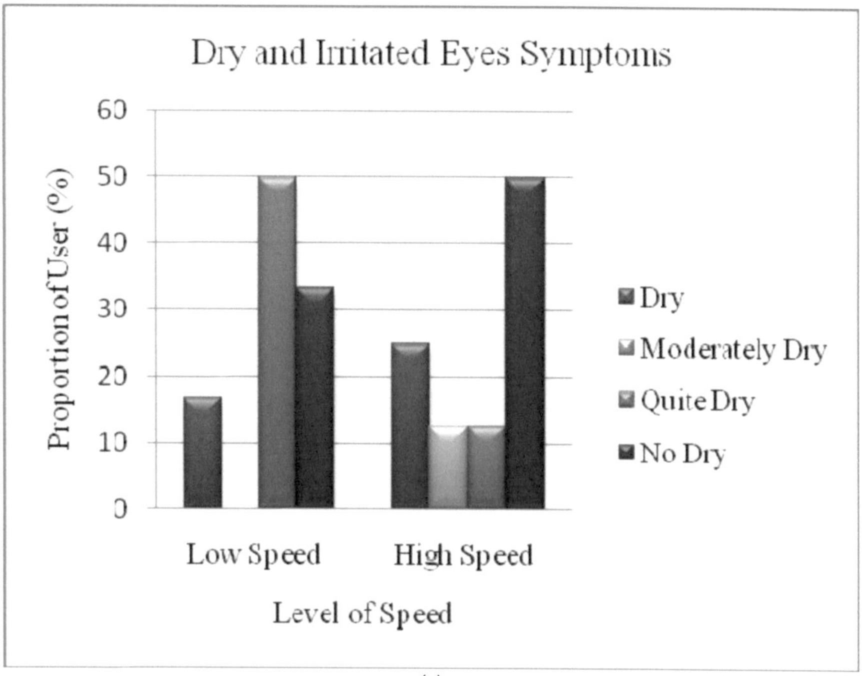

(c)

Fig. 6. (a) Level of eyestrain symptoms (b) Level of blurred vision symptoms (c) Level of dry and irritated eyes symptoms

Figures 7 (a), (b) and (c) shows the level of eyes symptoms for different resolution. To avoid eyestrain symptoms, high and low resolutions are preferred for LCD screen because more than

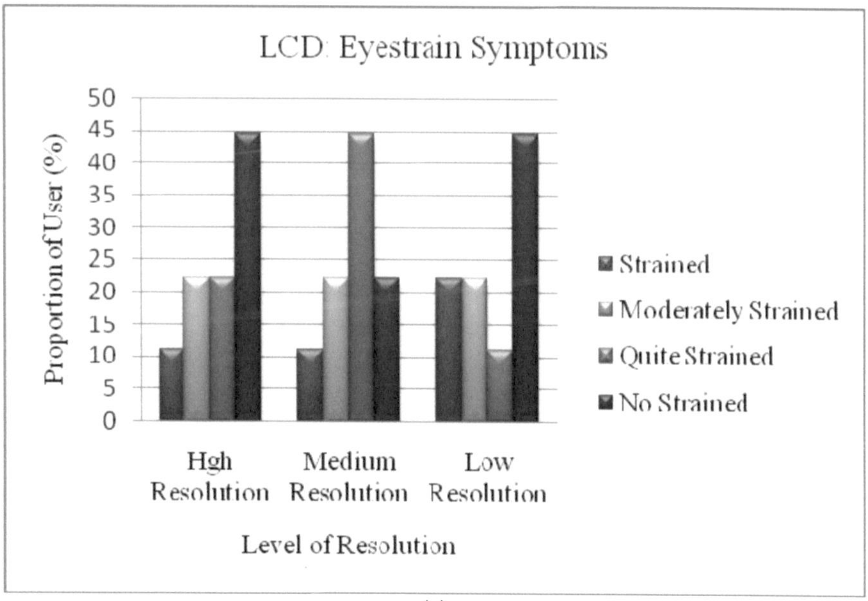

(a)

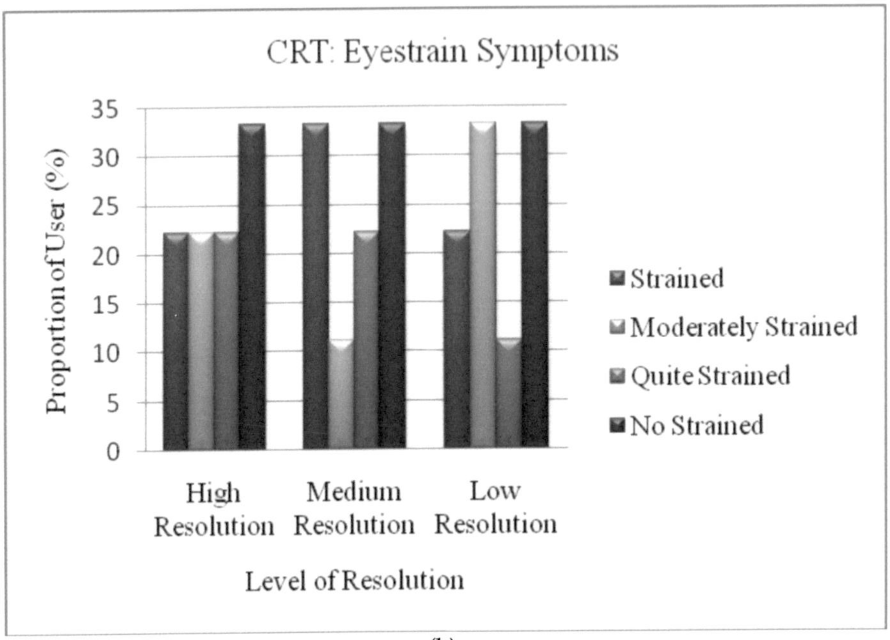

(b)

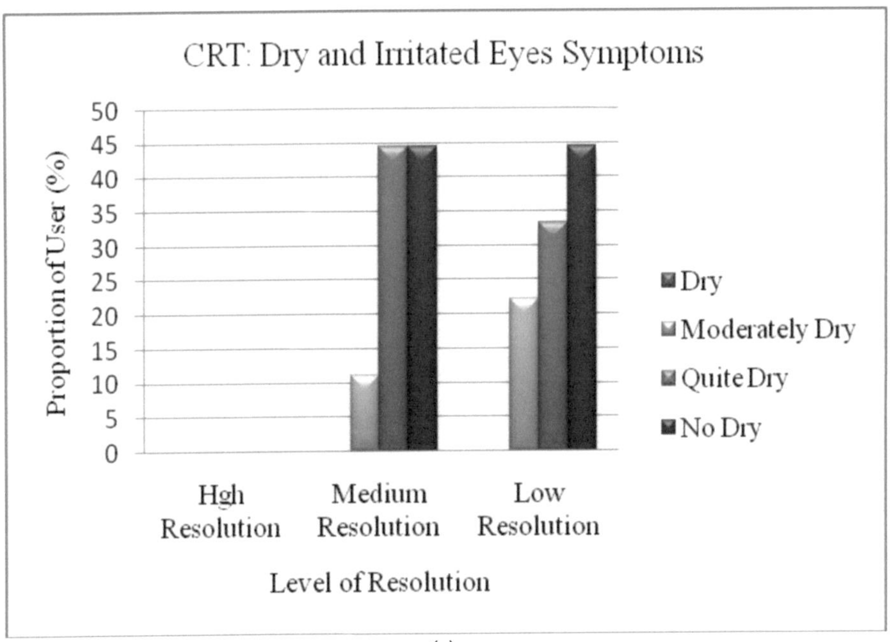

(c)

Fig. 7. (a) Level of eyestrain symptom on LCD (b) Level of eyestrain symptoms on CRT (c) Level of dry and irritated eyes symptoms on CRT

40 % of user did not experience any strain. But for CRT screen, all resolution level can be used because there were no incidence eyestrain symptoms or dry and irritated eyes symptoms.

4.7 Analysis of the contrast ratio between target and background

Figures 8 (a), (b) and (c) describes the level of incidence experienced by users for different contrast ratios. The result of statistical binomial test in Table 7 shows that eyestrain was

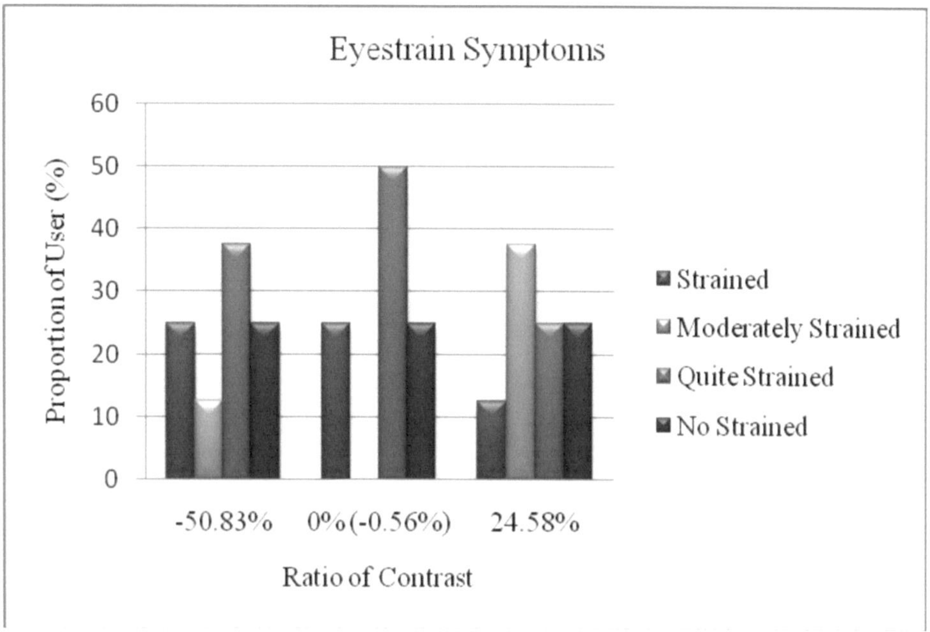

(a)

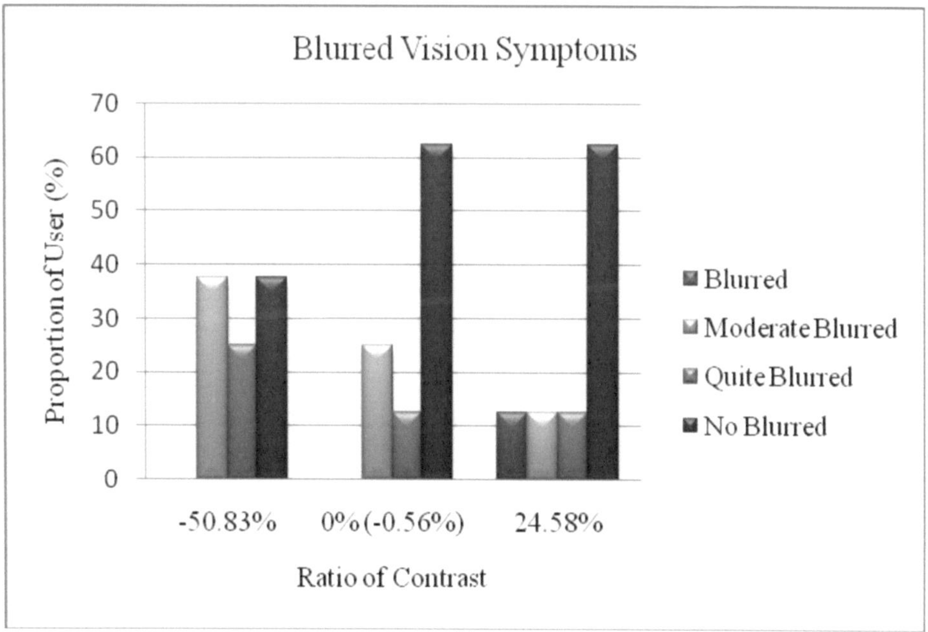

(b)

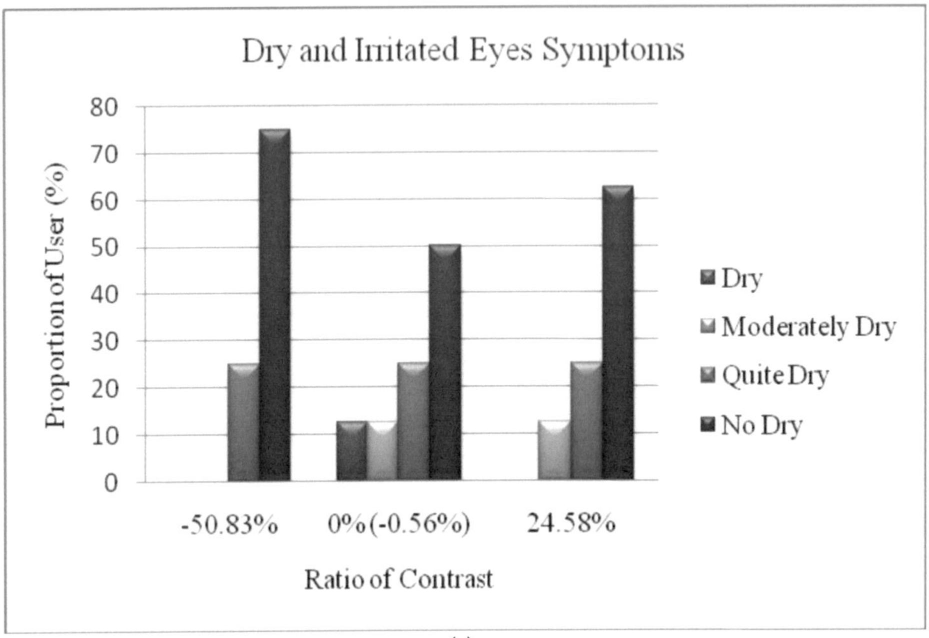

(c)

Fig. 8. (a) Level of eyestrain symptom (b) Level of blurred vision symptoms (c) Level of dry and irritated eyes symptoms

experienced by most users (75%) for all condition of contrast. While blurred vision was experienced by 63% of the users at -50.83% contrast ratios and dry and irritated eyes was experienced by 50% of the users at 0% (-0.56%) contrast ratios. This is due to the contrast condition affecting the ability of the eyes to distinguish the target from the background. Thus the contrast ratio should be considered as one of the attributes or variables in designing a virtual environment.

5. Conclusion

It can be concluded that:

1. The design of a virtual environment design is influenced by several attributes such as colour background, virtual lighting, field of view, flow rate, speed of virtual object, resolution of display and contrast ratio. These attributes significantly affect users particularly with eyestrain symptoms.
2. Blurred vision symptoms are significantly affected by several attributes of the VE design i.e. the red colour of the background, the field of view (FOV), the flow rate at ten seconds per piece (FR10), the speed of virtual object motion, and the contrast ratio at -50.83%.
3. Dry and irritated eyes symptoms are also significantly affected by several attributes of the VE design i.e. the virtual lighting at 10% and 100% levels of brightness, field of view (FOV) for all conditions, flow rate (FR) for all conditions, the speed of virtual motion for all speeds, the resolution of CRT screen at medium and low resolution and a contras ratio of 0%.

4. Virtual lighting at 100% level of brightness significantly affects visual symptoms, particularly light sensitivity symptoms of the users.

6. Acknowledgements

The authors wish to acknowledge all of our participants who made this investigation possible. Appreciation is also accorded to University of Malaya for funding this project as well as to the Islamic University of Indonesia Yogyakarta Indonesia.

7. References

Ahlstrom, G., Lowden, A., Malmkvist, H., Schenkman, B.,Stoehr, R., Weselka, R., 1992. Field study of a new type ofcomputer screen technology. In: Shieh, K.K., and Lin, C.C., (2000). Effects of screen type, ambient illumination, and color combination on VDT visual performance and subjective preference. International Journal of Industrial Ergonomics . 26. 527-536

Anshel, J., (2005). Visual Ergonomics Handbook. New York. Taylor & Francis Group

ANSI/HFES100.(2007).National Standars for Human Factors Engineering of Computer Workstations.HFES. p. 76

Barrett, Judy.(2004), Side effects of Virtual Environments: A Review of the Literature, DSTO-TR-1419,pp. 1-47.

Colombo, G., And Cugini, U.(2005).Virtual human and prototypes to evaluate ergonomics and safety.Journal of Engineering Design.16(2). 195 - 207.

Courtney, A.J., (1986). Chinese population stereotypes: color associations. Human Factors 28 (1), 97–99

Dukic, T., Rönnäng, M., And Christmansson, M.(2007). Evaluation of ergonomics in a virtual manufacturing process.Journal of Engineering Design.18(2). 125 - 137.

Grether, W.F. and Baker, C.A.(1972). Visual presentation of information. In: Tayyari, F. and Smith, J.L., (1997). Occupational Ergonomics; Principles and applications. London. Chapman & Hall.

Hu, B., Ma, L., Zhang, W., Salvendy, G., Chablat, C., Bennis, F.(2011).Predicting real-world ergonomic measurements by simulation in a virtual environment.International Journal of Industrial Ergonomics. 41. 64 - 71.

Lin, C.C.(2003).Effects of contrast ratio and text color on visual performance with TFT-LCD.International Journal of Industrial Ergonomics. 31. 65–72

Menozzi, M.,Napflin, U., Krueger, H.(1999). CRT versus LCD: A pilot study on visual performance and suitability oftwo display technologies for use in office work. Display.20. 3 - 10

Nichols, S.,(1999). Physical ergonomics of virtual environment use.Applied Ergonomics. 30. 79 - 90.

Pappas, M., Karabatsou, V., Mavrikios, D., Chryssolouris, G.(2005).Ergonomic evaluation of virtual assembly tasks. *Digital Enterprise Technology.*

Saito, S., Taptagaporn, S., Salvendy, G., (1993). Visual comfort in using different VDT screens. International Journal of Human Computer Interaction. 1 (4), 313-323

Shaikh, I., Jayaram, U., Jayaram, S., Palmer, C.(2004). Participatory ergonomics using VR integrated with analysis tools. Proceedings of the 2004 Winter Simulation Conference. USA.

Shieh, K.K., and Lin, C.C., (2000). Effects of screen type, ambient illumination, and color combination on VDT visual performance and subjective preference. International Journal of Industrial Ergonomics . 26. 527-536

Snyder, H.L., (1988). Image quality. In: Helander, M. (Ed.),Handbook of HumanComputer Interaction. Amsterdam. Elsevier

Stanney, K.M., Mourant,R.R., Kennedy, R.S.(1998). Human factors issues in virtual environments: A review of the literature. *Presence*. 7. 327-351.

Stewart, T.(1995). Ergonomics standards concerning human system interaction. AppliedErgonomic.26 (4). 271 - 274

Tayyari, F. and Smith, J.L., (1997).Occupational Ergonomics; Principles and applications. London. Chapman & Hall

Wilson, J.R.(1999).Virtual environment application and applied ergonomics.*Applied Ergonomics*.30. 3 – 9.

10

The Virtual Reality of Work – How to Create a Workplace that Enhances Well-Being for a Mobile Employee

Ursula Hyrkkänen[1], Suvi Nenonen[2] and Inka Kojo[2]
[1]*Aalto University and Turku University of Applied Sciences*
[2]*Aalto University*
Finland

1. Introduction

New developments in information and communication technology have changed the way people approach their life and work. Mobile virtual work is no longer bound to fixed locations as utilizing information and communication technology allows people to function freely in various environments. The employee is considered as mobile, when he works more than ten hours per week outside of the primary workplace and uses information and communication technologies for collaboration (Gareis et al., 2006; Vartiainen & Hyrkkänen 2010). Virtual reality (Fox et al., 2009), as an environment related to the new 'anytime anywhere work', can be called *the virtual workplace*. The virtual workplace provides connectivity through different size of devices and is accessed by different interfaces when supporting the performance of both individual and collaborative activities (Nenonen et al., 2009).

The interest of this article is the interrelationship between the physical and the virtual workplace not only with regard to their infrastructure, but also to their social and cultural contexts. Both prerequisites connected to the virtual workplace and its actual use can be challenging. It could be claimed, for instance, that simultaneous physical and virtual co-presence is generally not yet mastered in an effective way and that there still exist certain bottlenecks for a mobile employee in entering virtual reality.

Vischer (2007, 2008) has analyzed the workplace as a physical, functional and psychological entity in order to identify features related to comfort and fit between a workplace and an employee (fig 1). When the environment sets inappropriate or excessive demands to users, in spite of their adaptation and adjustment behaviors, it manifests the concept of misfit. In a good fit there is a balance between a person's abilities, skills, degree of control and decision latitude and the work environment's demands, complexity, expectations and challenges. The nature of person-environment transactions arouses the sensation of either comfort or stress. Comfort may be considered as the fit of the user to the environment in the context of work. (Vischer 2005, 2007, see also Dainoff et al. 2007.)

According to Vischer (2007), environmental comfort encompasses three hierarchical categories: the physical, functional, and psychological. Physical comfort relates to basic human needs, i.e. safety, hygiene and accessibility. These needs are responded to by applying building codes and standards. Functional comfort is defined in terms of support for users' performance in work-related tasks and activities. Psychological comfort is related to feelings of belonging, ownership and control over workspace. We have expanded the category of psychological comfort and fit also to cover the social factors, and named the third category psychosocial comfort and fit.

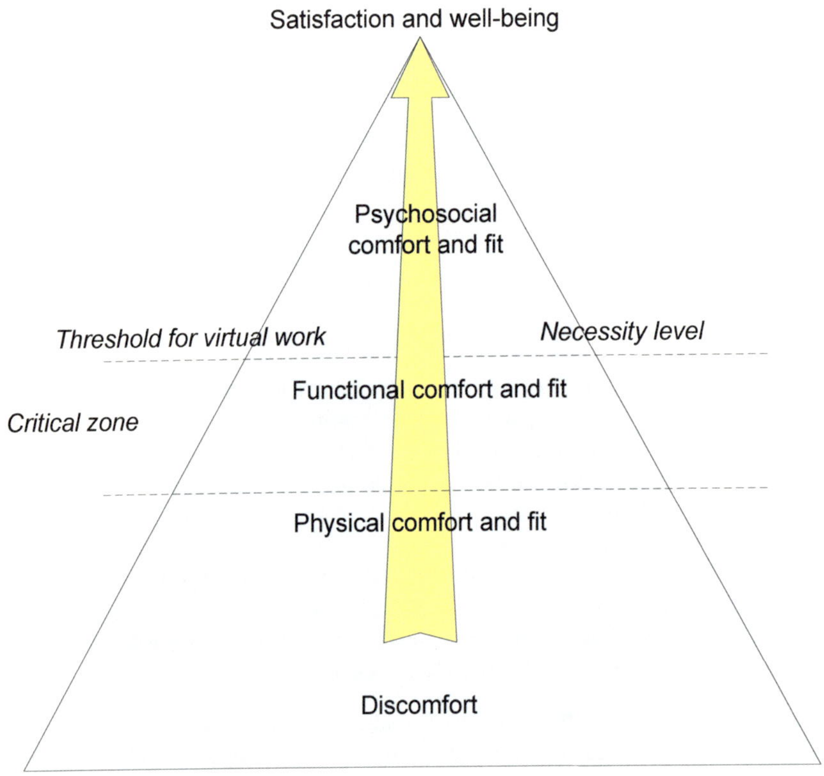

Fig. 1. Vischer's (2005) model of comfort and fit modified (Hyrkkänen & Nenonen, 2011) for assessing virtual work places

Vischer's user-centered model (2007) merges environmental aspects with psychological aspects in a dynamic way. Vischer has developed this abovementioned model for assessing the fit or misfit of physical workspace. We have tested and developed its applicability for assessing virtual places (see Hyrkkänen & Nenonen 2011). In this article, the virtual workplace will be analyzed as a three-level entity that enhances well-being from the point of view of the mobile employee.

The purpose of this chapter is to explore what are the elements of the virtual workplace that either hinder or enable productive mobile virtual work processes and well-being at work. The script will proceed as follows: first, there will be a broad literature inspection of the physical, functional and psychosocial elements of comfort and fit which either hinder or enable productive mobile virtual work. Secondly the method and findings of a preliminary study called "virtual me" will be presented for enlivening the literature review findings with vivid up to date data.

2. Background

The basic proposition in the background of this research follows the idea of Vischer's modified and tested model (Hyrkkänen & Nenonen 2011). The factors of fit and misfit are in the upcoming chapters examined from the physical, functional and psychosocial perspectives.

2.1 The elements of physical comfort and fit in the virtual workplace of a mobile employee

The elements of physical spaces and places impact on the possibilities for effective virtual work. Constraints of physical places hamper the mobile worker's way to virtual work places. It could be claimed that the access to the virtual reality is restricted in many ways by poor and out of date working environments, their lay outs, electrical designs and furniture. The reviewed articles demonstrated and confirmed this by describing many situations where the mobile employees met physical hindrances.

Despite the increase of "hot desking", many odd places are still offered for building up a work station, especially if the mobile employee is an occasional visitor (Hislop & Axtell, 2009; Mark & Su, 2010) at his own company's or customer's premises. At public places, mobile employees have even reported the need to compete for electrical power due to a limited amount of power outlets (Axtell et al., 2008; Brown & O'Hara, 2003; Forlano b, 2008; Mark & Su, 2010).

When executing the anywhere working style, the employee will undoubtedly encounter many physical places that are not in the first hand designed primarily for working purposes. This is likely to happen at airports, in different means of transportation, in cafeterias or in hotel rooms (Axtell et al., 2008; Breure & van Meel, 2003; Brown & O'Hara, 2003; Laurier, 2004; Laurier & Philo, 2003). Their furniture is primarily designed for travelling or for leisure time activities. They are hardly convertible for working. For example, in trains there are no flat surfaces large enough for laying down portable mobile devices (Perry & Brodie, 2006).

In the physical fit of virtual reality lies also the question of its appropriateness to the human sensory system. For example visual and auditory problems may arise. For ensuring the success of work, mobile employees carry many tools with them - including redundant tools to be on the safe side. To avoid letting the burden grow beyond measure, increasingly smaller-sized devices are selected. With small size you inevitably choose small displays - and visual difficulties. (Axtell et al., 2008; Brown & O'Hara, 2003; Felstead et al., 2005; Hislop & Axtell, 2009; Mark & Su, 2010; Perry et al., 2001; Perry & Brodie, 2006; Vartiainen & Hyrkkänen, 2010; Venezia & Allee, 2007.)

Noisy physical environments may disturb and interrupt concentrated working in virtual reality. Especially in public places, in trains and airplanes, tourists and neighbors near the mobile worker may disturb the work (Axtell et al., 2008; Breure & van Meel, 2003). On the other hand, a smooth level of discussing voices e.g. in a cafeteria may help the worker to relax and lose him/herself in virtual reality (Forlano, 2008a; Rasila et al. 2011).

The contradictory relation between the physical and virtual worlds might cause the misfit which may also lead to safety risks, e.g. when driving a car (Laurier & Philo, 2003; Perry &

Brodie, 2006). Switching concentration from driving to working with ICT-tools causes hazards and is therefore for safety reasons limited by law and norms. (Hislop &Axtell, 2009).

2.2 The elements of functional comfort and fit in the virtual workplace of a mobile employee

The functional fit or misfit of the workplace can be assessed by defining the degree to which occupants can either conserve their attention and energy for their tasks or expend it to cope with poor environmental conditions. Related to the functional fit of virtual places, the connectivity problems that cause disturbances and hindrances to virtual work flow are crucial. The maturity and sophistication of the ICT infrastructure is one of the key factors. For example, the Wi-Fi connections are not yet fully developed in all environments (Axtell, et al., 2008).

Some of the connectivity problems are derived from the limited skills of mobile workers in employing virtual settings and infrastructure (Hallford, 2005; Mann & Holdsworth, 2003; Mark & Su, 2010; Perry & Brodie, 2006; Vartiainen & Hyrkkänen, 2010; Venezia & Allee, 2007). Time constraints and tight schedules of mobile employees together with time-consuming downloads of connections and programs also make it unreasonable to start virtual work (Axtell et al., 2008; Brown & O'Hara, 2003; Breure & van Meel, 2005; Mark & Su, 2010; Perry et al., 2001; Perry & Brodie, 2006).

The security regulations of mobile employees' own or their customers' companies may hinder the access to and functioning in virtual places (Brown & O'Hara, 2003; Mark & Su, 2010;). In addition very expensive connections may present a barrier to employing functional connections (Axtell el al., 2008).

2.3 The elements of psychosocial comfort and fit in the virtual workplace of a mobile employee

In Vischer's (2005, 2007) environmental comfort model, psychological comfort links psychosocial aspects with environmental design and management of workspace through the concepts of *territoriality, privacy and control.*

A sense of territory is associated with feelings of belonging and ownership. Territoriality of the virtual work place may be considered as a different composition of public, semipublic and private virtual places. Public shared places and platforms include the internet, many applications of social media and interfaces which are open for everyone. Semipublic areas include applications and media channels which demand an identity but are still shared among a defined group of users. The private zone requires a personal key and passwords and the content is not shared or if so, the principles of sharing are decided by the individual user. Virtual territory is personalized by individual choices e.g. in screen savers, chosen applications and programs. The visual appearance is a significant factor indicating both individual ownership and social belonging e.g. to the organization (see Ettlinger 2008).

In many cases, the need for belonging will not come true in virtual spaces (Brown & O´Hara, 2003; Hallford, 2005; Mann & Hodsworth, 2003, Perry et al., 2001). The lack of belonging is affected also by limited access to colleagues and individuals, who are distant. This is the case of the mobile employee's physical world but also the case of virtual reality, e.g., when an employer attempts to avoid huge operating expenses (Axtell el al., 2008). Furthermore, the perceived problems of spreading tacit knowledge in virtual spaces (Hallford, 2005) can be seen as a factor of territoriality. The sense of presence is not easy to create.

According to Vischer (2007), privacy is best understood as the need to exercise control over one's accessibility to others. In virtual spaces and places there are, e.g., problems in controlling simultaneous co- and telepresence (Brown & O'Hara, 2003; Hallford, 2005; Green, 2002; Mark & Su, 2010; Tieze & Musson, 2005). In addition, the need for better privacy mastery is confronted (Axtell et al., 2008; Brown & O'Hara 2003; Breure & van Meel, 2003; Hislop & Axtell, 2009; Mark & Su, 2010; Perry & Brodie, 2006) e.g. when you are handling confidential things with your ICT tools.

In Vischer's model (2005), environmental control consists of mechanical or instrumental control, and empowerment. Instrumental control exists, if the employee masters his furniture, devices and tools. Empowerment as a form of environmental control arises from participation in the workplace decision making. The reviewed articles highlighted the lack of control in staying in virtual reality. The stress arose from expectations of continuous availability (Brown & O'Hara, 2003; Felstead et al., 2005; Hallford, 2005; Green, 2002; Mark & Su, 2010; Tietze & Musson 2005).

When comparing the factors identified in the reviewed articles to Vischer's psychosocial factors, the similarities are evident. Ensuring the psychosocial fit of a virtual workplace is the question of territoriality, privacy and control.

3. Method

In order to reflect the results of the literature review, a small scale empirical survey was carried out. The experience sampling method (ESM) was used as the research method. ESM refers to a technique that enables the capturing of people's behaviors, thoughts, or feelings as they occur in real time (Hektner et al. 2006).

The ESM research process consisted of five stages. In the first stage the design for the research was made and the diary booklet was designed and tested. In the second stage the subjects were contacted and the diary booklet was delivered to them. The sample of 20 employees (users) from different organizations participated. They were instructed to carefully enter all their actions and places they had been to in a diary booklet. The diary phase focused on what virtual devices and tools are used and for what purposes. In the third stage, the filled diary booklets were retrieved and familiarized with and the first interpretations were made. In the fourth stage, the interviews concerning the themes of fit and misfit in virtual work places were finalized and carried out with 10 users. The aim of the interview phase was to examine employees' experiences of fit or misfit concerning physical, functional and psychosocial features of their virtual workplace. In the fifth and final stage the final interpretation of the collected material was done with help of AtlasTi-program.

ESM can be seen as an application of a probes method. The probes method is a user-centered design approach and a qualitative knowledge gathering research tool that is based on user participation by means of self-documentation (Gaver et al. 1999; Gaver et al. 2004; Boeher et al. 2007; Mattelmäki 2008). The purpose of the method is to understand human phenomena and find signals of new opportunities by examining users' personal perceptions and background.

More precisely, probes are a collection of evocative assignments through which or inspired by which the users actively record requested material (Mattelmäki 2008). The most typical forms of traditional self-documentation are diaries and camera studies. The academic purpose of self-documentation is to examine the daily factors of human lives. (Graham et al. 2007; Mattelmäki 2008.) A relevant feature of self-documentation is collecting data from several situations that increase the reliability of the research (DeLongis et al. 1992). Self-documentation also minimizes the observers' possible influence on the person observed.

4. Results

Virtual devices and applications make it possible to work from almost any physical location. Some of the users started the working day in bed when waking up in the morning, by reading emails with their mobile phones and ended it in the same place before going to sleep. The use of virtual tools was constant: at all times, in all places, in work and in leisure. For instance, both making and answering work related phone calls and emails are done when shifting from one physical location to another in staircases, streets, cars, public transportation vehicles, taxis, airports and airplanes. The virtual tools are also used in the middle of different kind of work and leisure related events and meetings such as in lunch restaurants, cafés and bars, offices, seminar facilities, saunas and at home. As one user (U4) wrote in his diary: "I welcomed seminar guests and at the same time I answered some phone calls".

4.1 Physical comfort and fit in the virtual workplace of a mobile employee

The themes of discourse about physical comfort included tools and application for the virtual work as well as the places for the work including the theme of ergonomics (fig. 2). The employees used multiple physical places for work during their working days and the amount of different devices and applications that were utilized was numerous and varied from user to user. The most common virtual devices carried with were laptop and mobile phone. Some users also worked with table computers. The most common virtual application was the e-mail. Additionally, users applied a wide range of other applications. Some of them were used via the Internet e.g. Facebook, Skype, Google, blog, virtual newspapers and net banks. Some of them did not demand an internet connection like shared hard disk, virtual calendar and notebook, Microsoft Office programs and work specific applications such as ArchiCAD.

In many cases the virtual tools were utilized concurrently. The users had usually many applications open at the same time and they used them alternately. Some users also applied different devices for fulfilling the same task. As an example, a user (U6) was waiting for his next flight at the airport. The battery of his laptop was running low and he was charging it while waiting for the boarding call. When the call came the battery was 70% recharged. The user decided to answer some of the latest emails with the laptop and older ones with his mobile phone. The concurrent use of different devices requires a large enough flat surfaces to place the devices - this was not fulfilled especially in the means of transport or was hardly fulfilled in bus stations, railway stations or airports. Also the lack or paucity of functional power points or internet plug-ins or wireless webs was considered hampering the work especially during transitions. The inability to use the printers or totally non-working printers was a problem for some of the users.

The layouts of the physical workspaces were seen as a challenge in many cases. While on the move it was especially hard to find a place that supports quiet work or confidential discussions. For these reasons, working with certain tasks with virtual applications was considered difficult.

Also the decent ergonomics of the workplaces used was important. Many of the mobile employees mentioned the fatigue of musculoskeletal organs due to bad work postures. Inappropriate furniture and visual difficulties were the main causes for impairing working postures. On the other hand, some virtual tools allow flexible changes not only in the physical work position but also in bodily postures. According to the interview, the mobile phone appeared to be the most flexible virtual tool from this point of view.

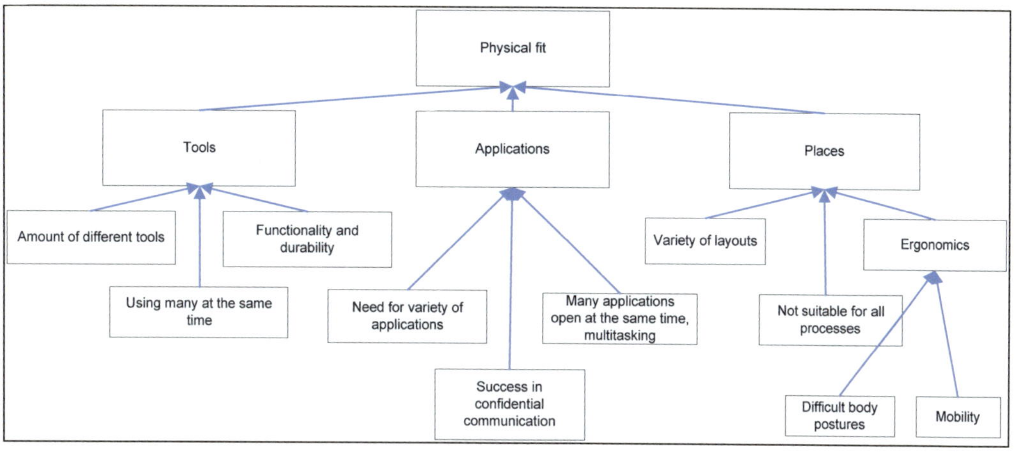

Fig. 2. The elements impacting the physical fit or misfit of virtual workplaces

4.2 Functional comfort and fit in the virtual workplace of a mobile employee

The leading themes of data included the connectivity and effective use of time (fig. 3). The most important thing when considering the nice and smooth i.e. functional use of virtual devices and applications seemed to be the availability, speed and functionality of the internet connection. Most of the notes in the diaries were somehow related to the use of an internet connection. Altogether, the internet connection, which was non-functional or difficult to access, was regarded as the key hindrance of productive knowledge work in virtual workplaces. There was a requirement that a quick and easily accessible internet connection should be available everywhere. This also presents requirements for the infrastructure of both virtual and physical places: they should guide you in getting quickly connected.

Because the workdays of the employees seemed to be busy with many things to do, the baseline assumption was that the use of virtual devices and applications is quick and smooth. If not, the irritation on account of wasted time increased, e.g., when sending emails took a few seconds instead of being instant. The interviewed subjects described the wasted time as a time that was spent with virtual tools but which did not directly contribute to completing the work related tasks and duties they were working with. An example of an experience of wasted time is a laptop that took 10 minutes to turn on. Another example is a situation where the user spent hours learning to use free program to find out if it is suitable for his purposes - it was not and the time was wasted.

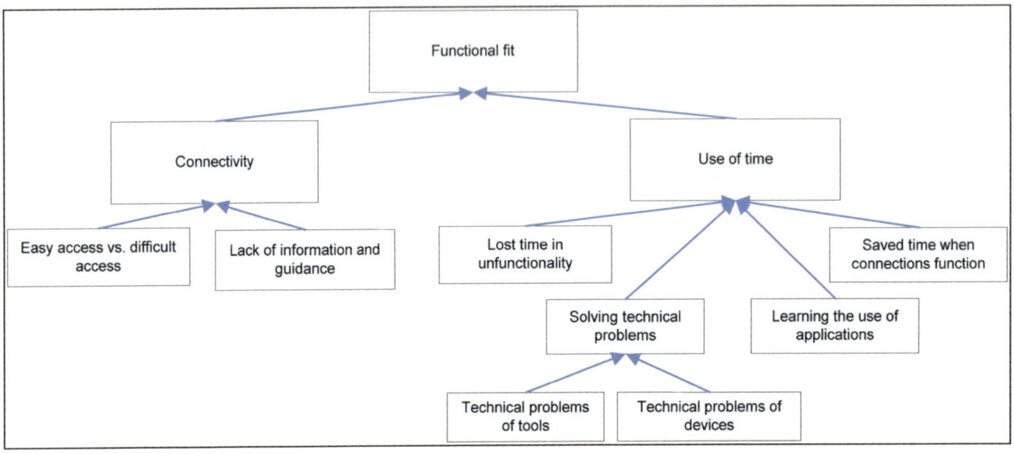

Fig. 3. The elements impacting the functional fit or misfit of virtual workplaces

4.3 Psychosocial comfort and fit in the virtual workplace of a mobile employee

The discourse concerning the psychosocial fit of virtual places dealt with the concepts of territoriality, privacy and control (fig. 4).

When the employees described the matters of territoriality, they stressed the importance of selecting the right virtual communication tools and channels. For example, sending emails was not the channel for enhancing **belonging**; more nuanced communication channels were selected and used.

The interviewed subjects described the virtual teambuilding methods that enhance belonging they have used or participated in. For this reason the normal working tools and applications were used for sharing work divergent matters. For example they shared photos of leisure time and discussed their holiday plans with live-meeting tools.

The managers of distributed teams expressed the essence to select and use the most suitable virtual behavior for enhancing the belonging of individuals. For example the calls "for no particular reason" played important role in enhancing employees' feeling of belonging.

According to the interview data, the concept of privacy consisted of three components. The interviewed described privacy through problems in simultaneous co- and telepresence, simultaneous use of many virtual communication and collaboration channels as well as problems followed from simultaneous use of work and leisure related virtual environments. The ensemble of the privacy was related to the concept of accessibility: the feeling of fit arose from the good control over the multidimensional opportunities to access both physical and virtual worlds.

Simultaneous co- and telepresence enabled simultaneous use of many communication and collaboration channels. For example, when taking part in a conference call without visual communication employees tend to do many other duties too, i.e., mute the microphone and communicate face to face with colleagues and send e-mails. Simultaneous use of many virtual communication and collaboration channels blur also the boundaries of work related and leisure related virtual places. While working in virtual places, many employees amused themselves by occasional visits in leisure related places, e.g., in their own Face book pages.

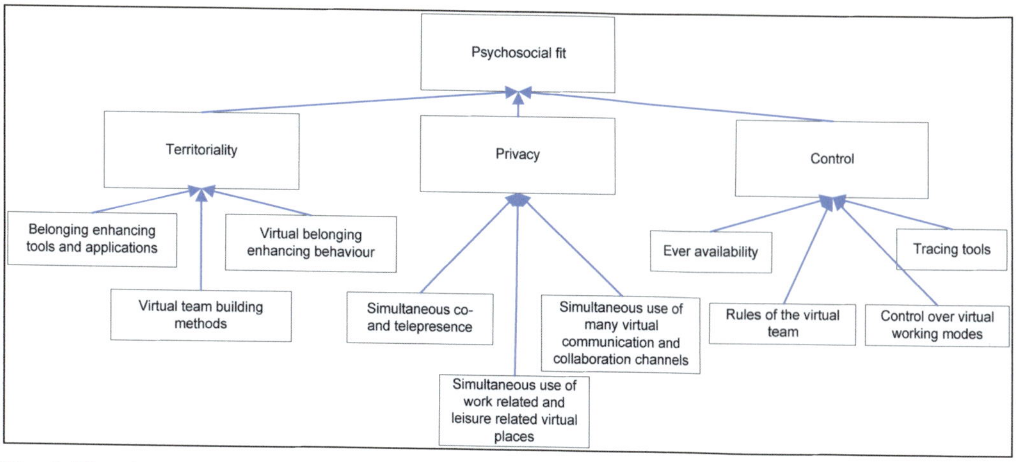

Fig. 4. The elements impacting the psychosocial fit or misfit of virtual workplaces

Taking over the fit of psychosocial elements in the virtual workplace the success in **control** is essential. The interviewed subjects defined the control to flow from the success in handling the demands of continuous availability, clear communication and collaboration rules inside the team as well as a good command over the different virtual working modes. They also pointed out the negative features of control. For example, the virtual tracing methods may also be used in a way that reflects a sign of distrust.

5. Conclusions

This research showed that Vischer's model (2005, 2007) of environmental fit is useful for a more detailed classification of virtual places and spaces. In virtual work the threshold of usability is at the functional level due to accessibility demands (see fig. 1). The work of a mobile employee will stop completely if the worker is not able to connect.

In order to develop well-functioning virtual workplaces for mobile employees, extensive attention should be paid to the whole system, within which employees confront their duties in different locations. Gaining comprehensive understanding on the context in which a given task is performed starts by forming questions first on the physical places and later on psychosocial themes. As such a vast field, the process demands profound multidisciplinary collaboration of different actors in organizations and support functions. The inspection of different fit levels is a useful tool for helping different authorities to explain their expertise in relation to other authorities. Gaps in management may also be demonstrated. There is a need for putting more emphasis in analyzing the non-visible work processes we have learned to conduct in virtual entity.

According to this research with Vischer ´s model as a frame of reference, it can be stated that

- At the level of physical fit, building codes and standards should be expanded to cover also the needs generated from the new working modes i.e. mobile work. The layouts of different premises should be clear and also instruct occasional visitors to quickly settle for working. The physical places should guide your route to virtual reality. Because the virtual reality is its own world with its voices and vistas, the disturbances caused by physical reality should be diminished, also when you are working in the places not primarily designed for work, i.e. trains, cafeterias, hotel rooms. This is a truly and demanding challenge for construction planning. The demands of performing mobile work should be taken into account also when designing furniture for premises not primarily aimed at working.
- At the level of functional fit, the access creates the threshold of work. Entering virtual work places i.e. the virtual reality of work is a question of existing and well functioning infrastructure. Moreover, questions concerning the easiness of connecting signals as well as of finding help and support in using information technology are essential. The transfer to virtual work places via well functioning infrastructures and applications must be attained regardless of the time and physical place. The operational environment of mobile employee should be portable as well as easy perceivable. (cf. Hyrkkänen et al, 2007.)
- Enhancing the fit at the psychosocial level, the mixture of physical and virtual worlds and simultaneous existence in both should be more effectively understood and supported. Particular and a lot of learning demanding challenge lies in controlling the simultaneous co- and telepresence, simultaneous use of many virtual communication and collaboration channels as well as simultaneous use of work and leisure related virtual channels. Although one of the major goals driving the development of virtual reality has been in providing a space for people to interact without the constraints of the physical world the fact seems to be that we can not totally rid ourselves form being physical as well (c.f. Fox et al, 2009). On that account, we have to learn to behave and work also in the interspace i.e. controlling simultaneous existence and belonging in the mixture of physical and virtual worlds. The integrated design, which seamlessly combines the physical and virtual places, needs to be developed further as well.

6. References

Axtell, C.; Hislop, D. & Whittaker, S. (2008). Mobile technologies on mobile spaces. Findings from the context of train travel. *International Journal of Human-Computer Studies* No.66, pp. 902-915

Boeher, K.; Vertesi, J.; Sengers, P. & Dourish, P. (2007). "How HCI Interprets the Probes", paper published proceeding *SIGCHI* 2007, April 28th - May 3rd, San Jose, California, ACM Press, New York, pp. 1077-1086

Breure, A. & van Meel, J. 2003. Airport offices: Facilitating nomadic worker. Facilities Vol.21 No.7/8, pp. 175-179

Brown, B. & O`Hara, K. (2003). Place as a practical concern of mobile workers. Environment and Planning No.35, pp. 1565-1587

Dainoff, M.; Mark,L.; Ye, L. & Petrovic, M. (2007). Forget about Aesthetics in Chair design: Ergonomics Should Provide the Basis for Comfort. In Dainoff, M.J. (ed.) *Ergonomics and Health Aspects of Work with Computers*. LNCS, Vol.4566, pp.19-25. Springer, Heidelberg

DeLongis, A., Hemphill, K. J. & Lehman, D. R. (1992). " A Structured Diary Methodology for the Study of Daily Events". Bryant, F. B., Edwards, J., Tindale, R. R., Posavac, E. J., Heath, L., Henderson, E., Suarez-Balcazar, Y. (Ed.), *Methodological Issues in Applied Psychology*, Plenium Press, New York, pp. 83-109

Ettlinger, O. (2008). *The Architecture of Virtual Space*. Ljubljana : Faculty of Architecture, 2008

Felstead, A.; Jewson,N. & Walters, S (2005). *Changing Places of Work*. New York, Palgrave macmilan

Forlano, L. (2008) a. Anytime? Aywhere?: Reframing Debates Around Municipal Wireless Networking. *The Journal of Community Informatics*, Vol.4, No1. Available from http://ci-journal.net/index.php/ciej/article/view/438/401

Forlano, L. (2008) b. Working on the move. The social and digital ecologies of mobile work places In Hislop (ed.) *Mobility and technology in the Workplace*. pp. 28-42. New York, Routledge

Fox, J.; Arena, D. & Bailenson, J.N. (2009). Virtual reality. A Survival Guide for the Social Scientist. Journal of Media Psychology Vol.21, No.3, pp. 95-113

Gareis, K.; Lilischkis, S. & Mentrup, A. (2006). Mapping the Mobile eWorkforce in Europe, in J. H. E. Andriessen and M. Vartiainen (Eds.), *Mobile Virtual Work. A New Paradigm?*, pp. 45-69. Springer, Heidelberg

Gaver, B.; Dunne, T. & Pacenti, E. (1999). "Cultural Probes", *Interactions*, Vol.6, No.1, pp. 21-29

Gaver, W.; Boucher, A.; Pennington, S. & Walker, B. (2004). "Cultural Probes And The Value Of Uncertainty", *Interactions*, Vol.11, No.5, pp. 53-56

Graham, C., Roundefield, M., Gibbs, M., Veter, F. & Cheverst, K. (2007). "How Probes Work". *Published proceeding at OZCHI* 2007, November 28 - 30th, Edelaide, Australia, ACM Press, New York, pp. 29-37

Green, N.: On the Move (2002). Technology, Mobility, and the Mediation of Social Time and Space. *The Information Society*, No18, pp. 281-292

Hallford, S. (2005). Hybrid workspace: re-spatialisations of work, organization and management. *New Technology, Work and Employment* Vol.20, No.1, pp. 19-33

Hektner, J.M., Schmidt, J.A. & Csikszentmihalyi, M. (Eds.). (2006). *Experience Sampling Method: Measuring the Quality of Everyday Life*. Sage Publications, Inc

Hislop, D. & Axtell, C. (2009). To infinity and beyond?: workspace and the multi-location worker. *New Technology, Work and Employment* Vol.24, No.1, pp. 60-75

Hyrkkänen, U. & Nenonen, S. (2011). The virtual workplace of a mobile employee - how does Vischer´s model function in identifying physical, functional and psychosocial fit? In J. A. Jacko (Ed.) *Human-Computer Interaction: Towards Mobile and Intelligent Interaction Environments*. Human-Computer Interaction, Part III, LNCS, Vol. 6763. Heidelberg: Springer. Available from URL:
< http://www.springer.com/computer/hci/book/978-3-642-21615-2

Hyrkkänen, U.; Putkonen, A. & Vartiainen, M. (2007). Complexity and Workload Factors in Virtual Work Environments of Mobile Work. In M.J. Dainoff (Ed.) *Ergonomics and Health Aspects*. HCII 2007, LNCS 4566, pp. 85-94. Springer, Heidelberg.

Laurier, E. (2004). Doing office work on the motorway. *Theory, Culture & Society* Vol.21 No.4/5, pp. 261-277

Laurier, E. & Philo, C. (2003). The region in the boot: mobilizing lone subjects and multiple object. *Environment and Planning* No.21, pp. 85-106

Mann, S. & Holdsworth, L. (2003). The psychological impact of teleworking: stress, emotions and health. *New Tecnology, Work and Employment* Vol.18, No. 3, pp. 196-211

Mark, G. & Su, N.M. (2010). Making infrastructure visible for nomadic work. *Pervasive and Mobile Computing* doi:10.1016/j.pmcj.2009.12.004. Available from http://www.elsevier.com/locate/pmc

Mattelmäki, T. (2008). *Design Probes* (2th edition), Publishing Series of University of Art and Design Helsinki, Vaajakoski, Finland.

Nenonen, S.; Airo, K.; Bosch, P.; Fruchter, R.; Koivisto, S.; Gersberg, N.; Rothe, P., Ruohomäki, V. & Vartiainen, M. (2009). *Managing Workplace Resources for Knowledge Work, the final report of ProWork-project,* Available from http://www.proworkproject.com/prowork/final-report (2009)

Perry, M. & Brodie, J. (2006). Virtually connected, practically mobile. In Andriessen & Vartiainen (Eds.) *Mobile Virtual Work. A New paradigm?*,pp.97-127. Springer, Heidelberg

Perry, M.; O'Hara, K.; Sellen, A.; Brown, B. & Harper, R. (2001). Dealing with Mobility: Understanding access anytime, anywhere. *ACM Transactions on Computer-Human Interaction (TOCHI)* Vol.8, No. 4, pp. 323-347

Rasila, H., Airo, K. & Nenonen, S. (2011). From Work Profiles to Worker Profiles. 6th Nordic Conference on Construction Economics and Organisation 13.-15.5.2011, Copenhagen, Denmark in *Proceedings of the 6th Nordic Conference on Construction Economics and Organisation – Shaping the Construction/Society Nexus : Volume 1: Clients and Users.*

Tietze, S. & Musson, G. (2005). Recasting the home-work relationship: A case of mutual adjustment? *Organization Studies* Vol.26, No.9, pp. 1331-1352

Vartiainen, M. & Hyrkkänen, U. (2010). Changing requirements and mental workload factors in mobile multi-location work. *New Technology, Work and Employment* Vol.25, No.2 pp. 117-135

Venezia, C. & Allee, V. (2007). Supporting mobile worker networks: components for effective workplaces. *Journal of Corporate Real Estate* Vol.9, No.3, pp. 168-182

Vischer, J.C. (2008). Towards an Environmental Psychology of Workspace: How People are Affected by Environments for Work. *Architectural Science Review* Vol.51, No.2, pp. 97-108

Vischer, J.C. (2007). The effects of physical environment on job performance: towards a theoretical model of workspace stress. *Stress and Health* No.23, pp. 175-184

Vischer, J.C. (2005). *Space meets status. Designing workplace performance.* Routledge, New York.